British Journal of **Educational Psychology**
Monograph Series II: Psychological Aspects of Education - Current Trends

Number 4

Student Learning and University Teaching

Edited by
Noel Entwistle and Peter Tomlinson

British Journal of Educational Psychology

'Psychological Aspects of Education – Current Trends'
Monograph Series

The *British Journal of Educational Psychology* hosts a series of annual conferences in the UK on psychological aspects of education where world-leading researchers provide inputs on the latest cutting-edge advances within their fields. The conferences are free of charge and the papers are published in a corresponding series of edited monographs.

No.1- **Learning and Teaching Reading**

No.2- **Development and Motivation – Joint Perspectives**

No.3- **Pedagogy – Teaching for Learning**

No.4- **Student Learning and University Teaching**

No.5- **Learning through Digital Technologies**

Cost: £15 (£40 for libraries/institutions)
To order, please contact the Commercial Sales Department, The British Psychological Society, St Andrews House, 48 Princess Road East, Leicester, LE1 7DR. Tel: +44 (0)116 252 9551, Fax: +44 (0)116 247 0787, email: sales@bps.org.uk or order online: www.bpsjournals.co.uk/bjepmonographs.

FORTHCOMING CONFERENCE—BOOK NOW FOR YOUR FREE PLACE
Learning and Teaching Writing
Oxford Brookes University, 28–29 June 2007
Contact: writing_conference@brookes.ac.uk for more information

Published in 2007 by The British Psychological Society, St Andrews House, 48 Princess Road East, Leicester LE1 7DR, UK.

ISSN 1476-9808 Monograph Series II: Psychological Aspects of Education - Current Trends
ISBN-13: 978-1-85433-444-2 Student Learning and University Teaching

www.bps.org.uk
Typeset in Europe by the Alden Group, Oxfordshire
Printed in Great Britain by Cambrian Printers, Aberystwyth

Contents

The
British
Psychological
Society

www.bpsjournals.co.uk

iv   **Brief biographies of speakers at the conference**

v   **Series preface**
Peter Tomlinson

1   **1 – Research into student learning and university teaching**
Noel Entwistle

19   **2 – Towards a pedagogical theory of learning**
Ference Marton

31   **3 – Theories of difficulty**
David Perkins

49   **4 – Academics' experiences of teaching and of their subject matter understanding**
Michael Prosser, Elaine Martin and Keith Trigwell

61   **5 – Variations in student learning and perceptions of academic quality**
John T. E. Richardson

73   **6 – The power of teaching – learning environments to influence student learning**
Jan D. Vermunt

91   **7 – Teaching – learning environments in contemporary mass higher education**
Dai Hounsell and Jenny Hounsell

113   **8 – Early career learning at work and its implications for universities**
Michael Eraut

135   **Reflections on papers 1, 3, 7 and 8**
Hazel Francis

147   **Reflections on papers 2, 4, 5, 6 and the conference as a whole**
Paul Ramsden

Brief biographies of speakers at the conference

Noel Entwistle is Professor Emeritus of Education at the University of Edinburgh and a past Editor of both the *British Journal of Educational Psychology* and *Higher Education*. His main research interests are in approaches to studying and influences on them. He was the Co-Director of the ETL project which looked at teaching-learning environments across four contrasting subject areas within the ESRC Teaching and Learning Research Programme (TLRP). E-mail: noel.entwistle@ed.ac.uk.

Michael Eraut is a Professor of Education at the University of Sussex and is currently Editor of *Learning in Health and Social Care* and is managing a TLRP project on learning in the early stages of professional employment within the fields of nursing, engineering and accountancy. His research interests in recent years have focused on non-formal learning and tacit knowledge within professional work from both theoretical and practical perspectives. E-mail: m.eraut@sussex.ac.uk.

Hazel Francis is an Emeritus Professor at the Institute of Education at the University of London, is a former Editor of the *British Journal of Educational Psychology* and was, until her retirement, a Pro-Director of the Institute. Her research interests have ranged widely within educational psychology, from the early years of learning to read, to the effects of genre on postgraduate students' ability to understand psychological texts. E-mail: h.francis@ioe.ac.uk.

Dai Hounsell is Professor of Higher Education at the University of Edinburgh and, until recently, was the *Higher Education* Editor with responsibility for articles on teaching and learning. For many years, he directed the university's Teaching, Learning and Assessment Centre. His main research interests are in assessment and feedback and the provision of effective teaching-learning environments, and he was the Co-Director of the ETL project. E-mail: dai.hounsell@ed.ac.uk.

Ference Marton is a Professor of Education at the University of Gothenburg and was, until recently, also attached to the University of Hong Kong. He is best known for introducing the distinction between deep and surface approaches and developing phenomenography as an influential research approach. In recent years he has been developing a theory of classroom learning based on establishing the necessary prerequisites for learning to take place – 'the space of learning'. E-mail: ference.marton@ped.gu.se.

David Perkins is a senior professor at the Graduate School of Education of Harvard University. He was Co-Director of Project Zero for more than 25 years and now serves as senior co-director. He has conducted long-term programmes of research and development in the areas of teaching and learning for understanding, creativity, problem-solving and reasoning. He co-directed a five-year project into Teaching for Understanding and is currently working on ways of encouraging thinking dispositions in students. E-mail: david_perkins@gse.harvard.edu.

Michael Prosser is currently Director of Research and Evaluation within the Higher Education Academy in 2005. He is an Associate Editor of the BJEP and has co-directed a series of major projects in teaching and learning in Australia, using phenomenographic analyses to explore approaches to teaching in relation to university teachers' understanding of their specialist areas. E-mail: mike.prosser@heacademy.ac.uk.

Paul Ramsden is the Chief Executive of the Higher Education Academy and a Visiting Professor at the Institute of Education, University of London. He was previously Pro-Vice-Chancellor (Teaching and Learning) at the University of Sydney and has been an Associate Editor of the BJEP. His best-selling book, *Learning to Teach in Higher Education*, is one of the classic texts on university teaching. E-mail: paul.ramsden@heacademy.ac.uk.

John T.E. Richardson is Professor of Student Learning and Assessment at the UK Open University, and is an Associate Editor of the BJEP. He is the author of *Researching Student Learning: Approaches to Studying in Campus-Based and Distance Education* (Buckingham: SRHE & Open University Press, 2000). He is currently examining evidence for causality in the relationships between students' approaches and their perceptions of the teaching they experience. E-mail: j.t.e.richardson@open.ac.uk.

Jan Vermunt is Professor of Teaching and Teacher Education at Utrecht University. His current research interests are in the interplay between teaching and learning processes, and encouraging self-regulated and cooperative learning. He is particularly interested in the development and implementation of new teaching, learning and assessment methods aimed at improving the quality of student learning processes. E-mail: j.d.vermunt@ivlos.uu.nl.

The
British
Psychological
Society

www.bpsjournals.co.uk

Series preface

The origin of this series of BJEP monographs lies in a striking but lamentable paradox. Its positive strand is well instanced and articulated by the influential volume: *How people learn: Brain, mind, experience and school* (1999) edited by John Bransford, Anne Brown and Rodney Cocking on behalf of the Committee on Developments in the Science of Learning of the US National Research Council. As the first chapter tells us:

> Thirty years ago, educators paid little attention to the work of cognitive scientists, and researchers in the nascent field of cognitive science worked far removed from classrooms. [. . .] The story we can now tell about learning is far richer than ever before, and it promises to evolve dramatically in the next generation. (Bransford, Brown and Cocking, 1999, p. 3)

The remainder of the book then provides an extremely readable and balanced review of current insights on learners and learning, focusing subsequently on implications of this research for the design of effective learning environments, including roles for technology and emphasizing the key role of teachers. As a widely accessible positive indication of, so to speak, 'what psychology now offers to education', it would be hard to better.

In the UK, on the one hand, there has been a welcome if gradual shift of concern from specification of national curricular goals, through assessment of their achievement, towards more recent emphasis on promoting such achievement through effective pedagogy (cf. Barber, 1998; Leach and Moon, 1999; Mortimore, 1999). On the other hand, by contrast, the paradox is that over precisely the same last couple of decades, the UK education system has been rapidly losing touch with the psychological insights our American colleagues (and Europeans and Australasians and others world-wide) have been increasingly celebrating as relevant to teaching. In particular, a variety of influences have led directly or indirectly to the initial teacher preparation sector in UK universities and colleges steadily losing precisely those staff whose psychological qualifications would enable it to be kept critically aware of these resources - in spite of efforts by The British Psychological Society to argue the case (cf. Tomlinson, Edwards, Finn, Smith & Wilkinson, 1992).

If the idea for the present series arose from the BJEP Editorial Board's desire to play some small part in ameliorating the situation just described, its conception and enablement were due to a stroke of financial good fortune whose provenance deserves recognition. Namely, although this Journal is now fully owned by The British Psychological Society, it was in fact published from 1935 onwards by an independent company, *British Journal of Educational Psychology Ltd*. Only in 1995 did the directors of that company decide to wind it up and to donate it and its considerable assets to the Society.

DOI:10.1348/000709906X162415

Acting according to the terms of this transfer, the Editorial Board of BJEP decided that in the face of the situation described above, it would be worthwhile to spend some of the funds at its disposal to mount a series of annual conferences in the UK on psychological aspects of education, in which world-leading researchers would be assembled to provide inputs on the latest cutting edge advances in their fields. Access to these inputs, particularly for educationists, would be maximised by making these conference events free of charge and by publishing the papers as a corresponding series of monographs. The Journal had already published a series of edited monographs in the 1980s, so it was decided that these collections of conference papers would comprise a new *British Journal of Educational Psychology Monograph Series II: Psychological Aspects of Education - Current Trends*.

As the present monograph reaches publication, five conferences have been held and a sixth and seventh are in preparation. Beyond these, this will be a rolling programme, but there seems little doubt, given the considerable recent expansion of psychological research in or of relevance to education, that over the coming decade we shall be able to hold events and publish monographs in some major areas and aspects of educational interest. So whilst the original impetus for the series was admittedly local, the monographs in the series should in return offer useful resources to the international community of those concerned with psychological aspects of education.

References

Barber, M. (1998). *The Learning Game*. London: Fontana.

Bransford, J. D., Brown, A. L., & Cocking, R. R. (Eds.). (1999). How people learn: Brain, mind, experience, and school. Committee on Developments in the Science of Learning of the US National Research Council, Washington, DC: National Academy Press.

Leach, J., & Moon, R. (Eds.). (1999). *Learners and pedagogy*. London: Paul Chapman in association with The Open University.

Mortimore, P. (Ed.). (1999). Understanding pedagogy and its Impact on learning. London: Paul Chapman.

Tomlinson, P. D., Edwards, A., Finn, G., Smith, L., Wilkinson, J. E. (1992). *Psychological aspects of beginning teacher competence. A submission by the British Psychological Society to the Council for the Accreditation of Teacher Education*. Leicester: British Psychological Society.

PETER TOMLINSON (University of Leeds, UK)

Student Learning and University Teaching, 1–18
BJEP Monograph Series II, 4
© 2007 The British Psychological Society

The
British
Psychological
Society

www.bpsjournals.co.uk

1 – Research into student learning and university teaching

Noel Entwistle*

University of Edinburgh, UK

This chapter provides an overview of research into student learning and university teaching as a framework through which to introduce earlier work carried out by the authors represented in this monograph. Teaching and learning in higher education can be seen as an interactive system that depends on the characteristics of the student, the specific nature of the subject matter, and the whole teaching-learning environment. Given the complexity of the whole system, the research described here inevitably concentrates on just parts of that whole, but together it provides a convincing portrayal of teaching and learning in higher education, with important implications for practice. The distinctive contribution of this chapter is to show how this research area reached its current stage of development and to present a heuristic model to summarize some of the most important influences on learning in higher education mentioned in the other chapters. It also indicates the need, in this area of research, to distinguish between *explanatory theories* (which increase our understanding of the interactions) and *action theories* (which guide practice and are couched in accessible language). It also suggests the importance of theories having not just relevance to practice but *pedagogical fertility* that will stimulate university teachers to think imaginatively about their own teaching. This leads to the idea of there being an *inner logic of the subject and its pedagogy*, implying that generic ideas about approaches to teaching have always to be reinterpreted within a specific disciplinary context, if they are to be recognized as valid by university teachers.

This monograph originates from a conference funded by the *British Journal of Educational Psychology* which was held at the University of Edinburgh in May 2005. The papers given at the conference were chosen to illustrate a range of approaches to research into student learning and university teaching, which related to each other coherently. The common theme of all the chapters is the attempt to understand the ways in which students or young professionals go about learning, studying and preparing for their future professional roles, along with descriptions of recent

*Correspondence should be addressed to Professor Noel Entwistle, Higher and Community Education, Moray House School of Education, The University of Edinburgh, Paterson's Land, Holyrood Road, Edinburgh EH8 8AQ, UK (e-mail: noel.entwistle@ed.ac.uk).

DOI:10.1348/000709906X166772

investigations that explore how teaching and other aspects of the learning environment influence those activities.

This introductory chapter is intended to provide a background to this area of research, partly by indicating how each chapter relates to the earlier studies of the authors, but also by tracing the development of thinking that underlies this research area as a whole. And this more general description is necessarily a personal account that reflects my own perceptions of what are the salient developments in this research area.

The contextual specificity of learning theories of learning

In educational research generally, there has been a growing acceptance that it is not sufficient to rely solely on theories of learning derived from mainstream psychology or sociology, although theories from both areas continue to offer important insights. Many years ago, the American psychologist George Kelly (who took a degree in Education at Edinburgh University) argued that psychological theories necessarily have a limited 'focus of convenience' (Kelly, 1955). Theories are derived from evidence collected using particular research designs and measurement techniques and within specific social contexts, and hence their applicability to other situations and circumstances cannot be assumed and often proves unconvincing.

There is also the problem of the welter of theories of learning that have accumulated over the years, without attempts to integrate them into a general theory. There is little evidence of cumulative development in theory to incorporate aspects of learning that earlier theories have correctly identified. We thus do not have any agreed theory of learning that could be applied with any confidence across the widely differing types of learning found in varying conditions and for a majority of learners. This is one of the reasons why the research into student learning and university teaching, represented by the papers presented at our conference, makes less use of mainstream theories of learning than might be expected.

Qualitative differences in understanding and learning

Thirty years ago, Ference Marton's research group in Gothenburg fundamentally changed the direction of research into student learning by publishing a series of articles in the *British Journal of Educational Psychology* (Fransson, 1977; Marton & Säljö, 1976; Svensson, 1977) on 'qualitative differences in learning'. At that time, neither the idea that qualitative differences in students' understandings of specific content could be rigorously investigated was accepted nor was there any recognition that the nature of the subject matter fundamentally affects the type of learning involved.

The original work of the Gothenburg group showed how to categorize the different levels of understanding shown by students who had read an academic article and also introduced the crucial distinction between deep and surface *approaches to learning* (Marton, 1976). It became clear that students' differing intentions in reading the article (to understand for themselves or to be ready to answer the expected questions) fundamentally influenced the specific learning processes these intentions brought into play, and therefore affected the extent to which conceptual understanding was achieved (Marton & Säljö, 1976). But *how* the learning was carried out (the approach) depended not just on the intention, but also on *what* was being learned (the content) and *where* the learning was taking place (the context). And this recognition of situated learning came long before its acceptance in mainstream psychology.

The identification of approaches to learning aroused considerable interest in Britain, leading to the publication of *The Experience of Learning* (Marton, Hounsell, & Entwistle, 1984), which described further developments by Swedish and British researchers. Subsequently, interest spread, first to Australia (Biggs, 1987; Ramsden, 1988; Trigwell & Prosser, 1991; Watkins & Hattie, 1985), then to South Africa (Meyer, 1988, 1991), Hong Kong (Kember, 1996) and The Netherlands (Vermunt, 1998), among other countries, and has also continued in Britain (e.g. Entwistle, 2000; Gibbs, 1992; Richardson, 2000).

Fundamental ideas about learning in educational contexts

One of the main functions of university education is to induct students into ways of thinking that are required if students are to become competent professionals in their chosen field – what has often been described as *academic discourse*. And, within that discourse, students have to become familiar with the academic meaning of a wide variety of interrelated concepts. One of the important contributions to the research area made by the Gothenburg research group was to establish ways of describing the different levels of understanding reached by students in carrying out academic tasks. This subsequently led Marton to focus his own research on the qualitatively different conceptions that students come to hold of key concepts in differing subject areas. To do this, he adapted the qualitative research methods used previously by his research group into a distinctive research approach called *phenomenography* (Marton, 1981). The essential features of this approach involve interviews, which encourage students to consider their learning experiences in successive steps as the researcher gently probes for deeper insights into those experiences. The analyses then separate out distinguishable categories, describe them through extracts from the interviews and consider the relationships existing between them (Marton & Booth, 1997). The findings from a wide range of studies into students' ways of understanding academic concepts have shown the importance of university teachers being aware of the contrasting conceptions of key concepts that exist among the students taking the courses they are teaching (Bowden & Marton, 1998).

Academic concepts are described in terms of the distinctive characteristics that define an agreed meaning that can then be communicated; but this process also drains them of their contextual links. Individual conceptions are formed from a much richer array of experiences, involving not just concepts which have been established previously, but also links to the specific context where they are being established, as well as relevant personal experiences and the feelings associated with them (Entwistle, in press). Once the agreed academic meaning of a concept has been firmly established in memory, it can be readily retrieved and used in new contexts, but this conception does not necessarily eliminate other conceptions, which may continue to coexist with it. This important conclusion relies on the work of Halldén (1999) who demonstrated how questioning can evoke alternative conceptions. Like Marton, he also drew attention to the different ways in which students conceived of the work they had been set in the classroom, and described the important implications these differences had for the subsequent processes of learning, and so on the outcomes of that learning. In student learning research, more general forms of conceptualizing have been demonstrated, with students holding differing conceptions of knowledge (Perry, 1970) and of learning (Säljö, 1979). And these differing conceptions are directly related to the ways in which students tackle academic tasks (Entwistle & Peterson, 2004).

Building on his work on phenomenography, Marton has recently been working on a 'variation' theory of learning specific to educational contexts, which is based on three elements – variation, discernment and simultaneity. One of the great difficulties students encounter in meeting a new topic is in distinguishing what is salient from what is incidental. And yet understanding depends on seeing what are the defining features of a concept or phenomenon that is being introduced and the function of formulations that make sense of sets of related aspects or observations. Students have to encounter the variety of aspects involved (*variation*), and they also have to be able to *discern* which are the key features. And discernment goes beyond being told what is important; it depends on the students' active use of prior knowledge and experience to determine the critical features. The salient variations may be met in everyday living, or may be systematically provided by a teacher; but without the opportunity to see these variations, critical features cannot be recognized. Moreover, the academic learning process involves not just being able to hold the key features in the mind *simultaneously*, but also depends on being prepared actively to explore the interconnections that create a firm understanding of the concept, phenomenon or process (Marton & Pang, 2006). It is this theory of learning that Marton described in his presentation to the conference and is explained in the next chapter.

Teaching for understanding and theories of difficulty

David Perkins and his colleagues, working within the multifaceted Project Zero in the Harvard Graduate School of Education, have also been exploring a range of aspects of learning, thinking and teaching in differing educational contexts, drawing on established psychological constructs, but also introducing ideas that have emerged from research within specific educational contexts (see www.pz.harvard.edu). Although much of the work relates to school or to the workplace, the ideas developed have also influenced thinking in higher education, particularly through the *Teaching for Understanding* curriculum framework (TfU) (Wiske, 1998). This emerged from a major project, actively involving teachers, which sought to redirect teaching in ways which made understanding a more explicit goal. It was rooted in a particular view of understanding, which was later taken up by Biggs (1996) in developing his ideas about constructive alignment, as we shall see later on. Perkins described understanding in the following terms:

> Understanding is being able to carry out a variety of actions or 'performances' that show one's grasp of a topic and at the same time advance it . . . Our 'performance perspective', in brief, says that understanding is a matter of being able to do a variety of thought-demanding things with a topic – like explaining, finding evidence and examples, generalizing, analogizing and representing the topic in a new way . . . It is being able to take knowledge and use it in new ways. (Perkins & Blythe, 1994, p. 6)

Within the TfU framework, teachers begin by setting up clearly defined understanding goals and describe *generative topics* in ways that make them open-ended, encouraging student research and discussion. This focus on understanding is kept firmly in the students' minds using *throughlines* that describe the overarching goals of the course in terms the students can easily grasp, and these are revisited each time a new topic is introduced. Comments from the teachers involved in this project help to make these terms clearer:

> *Generative topics* are issues, themes, concepts, ideas, and so on that provide enough depth, significance, connections, and variety of perspective to support students' development of powerful understandings . . . Generative topics . . . are central to one or more disciplines or domains, they are interesting . . . [and] accessible to students . . .

> *Throughlines* need to capture the essence of a whole course . . . [and] are often rooted in deeply held but rarely articulated beliefs and values about both the subject matter and the teaching and learning processes . . . They help students see the purposes that underlie their daily work, make connections among various topics and assignments, and track their own developing understandings (Blythe *et al.*, 1998, pp. 18, 25, 41.

The framework sees understanding not just as an outcome of learning but also as part of the process, and therefore encourages teachers to set work that involves *understanding performances* through which students can both develop their own understanding and demonstrate it.

This concern with understanding has led to questions about why students often fail to develop effective understanding, even when the teaching has been quite well designed. In most subjects, there remain areas of *troublesome knowledge* that students find difficult, and that was the area that Perkins addressed in his contribution to the conference. Previously, he had established certain types of knowledge which often form 'trouble spots' for students (Perkins, 2006), such as conceptually challenging concepts (Newton's laws of motion), or established ways of thinking which conflict with academic perspectives ('presentism' in historical interpretations). In Chapter 3, Perkins develops these ideas further by describing differing reactions that staff have to the identification of difficulties, and their implications for the design of teaching.

Subject knowledge and approaches to teaching

Michael Prosser and his collaborators have carried out a series of influential projects in Australia, many of which have been directly influenced by phenomenography or by variation theory. Trigwell, Prosser, and Taylor (1994) used phenomenographic analyses of interviews with university teachers to build on previous work describing contrasting approaches to teaching (Dall'Alba, 1991). Clear parallels emerged between the approaches to studying previously identified among students and the approaches to teaching adopted by staff. Among lecturers, one of the main distinctions was between those who saw the subject mainly from their own perspective as subject specialists and transmitted information that students were expected to absorb (information transmission, teacher-focused) and those who saw the subject in more relativistic terms and encouraged students to change their conceptions of the subject matter through more open ways of teaching (conceptual change, student-focused; Prosser & Trigwell, 1999). Trigwell, Prosser, and Waterhouse (1999) reported the use of questionnaires to provide scores on approaches to studying and approaches to teaching, which showed that lecturers who describe their teaching as mainly involving information transmission are more likely to have classes adopting surface approaches to learning than those whose teachers are emphasizing conceptual change.

Even though a course team may be encouraging conceptual development, students may still encounter difficulties with specific topics, and it is here that

Marton's variation theory comes into play. Cope and Prosser (2005), for example, have reported a study which looked at a single topic – information systems – that students found particularly difficult. They showed that the teaching of the topic could be improved by identifying, and focusing on, its 'educationally critical aspects'. In their study, Cope and Prosser identified different levels of understanding shown by students and considered these in terms of the distinction introduced by Entwistle and Smith (2002), between the students' personal understandings and the *target understanding* set by the teacher.

> A learning experience can be analysed and described in terms of related 'what' and 'how' components. The 'what' component concerns the level of understanding of the phenomenon developed as a consequence of the learning experience. The 'how' component concerns the approach used to learn about the phenomenon . . .

> The study extends the notion of target understanding . . . [by] describing a scholarly learning experience to which students should aspire . . . incorporating both the target understanding *and* the specifics of an optimal approach to [reaching it] . . . Importantly, the study also . . . [identifies] the [educationally critical] aspects of the scholarly learning experience which need full emphasis if a target understanding is to be reached. (Cope & Prosser, 2005, pp. 346, 352)

Prosser and his co-workers (Prosser, Martin, Trigwell, Ramsden, & Lueckenhausen, 2004) have subsequently developed links with subject matter further by bringing together the ways in which academic staff think about their teaching, their subject area and their own research. Using phenomenographic analyses, relationships between categories show clear connections in their conceptualizations, as is explained in Chapter 4. In this chapter, the authors contrast the types of model used in research on student learning. Some studies see the relationships between teaching and learning as causal, with teaching leading directly to changes in students' learning. Others, as we shall see, envisage two-way relationships between the teaching–learning environment and the characteristics of students within an interacting system. However, within phenomenography, the relationships are seen as 'relational', with the nature of the relationships being altogether more fluid as the perspective and the focus of the analysis change.

Relationships among conceptions, perceptions and approaches

Although the relationships between approaches to learning and self-rated teaching approaches have been demonstrated, most of the research has looked at students' *perceptions* of the teaching they have experienced. Ramsden and Entwistle (1981) conducted one of the first of these studies and, using both questionnaires and interviews, they established that there were marked differences among students in their perceptions of the same teaching. Moreover, those perceptions were related to their approaches to studying. In the interviews, the main characteristics of what students generally perceived as 'good teaching' involved clarity, level, pace and structure in the lectures, while Entwistle (1998) suggested that it was the three remaining characteristics (the 'three Es') - explanation, enthusiasm and empathy - which were most likely to evoke a deep approach to learning among students.

While these relationships have been known for some time, the use of correlational analysis to establish them leaves open the important issue of causality. To what extent do the links indicate that students with established study habits perceive the teaching they experience in contrasting ways, or is it the teaching itself which is responsible for the observed changes in approaches? It was clear from an early stage in this research that one of the strongest influences on approaches would be the assessment procedure adopted. In one of the few experiments carried out, Thomas and Bain (1984) showed that shifting the assessment of a course unit from essay-type questions to MCQs moved the class as a whole away from deep and towards surface approaches, and when the assessment methods were changed back again, the opposite effect was demonstrated. However, while the overall means shifted up or down, the rank order of individual students stayed much the same. This indicated that there must be considerable stability in the tendency of individual students to adopt deep or surface approaches, but that, nevertheless, differences in assessment still have marked effects on the approaches adopted by the class as a whole. Subsequently, it has become clear that the effects on approaches to learning come not just from specific teaching or assessment methods, but rather from the whole teaching–learning environment that students experience.

John Richardson has been carrying out an extensive set of studies using inventories to investigate aspects of student learning among a wide variety of students, exploring the relationships found among specific groups of students (e.g. deaf students) and with contrasting types of teaching (conventional and distance learning; Richardson, 2000). Recently, he has been using a shortened version of the *Approaches to Studying Inventory* (ASI) and a revised version of it (RASI; Tait, Entwistle, & McCune, 1998) to distinguish differing approaches to studying, and relating these to the scales within the *Course Experience Questionnaire* (CEQ). The CEQ was developed by Ramsden (1991) to capture students' perceptions of the teaching they have experienced, producing separate scores on *clear goals and standards, good teaching, generic skills, appropriate assessment* and *appropriate workload*, although these can also be combined to produce a composite score representing students' perceptions of 'academic quality'.

> The findings of the present investigation are striking in view of the level of overlap between responses to the RASI and responses to the CEQ: . . . there exists an intimate relationship between students' approaches to studying in higher education and their perceptions of the academic quality of their courses. This in-turn is consistent with the idea that approaches to studying depend on the perceived content, context and demands of the learning task . . . Even so, the finding of an overlap between students' scores on the CEQ and their scores on the RASI is purely correlational in nature. In itself, it says nothing about either the existence or the direction of a causal relationship between approaches to studying and perceptions of the academic environment. It is possible, indeed, that students' approaches to studying influence their perceptions of the learning context: that students evaluate their courses more favorably *because* they have adopted more congenial ways of studying. (Richardson, 2005, p. 20)

More recently, Richardson has used a series of studies to obtain much firmer evidence of the nature of the relationship between variations in students' learning and their perceptions of the courses they have experienced. In his presentation to the conference, he identified four theoretical ways of accounting for the relationships, and in Chapter 5 he refers to empirical evidence to test each of these possibilities, suggesting that the relations almost certainly operate in both directions – perceptions of teaching affecting approaches to learning, and prior approaches also influencing future perceptions. This conclusion helps to justify interactive models which depend on a whole series of two-way relationships between variables describing students and those indicating aspects of the teaching–learning environment.

A teaching–learning environment as an interactive system

A teaching-learning environment includes all the components experienced by students which are intended to help them to learn more effectively – the various teaching activities, the learning materials made available, the support provided by tutors or demonstrators, as well as the assignments students are required to complete and the assessment procedures adopted. The extent to which these components work in consort has an important effect on student learning, as do the perceptions students have of the environment acting as an interactive whole.

In the field of personality research, Magnusson (1984) argued that it was important not just to know that the environment influenced people's behaviour, but also to be able to map the various characteristics of the environment which had those influences. He thought that it ought to be possible to find such characteristics in similar ways that psychologists had previously identified the main individual differences among people. And in the field of organizational behaviour, Checkland (1981) introduced the idea of 'soft systems analysis' which explained how detailed observation, and discussion with the various groups of workers involved, could be used to develop a conceptual framework describing the interplay between the most influential factors affecting organizational effectiveness. This framework could then be used to guide ways of improving the efficiency and productivity of the organization.

Putting these two ideas together, Entwistle (1987) developed a heuristic model of the teaching-learning process in higher education as a system, showing the interaction between student characteristics and what research at that time had shown to be some of the most influential characteristics of the teaching-learning environment affecting the quality of student learning. This environment was shown as being split between two main areas, the one relating to the teaching activities which are closely related to the subject matter and the other covering assessment and aspects that are more affected by departmental and institutional policies and the provision of resources. A recent version of this model will be introduced later on Figure 1.

Eizenberg (1988) subsequently showed how the components within a teaching-learning environment can combine to support or inhibit effective student learning, and also how one element failing to fit in with the rest of the system may prevent students adopting deep approaches. Biggs (1993) used general systems theory to argue for a conceptual framework – the 3P model – which linked the 'presage' factors that preceded a student's entry to a course with the 'processes' of learning subsequently adopted which, in-turn, affected the 'product' – the learning outcomes achieved through studying. He subsequently drew on Perkins' ideas about teaching for understanding to introduce the influential concept of *constructive alignment* (Biggs, 1996) which linked together aspects of the TfU framework with Eizenberg's recognition of the importance, within an interacting network of cause and effect, of matching teaching and assessment closely to the main course objectives.

Biggs (2003) explained the importance of constructive alignment in the following terms:

> In deciding on teaching methods to use that address the objectives, we need a theory of learning and teaching. Hence [the term] 'constructive alignment' [is used to describe] a marriage between a constructivist understanding of student learning, and an aligned design for teaching . . . It is easy to see why alignment should work. In aligned teaching, there is maximum consistency throughout the system. The curriculum is stated in the form of clear

objectives, which state the level of understanding required rather than simply a list of topics to be covered. The teaching methods are chosen that are likely to realize those objectives; you get students to do the things that the objectives nominate. Finally, the assessment tasks address the objectives, so that you can test to see if the students have learned what . . . they should be learning. . . . The students are 'entrapped' in this web of consistency, optimizing the likelihood that they will engage in the appropriate learning activities, but paradoxically leaving them free to construct their knowledge (p. 27).

The effects of differing teaching–learning environments

The previous section provides a background to Chapters 6 and 7 which push the theoretical discussions and empirical findings even closer to the experiences of staff and students in actual teaching–learning environments. Much of the work of Jan Vermunt and his co-researchers has involved the development and use of questionnaires which, although using a different conceptual framework to the ones mentioned earlier, produce findings which are broadly similar (Vermunt, 1998, 2005). They have reported four main qualitative differences in how students learn: *meaning-directed* (like deep), *reproduction-directed* (like surface), but also *application-directed* which involves a vocational and practical orientation to studying, and *undirected learning* – studying without any clear purpose.

A particular feature of this work has been the emphasis on *study regulation* (Vermunt, 1998), which has been developed from a range of ideas drawn from educational psychology that indicate what affects the likelihood that students will direct their effort towards effective study activities. Internal regulation controls the balance between cognitive, affective and metacognitive processes in learning, while external regulation comes from the particular approaches to teaching adopted, but also through instructional materials and computer-based learning systems. An important aspect of any teaching-learning environment is the balance that is achieved between external and internal regulation, with external control being necessary in the early stages of a degree course, but diminishing as the student becomes more experienced in independent studying.

Vermunt and Verloop (1999) have gone on to examine the match between the environments provided by staff and the learning patterns shown by students, and introduce the contrast between *constructive and destructive friction* in the effects of teaching–learning environments on student learning.

> Teaching strategies and learning strategies are not always compatible. Between students' self-regulation and teachers' external regulation of learning processes, complex interplays may take place. *Congruence* occurs when students' learning strategies and teachers' teaching strategies are compatible; *friction* occurs when this is not the case . . . From the viewpoint of influence on the learning and thinking activities students employ, *constructive* and *destructive* frictions may be discerned. Constructive frictions represent a challenge for students to increase their skill in a learning or thinking strategy. These may be necessary to make students willing to change and to stimulate them to develop skill in the use of learning and thinking activities they are not inclined to use on their own. Destructive frictions may cause a decrease in learning or thinking skills. Here, existing learning and thinking skills are not called upon or potential skills are not developed. (Vermunt & Verloop, 1999, p. 270)

Vermunt develops these ideas further in Chapter 6, with a particular emphasis on the implications for teaching and curriculum design. He examines the extent to which differing teaching-learning approaches are regulated by the teacher or require the students to regulate their own studying, and concludes that many traditional approaches fail to encourage the independence in learning that people need to develop to be effective in work situations and in everyday life.

In Chapter 7, Dai Hounsell reports some of the findings from a national 4-year study in UK which looked at ways of *Enhancing Teaching-learning Environments in Undergraduate Courses* – the ETL project (www.tla.ed.ac.uk/etl). This project is distinctive insofar as it focused systematically on the differences in the teaching-learning environments found in four contrasting academic disciplines – electronic engineering, biological sciences, economics and history. It also involved academic staff actively in discussing analyses of students' reactions to their course units obtained from detailed questionnaires and group interviews that led to *collaborative initiatives* designed to overcome specific difficulties experienced by students. The great advantage in this approach is that students' experiences are weighed against an expert appreciation of the subject area and judged in relation to the pressures and constraints under which academics are working.

In UK, considerable emphasis has been put on the importance of defining specific *intended learning outcomes* for every module or course unit. However, when academic staff were interviewed, they did not refer to these more bureaucratic requirements, but to what they saw as the main *ways of thinking and practising in the subject* (WTPs; McCune & Hounsell, 2005), and that concept became one of the key ways of considering differences between subject areas.

> Bearing in mind the literature about disciplinary differences, and also our initial analyses of interviews with staff in the earlier stages of the ETL project . . . the ETL team coined the phrase 'ways of thinking and practising' (WTP) in a subject area, to describe the richness, depth and breadth of what students might learn through engagement with a given subject area in a specific context. This might include, for example, coming to terms with particular understandings, forms of discourse, values or ways of acting which are regarded as central to graduate-level mastery of a discipline or subject area. (McCune & Hounsell, 2005, p. 257)

The ETL project also introduced the notion of *threshold concepts* (Myer & Land, 2006), being concepts, which serve as portals to important topic areas, opening up the subject for students in important ways, but which are often found to be particularly difficult by students. Recently, it has been suggested that there are also threshold ways of thinking which serve the same purpose at the level of the discipline as a whole (Davies & Mangan, 2005).

Building on Biggs' notion of constructive alignment, and on earlier work on the interaction between the different elements in the teaching-learning environment, the project also demonstrated the importance of various forms of *congruence*, or the lack of it, within undergraduate courses. Biggs had stressed the need for teaching activities and assessment procedures to be constructively aligned with understanding aims, but the ETL project has added to the complexity by drawing attention to the other components that also have to be taken into account, including the students' backgrounds and aspirations, course organization and management, the curriculum aims, scope and structure, and the learning support provided. The term 'congruence' was chosen to avoid the implied linearity of the word 'alignment'.

A further form of congruence is one which builds on earlier research into the effects of the feedback given by staff to students on their assignments and, in particular, how students interpret the comments they are given on their work (Hounsell, 1987). In the early stages of a degree, students often fail to understand the meaning of comments from staff, because, to do so, they would have to have the more sophisticated understanding of the academic discourse they are still in the process of acquiring.

> It appears as though tutors' comments often amount to summary judgments rather than specific diagnoses, alluding to an academic form of discourse which is largely tacit and thus invisible to students who have not already perceived its distinctive features . . . At the core of the problem is what Bruner has described . . . as *telling* out of context rather than *showing* in context. Yet even where well-documented comments have made the diagnosis readily comprehensible, the gulf which lies between diagnosis and remedy may remain unbridged and, for some students, unbridgeable without sustained support (Hounsell, 1987, pp. 251–252).

Learning within professional environments

The final chapter introduces research in a quite different, yet complementary, area. Michael Eraut and his co-workers have been systematically exploring the nature of learning that young professionals experience in the workplace and the extent to which those contexts allow and encourage learning to continue in an effective way. They have shown that there are important differences in the nature of learning at university and in the workplace, even when the university course is preparing for a profession (Eraut, 2000, 2004).

One important distinction to be made is between *cultural knowledge* and *personal knowledge*. Cultural knowledge within universities is largely provided in the academic codified form required for publication. Although codified knowledge of various forms is also found in the workplace, there is also a great deal of knowledge used there which is informal and tacit. While codified knowledge can be acquired from reading books or listening to lectures, tacit knowledge comes from experience and discussions within the relevant professional context. It thus follows that students preparing for the professions need to experience both forms of learning.

Just as the student learning research has brought out the importance of the teaching–learning environment and how the constituent components interact coherently, the research into workplace learning has been following a similar trajectory. Eraut (2004) has analysed the strong influences of the workplace situation on the possibilities for learning, but rejects any exclusively social emphasis, stressing the equal importance of personal knowledge. Workplace learning, as with student learning, depends on the prior knowledge and experience of the individual, as well as the opportunities provided by communal activity in the professional setting: it is in the interaction between the two that learning takes place.

> As a counterpart to cultural knowledge, I define *personal knowledge* as what individual persons bring to situations that enables them to think, interact and perform . . . It includes not only personalized versions of public codified knowledge but also everyday knowledge of people and situations, know-how in the form of skills and practices, memories of episodes and events, self-knowledge, attitudes and emotions . . . While remaining a strong supporter of the concept of situated learning, I strongly dissent from those theorists . . . who attempt to eradicate the individual perspective on knowledge and learning. Their research . . . fails to recognize the need for an individually situated (as well as a socially situated) concept of knowledge in the complex, rapidly changing, post-modern world. Individuals belong to several social groups in which they both acquire and contribute knowledge, and their experiences of multiple group membership cannot be ring-fenced . . . There will also be aspects of a person's knowledge that have been constructed

through lifelong learning and have become unique to them, i.e. outside the circle of shared cultural knowledge, because of the unique set of situations in which they have participated. (p. 202)

The research that Eraut describes in his chapter identifies the different kinds of learning which take place in the workplace, many of which also occur in university settings. But the education currently provided in universities does not offer enough opportunities for the collaborative, team-based learning which is so important in work situations. The findings of this study show parallels between *learning factors,* through, for example, the challenge and value of the work or the feedback and support provided, and *context factors* that include the allocation and structuring of the work and the encounters and relationships with others.

Towards an integrative framework in research into teaching and learning in higher education

The philosopher of science, Rom H rré (2002), recently set out the main characteristics for deciding whether a subject area has developed into a science, as he considered what steps cognitive science might take in that direction. He saw this process as depending on two main 'projects'.

> There must be a way of identifying and classifying the phenomena to be studied. There must also be a way of thinking about the processes by which those phenomena come into being, and so explaining them. The classifying job needs a system of categories and kinds, expressed in the concepts of taxonomy. The explaining job needs a picture or model of the mechanisms involved . . . Such 'models of mental processes' have no existential implications. They are pragmatically helpful ways of presenting what we know about the phenomena in question . . . (pp. 16, 17)

In cognitive science, Harré sees the important step as being bringing together descriptions of the mental lives of people with those of the neurological mechanisms which give rise to the experiences of perceiving, thinking and feeling. In research into teaching and learning in higher education, we have to bring together observed and experienced teaching and learning processes, the distinctive nature of academic subject areas, and the varying teaching–learning environments which are related to high-quality learning outcomes. But, in education, there are other considerations to be kept in mind. The conceptual frameworks and models developed must be easily understood by both teachers and students, for whom the detailed conceptualization is not relevant to their ability to work effectively, and the language should not be unnecessarily technical. Perkins (2002) has suggested that we need to extract from the explanatory theories that researchers develop a pragmatic essence that can form an 'action theory'. He envisages a 'toolkit' made up of a limited set of ideas which have been shown to have a major influence on the quality of learning and suggests that these have also to be expressed in terms of an 'action poetry', that is within a terminology which is easily accessible to practitioners. Beyond that, the power of the theory depends on its *pedagogical fertility* (Entwistle, 1994): it should have an immediacy for teachers which sparks off ideas about teaching and learning that have practical consequences.

   Figure 1 is an attempt, based on earlier heuristic models (Entwistle, 1987, 1998), at specifying a set of concepts that describe the interactions between student characteristics, subject-based teaching activities and other aspects of the overall teaching-learning environment provided for students, and experienced by them in

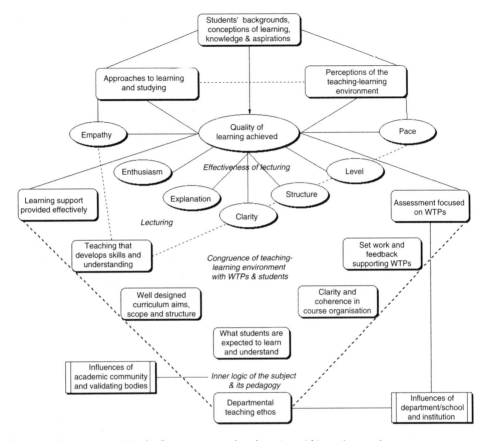

Figure 1. Heuristic model of influences on student learning within an interactive system.

differing ways. Ideally, the model would be presented through the web in ways that would have links to the specific concepts and categories that are implied within each box, and then on to the specific research findings that justify the influences suggested. These components and their probable effects on the quality of student learning remain implicit in Figure 1, except in relation to face-to-face teaching.

The aspects related to face-to-face teaching, shown in the elliptical boxes around the centre, bring together ideas from several of the authors contributing to this monograph. The broader description of the teaching–learning environment shown in the other rectangular boxes in the bottom half of the diagram draws substantially on the elements identified within the ETL project (Entwistle, 2003) which need to be congruent with the main understanding aims (seen as covering knowledge, skills, ways of thinking within the discipline – the WTPs), but also includes other ideas introduced in this overview. However, the phenomenographic research, and its later developments by Marton and Prosser and their colleagues, draws attention to the crucial importance of the subject matter in determining how teaching influences student learning.

In the one topic area within the ETL project where it was possible to explore the teaching of a specific topic area across several contrasting settings, the distinctive teaching methods being used seemed to reflect an *inner logic of the subject and its pedagogy*, linking teaching and learning to the WTPs identified within that area (Entwistle, Nisbet, & Bromage, 2006). The findings suggest that generic approaches to teaching which are believed to have substantial advantages in promoting deep approaches to learning have to be carefully adapted to the particular demands of the subject area, and even to the specific topic, before their beneficial effects are likely to be found. While this concept, linking WTPs and specific teaching–learning activities, resonates with the notion of congruence, it has its roots more firmly in the specific subject area, and thus strengthens the idea of *signature pedagogies* discussed recently by Shulman (2005). He and his colleagues have been investigating several professional areas in universities and have been struck by the existence of methods of teaching that have evolved to encourage the specific kinds of thinking that are characteristic of each profession.

> What I mean by 'signature pedagogy' is a mode of teaching that has become inextricably identified with preparing people for a particular profession. This means it has three characteristics: first, it's distinctive of that [specific] profession . . . Second that it is pervasive within the curriculum, so that there are certain continuities that thread through the programme that are part of what it means to 'think like a lawyer' or 'think like a physician'. . . There are certain kinds of thinking that are called for in the rules of engagement of each course, even as you go from subject to subject. The third feature is another aspect of pervasiveness, which cuts across institutions and not only courses. Signature pedagogies have become essential to general pedagogy of an entire profession, as elements of instruction and of socialization.

This selection of concepts reflects my own way of explaining the interactions identified in the research; other participants in university education will, no doubt, have differing views about which aspects of the overall picture are most important. Educational psychologists, for example, will draw on cognitive psychology for information about the structure and working of memory, the fundamental learning processes and the stability and variability of individual differences: their perspective thus foregrounds the individual student. In contrast, university teachers, through their classroom experience, inevitably concentrate on their own teaching activities and the effects these are having on their students, although when discussing course development or departmental policy, they are likely to take a broader view (McAlpine *et al.*, 2006; Norton, Richardson, Hartley, Newstead, & Mayes, 2004). Students have very clear views about any aspects of the teaching which they find to interfere with their learning, but they are novices in regard to the subject content and hence cannot see the subject as a whole in the ways that staff do. Educational developers will generally see the effects of the overall teaching–learning environment as crucial, while considering fundamental cognitive processes or the limitations of short-term memory, as less relevant.

Each perspective provides an equally valid way of considering some aspects of teaching and learning in higher education, but it is impossible, due to the limitations of our own mental functioning, to hold them all in awareness simultaneously. The best we can do is to select aspects generally considered to be influential in university teaching and choose concepts which fit into a coherent whole that makes sense to the participants. The way in which the concepts create that whole can be suggested through a conceptual model, such as Figure 1, and yet that remains no more than a first-order approximation to the overall complexity and subtlety of the real-world interacting system.

In considering the validity of Harré's plea for a more scientific approach within cognitive science for our own field, we have to remain cautious, as his interpretation of 'science' is couched within a particular view in which linear causal relationships dominate. In research into student learning, the more complex conceptualization from phenomenography encourages us to see the relationships as being much less clear-cut, being relational rather than either causal or two-way interactions, where the perceptions of the individual can vary across situations, affecting the salience of the relationships identified. Nevertheless, the conceptual frameworks emerging from this research area do provide a way of thinking for university teachers, which is likely to improve the quality of student learning, while the findings also suggest a set of guidelines about the generic approaches that would be worth considering for adaptation to the particular requirements of their own discipline.

References

Biggs, J. B. (1987). *Student approaches to learning and studying*. Hawthorn, Victoria: Australian Council for Educational Research.

Biggs, J. B. (1993). From theory to practice: A cognitive systems approach. *Higher Education Research and Development, 12*, 73-86.

Biggs, J. B. (1996). Enhancing teaching through constructive alignment. *Higher Education, 32*, 1-18.

Biggs, J. B. (2003). *Teaching for quality learning at university* (2nd ed.). Buckingham: SRHE and Open University Press.

Blythe, T., and associates (1998). *The teaching for understanding guide*. San Francisco: Jossey-Bass.

Bowden, J., & Marton, F. (1998). *The university of learning: Beyond quality and competence in higher education*. London: Kogan Page.

Checkland, P. (1981). *Systems thinking, systems practice*. London: Wiley.

Cope, C., & Prosser, M. (2005). Identifying didactic knowledge: An empirical study of the educationally critical aspects of learning about information systems. *Higher Education, 49*, 345-372.

Dall'Alba, G. (1991). Foreshadowing conceptions of teaching. *Research and Development in Higher Education, 13*, 293-297.

Davies, P., & Mangan, J. (2005). *Threshold concepts and the integration of understanding in economics*. IEPR Working Paper 2005/19 (Stoke-on-Trent, Staffordshire University, UK) at http://www.staffs.ac.uk/schools/business/iepr/publications/Working-papers.html

Eizenberg, N. (1988). Approaches to learning anatomy: Developing a programme for preclinical medical students. In P. Ramsden (Ed.), *Improving learning: New perspectives* (pp. 178-198). London: Kogan Page.

Entwistle, N. J. (1987). A model of the teaching-learning process. In J. T. E. Richardson, M. W. Eysenck, & D. Warren-Piper (Eds.), *Student learning: Research into education and cognitive psychology* (pp. 13-28). Buckingham: SRHE and Open University Press.

Entwistle, N. J. (1994). Generative concepts and pedagogical fertility: Communicating research findings on student learning. Presidential address to the European Association for Research on Learning and Instruction. *EARLI News*, June, 1994, 9-15.

Entwistle, N. J. (1998). Improving teaching through research on student learning. In J. J. F. Forest (Ed.), *University teaching: International perspectives*. New York: Garland.

Entwistle, N. J. (2000). Approaches to studying and levels of understanding: The influences of teaching and assessment. In J. C. Smart (Ed.), *Higher education: Handbook of theory and research* (Vol. XV, pp. 156-218). New York: Agathon Press.

Entwistle, N. J. (2003). *Concepts and conceptual frameworks underpinning the ETL project*. ETL Occasional Reports, 3 at http://www.tla.ed.ac.uk/etl/publications.html

Entwistle, N. J. (in press). Conceptions of learning and the experience of understanding: Thresholds, contextual influences, and knowledge objects. In S. Vosniadou, A. Baltas, & X. Vamvakoussi (Eds.), *Reframing the problem of conceptual change in learning and instruction*. Oxford: Pergamon.

Entwistle, N. J., Nisbet, J. B., & Bromage, A. (2006). *ETL subject area report on electronic engineering* at http://www.tla.ed.ac.uk/etl/publications.html

Entwistle, N. J., & Peterson, E. R. (2004). Conceptions of learning and knowledge in higher education: Relationships with study behaviour and influences of learning environments. *International Journal of Educational Research, 41*, 407-428.

Entwistle, N. J., & Smith, C. A. (2002). Personal understanding and target understanding: Mapping influences on the outcomes of learning. *British Journal of Educational Psychology, 72*, 321-342.

Eraut, M. (2000). Non-formal learning and tacit knowledge in professional work. *British Journal of Educational Psychology, 70*, 113-136.

Eraut, M. (2004). Transfer of knowledge between education and workplace settings. In H. Rainbird, A. Fuller, & H. Munro (Eds.), *Workplace learning in context* (pp. 201-221). London: Routledge.

Fransson, A. (1977). On qualitative differences in learning. IV – Effects of motivation and test anxiety on process and outcome. *British Journal of Educational Psychology, 47*, 244-257.

Gibbs, G. (1992). *Improving the quality of student learning*. Bristol: Technical and Educational Services.

Halldén, O. (1999). Conceptual change and contextualisation. In W. Schnotz, S. Vosniadou, & M. Carretero (Eds.), *New perspectives on conceptual change* (pp. 53-66). Oxford: Pergamon.

Harré, R. (2002). *Cognitive science: A philosophical introduction*. London: Sage.

Hounsell, D. J. (1987). Essay-writing and the quality of feedback. In J. T. E. Richardson, M. W. Eysenck, & D. Warren-Piper (Eds.), *Student learning: Research into education and cognitive psychology* (pp. 109-119). Buckingham: SRHE and Open University Press.

Kelly, G. A. (1955). *The psychology of personal constructs*. New York: Norton.

Kember, D. (1996). The intention to both memorise and understand: Another approach to learning? *Higher Education, 31*, 341-354.

Magnusson, D. (1984). The situation in an interactional paradigm of personality research. In V. Sarris & A. Parducci (Eds.), *Perspectives in psychological experimentation: Towards the year 2000* (pp. 211-233). Hillsdale, NJ: Erlbaum.

Marton, F. (1976). What does it take to learn? Some implications of an alternative view of learning. In N. J. Entwistle (Ed.), *Strategies for research and development in higher education* (pp. 32-43). Amsterdam: Swets & Zeitlinger.

Marton, F. (1981). Phenomenography: Describing conceptions of the world around us. *Instructional Science, 10*, 177-200.

Marton, F., & Booth, S. (1997). *Learning and awareness*. Mahwah, NJ: Erlbaum.

Marton, F., Hounsell, D. J., & Entwistle, N. J. (Eds.). (1984). *The experience of learning*. Edinburgh: Scottish Academic Press (Second edition, published in 1997 but now out of print, is available at http://www.tla.ed.ac.uk/resources/EoL.html).

Marton, F., & Pang, M. F. (2006). On some necessary conditions of learning. *Journal of the Learning Sciences, 15*, 193-220.

Marton, F., & Säljö, R. (1976). On qualitative differences in learning: I. Outcome and process. *British Journal of Educational Psychology, 46*, 4-11.

McAlpine, L., Weston, C., Berthiaume, D., & Fairbank-Roch, G. (2006). How do professors explain their thinking when planning and teaching? *Higher Education, 51*, 125-155.

McCune, V., & Hounsell, D. J. (2005). The development of students' ways of thinking and practising in three final-year biology courses. *Higher Education, 49*, 255-289.

Meyer, J. H. F. (1988). Student perceptions of learning context and approaches to studying. *South African Journal of Higher Education, 2*, 73-82.

Meyer, J. H. F. (1991). Study orchestration: The manifestation, interpretation and consequences of contextualised approaches to studying. *Higher Education, 22,* 297-316.

Meyer, J. H. F. & Land, R. (Eds.). (2006). *Overcoming barriers to student understanding: Threshold concepts and troublesome knowledge.* London: Routledge.

Norton, L., Richardson, J. T. E., Hartley, J., Newstead, S., & Mayes, J. (2004). Teachers' beliefs and intentions concerning teaching in higher education. *Higher Education, 50,* 537-571.

Perkins, D. N. (2002). *King Arthur's round table: How collaborative conversations create smart organisations.* New York: Wiley.

Perkins, D. N. (2006). Constructivism and troublesome knowledge. In R. Land & J. H. F. Meyer (Eds.), *Overcoming barriers to student understanding: Threshold concepts and troublesome knowledge.* London: Routledge.

Perkins, D. N., & Blythe, T. (1994). Putting understanding up front. *Educational Leadership,* February, 1994, 4-7.

Perry, W. G. (1970). *Forms of intellectual and ethical development in the college years: A scheme.* New York: Holt, Rinehart and Winston.

Prosser, P., Martin, E., Trigwell, K., Ramsden, P., & Lueckenhausen, G. (2004). Academics' experiences of understanding of their subject matter and the relationship of this to their experiences of teaching and learning. *Instructional Science, 31,* 1-21.

Prosser, M., & Trigwell, K. (1999). *Understanding learning and teaching: The experience of higher education.* Buckingham: SRHE and Open University Press.

Ramsden, P. (Ed.). (1988). *Improving learning: New perspectives.* London: Kogan Page.

Ramsden, P. (1991). A performance indicator of teaching quality in higher education: The course experience questionnaire. *Studies in Higher Education, 16,* 129-150.

Ramsden, P., & Entwistle, N. J. (1981). Effects of academic departments on students' approaches to studying. *British Journal of Educational Psychology, 51,* 368-383.

Richardson, J. T. E. (2000). *Researching student learning: Approaches to studying in campus-based and distance education.* Buckingham: SRHE and Open University Press.

Richardson, J. T. E. (2005). Students' perceptions of academic quality and approaches to studying in distance education. *British Educational Research Journal, 31,* 1-21.

Shulman, L. (2005). *The signature pedagogies of the professions of law, medicine, engineering and the clergy: Potential lessons for the education of teachers.* Paper presented at a workshop held at the U.S. National Research Council's Center for Education, February 6-8, 2005, and posted at the website of the Carnegie Foundation for the Advancement of Teaching at http://hub.mspnet/index.cfm/11172

Svensson, L. (1977). On qualitative differences in learning. III - Study skill and learning. *British Journal of Educational Psychology, 47,* 233-243.

Säljö, R. (1979). *Learning in the learner's perspective. I. Some common-sense conceptions* (Report 76). Gothenburg: University of Gothenburg, Department of Education.

Tait, H., Entwistle, N. J., & McCune, V. (1998). ASSIST: A reconceptualisation of the approaches to studying inventory. In C. Rust (Ed.), *Improving student learning: Improving students as learners.* Oxford: The Oxford Centre for Staff and Learning Development, Oxford Brookes University.

Thomas, P. R., & Bain, J. D. (1984). Contextual dependence of learning approaches: The effects of assessments. *Human Learning, 3,* 227-240.

Trigwell, K., & Prosser, M. (1991). Improving the quality of student learning: The influence of learning context and student approaches to learning on learning outcomes. *Higher Education, 22,* 251-266.

Trigwell, K., Prosser, M., & Taylor, P. (1994). Qualitative differences in approaches to teaching first-year university science. *Higher Education, 27,* 75-84.

Trigwell, K., Prosser, M., & Waterhouse, F. (1999). Relations between teachers' approaches to teaching and students' approaches to learning. *Higher Education, 37,* 57-70.

Vermunt, J. D. (1998). The regulation of constructive learning processes. *British Journal of Educational Psychology, 68,* 149-171.

Vermunt, J. D. (2005). Relations between student learning patterns and personal contextual factors and academic performance. *Higher Education, 49*, 205-234.

Vermunt, J. D., & Verloop, N. (1999). Congruence and friction between learning and teaching. *Learning and Instruction, 9*, 257-280.

Watkins, D., & Hattie, J. (1985). A longitudinal study of the approaches to learning of Australian tertiary students. *Human Learning, 4*, 127-141.

Wiske, M. S. (Ed.). (1998). *Teaching for understanding: Linking research with practice*. San Francisco: Jossey-Bass.

Student Learning and University Teaching, 19–30
BJEP Monograph Series II, 4
© 2007 The British Psychological Society

The British Psychological Society

www.bpsjournals.co.uk

2 – Towards a pedagogical theory of learning

Ference Marton*

University of Gothenburg, Sweden

This chapter describes the early stages of developing a theory of learning, which offers an alternative perspective to those currently underpinning teaching and learning. It is not specific to higher education; indeed, it has been developed mainly from work at school level. However, the ideas are sufficiently general to apply to teaching and learning at university level, and there are already some examples of research in universities based on the theory. As it is still being developed, the status of 'theory' has yet to be attained: what is offered is better thought of as a 'framework', a way of thinking about learning within educational contexts. Its importance lies in directing the teacher's attention to the specific *object of learning* – the actual content of what the student is expected to learn. The theory also suggests in general terms what is needed to make learning possible, and so is a *pedagogical* theory which has generally been referred to as *variation theory*, for reasons which will become clear.

The work had its roots in the phenomenographic research which described the different ways in which students see and make sense of important concepts, principles or phenomena met in their studying (Marton & Booth, 1997). Typically, these investigations identified five or more distinct conceptions existing among the groups of students interviewed. However, at that stage, the research was essentially descriptive and did not provide direct help for teachers about the implications of these importantly different conceptions for teaching. The new theory helps to explain how we learn to make sense of the world around us in terms of different phenomena, aspects and categories. It describes how we learn to see the world in different ways and is complementary to both phenomenography and other theories of learning. Above all, it involves teachers in thinking critically about how they present topics and what they have to do to ensure that learning is made easier for the students.

One of the problems with traditional ways of thinking about learning is that human memory has been viewed in too mechanistic a way, imagined as various 'boxes' which can be accessed as required to transfer previously coded material from long-term memory into working memory. Our approach is to think in terms of *awareness*, and to

*Correspondence should be addressed to Professor Ference Marton, University of Gothenburg, Box 300, 405 30 Gothenburg, Sweden (e-mail: ference.marton@ped.gu.se).

DOI:10.1348/000709906X162433

recognize that our perception of past events, and hence our memories, are continuously being modified, by reflecting on those events in the light of new experiences. Therefore, our theory begins by exploring the nature of the awareness involved in coming to see a phenomenon or topic in an importantly new way, and leads to questions about what we need to do in order to learn how to handle new situations in more powerful ways. If we are able to handle a situation in a more powerful way, we must first *see* it in a powerful way, that is discern its critical features and then take those aspects into account by integrating them together into our thinking simultaneously, thus seeing them holistically. In addition, to discern those critical features, we must have experienced a certain pattern of variation and invariance in the object of learning. A medical student, for example, has to listen to the hearts of many different patients before any sense can be made of the differences heard, while to say anything interesting about the taste of a certain wine, we must first have tasted many different wines.

The practical meaning of the theory changes with the specific object of learning. The most fundamental thing about learning is that we learn different things. A pedagogical theory, which is to be practically efficient, must be sensitive to *what* is learned and this is exactly what variation theory provides. It focuses on the significance of experiencing the *variations* in an object of learning without which understanding is logically impossible. To learn about the meaning of democracy, for instance, students have to experience a certain pattern of variation and invariance. They must familiarize themselves with forms of government other than democracy and also with different forms of democracy. To develop empathy, though, a quite different pattern of variation and invariance is necessary. They must have tried to see the same thing from different perspectives and different things from the same perspective, while to understand the idea of the mathematical proof they must have seen two different proofs, at the very least. The aim of the our theory is to make theoretical tools available for analysing the extent to which the necessary conditions for achieving specific aims for learning are present in certain situations. Then, these tools can also be used to create necessary conditions to achieve those aims.

Discussions on learning and teaching in educational institutions are often about what general conditions are favourable, or not, for learning, but variation theory is different. When questions are raised about why students succeed or not, it is – as a rule – assumed that it is possible, in principle, for all students to learn what is being taught. However, this rarely happens in practice. Nobody can learn to solve new problems if they have never encountered any problem for themselves, without a teacher being there to explain how it is supposed to be solved. Nor can anybody adjust their way of expressing themselves in written language to different situations if they have previously written for only one situation. If the teacher gives a proof of the Pythagoras theorem on the board, and does only that, the students will find it impossible to understand the meaning of 'to prove a mathematical proposition', as then the *idea* of a mathematical proof cannot be distinguished from a single proof for a specific proposition. At least two proofs are needed to do that, and at least two different proofs are required if the same proposition is to evoke the idea that there might be different proofs for the same proposition.

Learning and discernment

Learning to discern the critical features of concepts, of problems or situations, is a crucial form of learning in higher education. In addition, it is an ability many students find it difficult to acquire within academic disciplines. Learning to discern, distinguish, make new distinctions, in a metaphorical sense, amounts to learning to 'see', and more importantly, to see in a different and more revealing way. Our capacity to discern and focus on different aspects of an idea or topic is quite limited. We discern and focus on only a few aspects at the same time, and people differ in the aspects they see as salient. A way of seeing can be defined in terms of the aspects which are discerned and focused on simultaneously, and so people may share the same perception, or may have quite different ones.

Variation theory is concerned with learning to see something in a new way, but there are, of course, other important forms of learning. We not only need to learn to tell colours apart, but we must also be able to name them in a consistent way. We not only need to understand the idea of democracy, but we also have to remember what specific forms exist in different countries. Understanding the idea of mathematical proof is not sufficient as we also have to be able to spell 'Pythagoras'. Education involves learning facts and details, but here we are concerned only with the type of learning that involves changing our way of seeing important aspects of the world around us.

Variation and simultaneity

To be able to discern differences, we must first experience variation. However, that variation must also be experienced in ways which enable us to compare the instances alongside each other, in other words, simultaneously. To experience green as distinct from red, both colours must be present, together, in our awareness. If we were to focus on them one at a time, without being aware of, or remembering, the other, we could never experience any difference, any variation. If a woman seems tall to us, she does so against the background of all other women whom we have met before and who, so to speak, co-exist with her in our awareness. This kind of simultaneity in experience, a kind of simultaneity over time, is also needed if we are to experience a melody. The different tunes must co-exist in our awareness, otherwise we would hear each tune by itself and not any distinguishable melody.

However, there is another kind of simultaneity which is necessary for seeing something in a certain way. As there are generally several characteristic features that we must discern and focus on in order to see something in a certain way, *simultaneity* is necessary in the experience of those different aspects at the very same point in time, that is not *over* time but *in* time. If two people look at the same thing and discern the same critical features, but one of them is focusing on all these features simultaneously, while the other does so one at a time, the two people see the same thing in two very different ways.

The object of learning and the space of learning

Learning is always the learning of something. This something, as we have seen, is the *object of learning*. This is often seen simply in terms of content: equations of the second degree, photosynthesis, forms of government, the most frequent religions and so on. These certainly can be objects of learning, but we need to draw attention to different senses in which an object of learning can exist in classroom contexts.

The content of learning can be seen as the *direct object of learning*, but often the teacher expects the student to learn how to use that object or work with it in some way. If the students' attention is to be focused on what they are expected to learn, the teacher has also to be concerned with the capability that the students are meant to develop. What are they expected to be able to do with the direct object? The nature of the intended capability is the *indirect object of learning*. The object of learning as a whole thus comprises the indirect and the direct object – the *how* and the *what* of learning, as described in phenomenography (Marton & Booth, 1997). The object of learning brings together capabilities and content, for example, '*to be able to solve* equations of the second degree', '*to understand* photosynthesis', '*to be able to see* similarities and differences between different forms of governments', '*to be able to see* different religions *in terms of* what unites them and what sets them apart'. The capabilities, 'to be able to solve . . .', 'to understand . . .', 'to be able to see . . . in terms of . . .', are the indirect objects.

At this stage, what we have is an object of learning seen from the teacher's perspective – the *intended object of learning*. However, the intended learning objective has to be realized in practice. The object of learning is not only about what *should* be learned but also what *can* be learned in the situation as it exists in the classroom. Although there is great emphasis these days on formulating precise learning objectives or 'intended learning outcomes', it is not the objectives, as words, that affect the students; it is how the object of learning is presented and brought to life within a lecture, tutorial or other teaching–learning activities – what the students encounter is what makes it *possible* for them to learn. We call this the *enacted object of learning*, which is constituted by the teacher and students together, within a teaching–learning event. The actions of the teacher and the students together create a 'space' within which learning can take place, as described more fully in *Classroom Discourse and the Space of Learning* (Marton & Tsui, 2004).

In order to find effective ways of arranging for learning, researchers first need to address *what* it is that should be learned in each case, and find the different conditions that are conducive to different kinds of learning. It is only when we have a fair understanding of what learners are expected to learn, what they actually learn in those situations and *why* they learn something in one situation but not in another that pedagogy becomes a reasonably rational set of human activities. In other words, we need to become more analytical and systematic in ensuring that we are setting up situations in which it *really* is possible for students to learn. And for this, it is important that the enacted object of learning can be described in terms of a theory. And that such a theory should make clear for the students what is worth noticing and what is not.

The enacted object of learning should thus indicate what aspects of the object of learning are possible to learn under given conditions. Therefore, following our previous argument, for every object of learning it must be possible to identify a certain pattern of variation and invariance that the learners must experience in order to learn effectively. This does not imply that this is the *only* necessary condition, as there is a mutual responsibility in teaching and learning between the teacher and the students. It is also necessary that the students actively focus their attention on the object of learning. These two conditions are not independent of each other: students are able to focus their attention better on the object of learning if the conditions provided make it possible for them to make sense of it, to 'appropriate' it. However, here we are concentrating on just the pattern of variation which is a necessary, but not sufficient, condition for learning to happen.

The enacted object of learning has been described, so far, from the point of the view of an outside observer who is looking at the scenario from a theoretical perspective. However, we must also ask what the object of learning is like from the point of view of the students, in other words the *lived object of learning*. If we are to discover how certain ways of seeing develop, we must consider what aspects of the object of learning the students discern and focus on simultaneously. In other words, it is a description of how the researcher aided by these theoretical tools perceives the students' ways of experiencing the object of learning (i.e. what aspects they discern and focus on simultaneously).

As we have seen, learners can discern a certain aspect of the object of learning if they experience variation in a dimension of that aspect. When students discern and focus on those critical aspects of the object of learning, which are possible to recognize in a particular situation, their lived object of learning becomes equivalent to the enacted object of learning. Such an identity is far from always the case, however, as students do not always make use of all the possibilities that the situation affords.

We have now pointed to three different forms of the object of learning and their equivalents:

> *intended object* – learning objective;
> *enacted object* – the space of learning;
> *lived object*   – outcome of learning.

Of course, we might try to do without the term 'the object of learning', but we want to emphasize that we have to deal with three distinct forms of this same thing. But what is this 'same thing'? The object of learning comprises all the possible dimensions that in principle could be discerned, but, as we can never specify all the different ways in which something can be seen, 'the object of learning' remains a theoretical concept of which the different forms are just parts.

What is critical for students' learning?

Pedagogical discussions are often about how learning is organized. What is the best way of going about lectures, group work, individual studies and so on? How good is project work, problem-based learning? By now it should be obvious that, first, a certain way of organizing learning cannot be the best for all forms of learning, that is the best regardless of the purpose. Secondly, it should be obvious that it is important *how* the content is taught. In problem-based learning, even with the same learning objectives, the quality of the problems and thereby the student's learning, may vary a great deal. That is true also of other forms of teaching, such as the lecture, where the same content may be dealt with in entirely different ways, with consequent differences in the students' learning.

We have carried out a large number of studies in Hong Kong schools since 1998 (Chik & Lo, 2004; Marton & Tsui, 2004). In all of these, we have studied how the same object of learning is handled in different classrooms (two or more) and in most cases we have also investigated the learning results and made comparisons between classes, trying to understand the differences found. In every study, we managed to establish a close relationship between how the object of learning was handled and what the students learned from the lessons, that is between the enacted and the lived objects of learning. In some classes, the lessons proved to have a higher 'learning value' for a certain object of learning than in others, as the students could appropriate the object of learning much better. When we compared lessons with the same intended object of learning but which differed in terms of learning value, we found that the variation in results is a function of the *variation provided* in the pedagogical dimension of the content or subject. We can never say that a lesson is better than another lesson in any absolute sense, but we can say that one is a better resource for a specific learning aim than the other.

Although most of the work using variation theory has been carried out in schools, we can give two illustrations of studies in higher education which have made use of at least some of the evolving principles. The first comes from research into medical education, while the second is drawn from a doctoral thesis that looked at differences among university teachers of accounting.

Medical education

This study was not based on the variation theory itself, but the method used involved comparing and contrasting critical features of an object of learning. Hatala, Brooks, and Norman (2003) compared two conditions for learning interpretation skills for ECGs. Following a sequential presentation of three typical ECG diagnoses (myocardial infarction, ventricular hypertrophy and bundle branch blocks), illustrated by two examples each, two groups of students engaged in the practice of those diagnoses under two different conditions. One of these was called 'non-contrastive': the students had to examine 4 new cases exemplifying each diagnosis, for one diagnostic category at a time (12 cases all together). In the other condition, called 'contrastive', the same 12 cases were mixed and the students were encouraged to compare them. In the non-contrastive condition, the students were primarily focusing on what was common for each diagnostic category, while in the contrastive condition the students focus was necessarily on how the diagnostic categories differed. When using six novel cases to be diagnosed as a test, students from the contrastive group clearly outperformed those from the non-contrastive group.

> [In the contrastive practice], students were encouraged to compare and contrast the difference in the features between the competing diagnoses . . . [and this proved relatively] more effective in helping students notice the types of features that discriminate between competing diagnostic alternatives. . . . The contrastive approach should be applicable to other perceptual and/or diagnostic domains where noticing features is an important component of the task, and the list of competing alternatives for a given diagnosis is limited.
> (Hatala et al., 2003, pp. 23–24)

Accountancy education

In this second example, it is possible to interpret the study more directly in the light of variation theory. The focus was on how differences in the ways in which the topic was treated affected what students came to understand about the topic. Rovio-Johansson (1999) followed three lecturers teaching accounting at university level, video-recording three parallel 2-hour lectures for each one of the three different topics. After each lecture, she interviewed five students about the topic dealt with. From analyses of the data, she could detect a pattern running through the three teachers' ways of teaching. As Bowden and Marton (1998) explained in commenting on an earlier phase of the study, one of the lecturers addressed the topics at a concrete, technical level, aiming at the development of the students' capability to solve certain types of problem, defined in advance. The second tried, throughout the lecture, to situate each topic within a theoretical framework, aiming at a deep understanding of the concepts and principles used, while the third lecturer moved between general formulations and specific instances of the same problems, aiming at developing students' capabilities for making and grounding rational economic decisions.

These differences can be illustrated in relation to the first topic investigated – the limiting factor in production. This refers to the factor in the production process, which limits the total capacity (given that there are relatively greater resources available as far as the other factors are concerned). The three teachers planned the lecture together. After an introduction, a problem was presented and worked through by the teachers. Discussion, mainly carried through by the teacher, followed and the lecture was concluded. In the problem, the limiting factor, which in this case was the machine hours available, was identified. Then, a decision had to be made about how to decrease the demands on machine hours by buying something ready-made instead of producing it 'in-house'. The choice had to be based on optimal contribution to profit.

There were clear-cut differences found among the three teachers, even though the content of the lecture was well defined, and the staff had planned it together and worked through the very same problem. Furthermore, the content of the lecture could be considered fairly elementary and straightforward. Still, the differences were striking. The first teacher talked about the problem, while going through the solution on the board, concentrating on the problem in isolation. The teacher moved between the actual production process referred to in the problem and the method for dealing with the problem. The focus was thus on the problem-solving process, rather than on a specific solution within a defined context.

The second teacher opened up several dimensions of variation in the introduction and talked about different cost concepts, not only the ones immediately relevant to the actual problem, and about different ways of deciding what costs to allocate to different component parts in the production process. This teacher also pointed out the relativity of the system of accounting itself, explaining that different systems will give you different kinds of information, and therefore 'opening up' a dimension of a variation corresponding to how the system for calculating the outcome was set up, by showing that it could be done in different ways.

The third teacher gave a variety of different examples from several companies (this is certainly a dimension of variation) and opened up a dimension of variation corresponding to the way in which costs are determined. Like the second teacher, he also went through the different cost concepts and not only those which applied to costing in the actual case. Furthermore, he made the point that there are other ways for setting prices in addition to calculus, and that finding the appropriate way may vary from case to case.

Therefore, there were differences in what was taken for granted and what was opened up as a dimension of variation. These differences were reflected in the interviews with the students. While four out of the five students who had listened to the first teacher focused on the specific example given, when discussing the limiting factor, they all talked about 'machine hours'. In contrast, the students who had listened to the other two teachers dealt with the question in more general terms. Also, there were distinct differences in how the students went about solving the problem about the limiting factor during the interview. Although, to solve the problem, it was essential to discern the effect of the limiting factor on the relationship between profitability and profit, students who had been listening to different lecturers approached the problem differently. Students of the first teacher saw the problem from a point of view of the effect of the limiting factor on the relationship between the process of production and the contribution to profit; students of the second teacher concentrated on the effect of the limiting factor on the relationship between costs or expenses (such as variable and incremental expenses) and on contribution to profit, while students of the third teacher were more concerned about the effect of the limiting factor on the relationship between costs and pricing and on contribution to profit (Rovio-Johansson, 1999).

From this example, we can argue that it is not so much how the *teaching* is organized (in lectures, project work, problem-based learning, etc.), but how the *content* is organized that is of decisive importance for the students' learning. The point is not, however, that a particular form of organization (pattern of variation and invariance) is better than another in general, nor that more variation is better than less variation. The point is that *what varies, and what is invariant*, are the most important aspects of how the content is organized; and how the content is organized decides on what conditions learning might or might not take place. (For a detailed treatment of the actual theory of learning, see Bowden & Marton, 1998; Marton & Tsui, 2004).

Differences between conditions and between individuals

In the detailed studies in school classrooms in which we had deliberately set up conditions to test variation theory, not all students in the experimental groups managed to learn effectively, while some students in the comparison groups, in which, according to variation theory, it ought to have been impossible to learn, still managed to learn. This is hardly surprising, of course, but it does seem problematic for the theory. And yet, we must remember that the expression 'impossible to learn' is used in the sense of 'impossible to discern', and 'impossible to discern' means 'impossible to discern from what the learner could experience and discern *in that particular situation*'. Still, it is of course, entirely possible that some students have already been able to discern a certain aspect which is invariant in the specific situation. For example, someone who has seen different colours before would, of course, notice that everything has the same green colour in a room without any contrasts at all. The contrast resides in previous experiences which are present in awareness together with all the green here and now.

It is also possible that a learner can discern something which has never been discerned before and which is not possible to discern in the actual situation. Take, for instance, the object of learning 'to understand the idea of mathematical proof', at its most basic level. Obviously, it takes two instances at least to separate the idea of mathematical proof from the specific proof that the student has happened to encounter. Imagine, for instance, a lecture in which only one proof is presented and thus the separation of the idea of proof from the actual proof is not made possible. However, think of a student who has seen only one mathematical proof before and thus never been aware of the idea of mathematical proof. Now if that student encounters another example and if, at the same time, is aware of the proof seen before, all of a sudden it becomes possible to separate the proof from the idea of the proof. This oversimplified example points to an interesting principle, namely the complementarity between the variation experienced by the students previously and the variation they can experience in a certain situation. If, after a lecture, a student can discern a certain critical aspect of the object of learning, that could be because it had been done before, because it had been learned during the lecture or because a combination of experiences before and during the lecture had created the necessary conditions.

Making learning possible

If we can tell whether or not learning is possible under certain given conditions, then we should also be able to create the conditions that make learning of a certain kind possible. Doing so also implies putting the theory to the test. Some such attempts have been made and with remarkable results. These studies (Holmqvist, Gustavsson, & Wernberg, 2005; Lo, Pong, & Chik, 2005; Marton & Pang, 2006) show, first, that when the learners have the opportunity to experience the pattern of variation necessary for learning something, they are successful to a much greater extent than when the necessary pattern of variation has not been provided. This may sound tautological, but it did show, first, that there is a certain necessary pattern of variation for every object of learning to which students are introduced, and secondly, that an appropriate pattern of variation has been found in each particular case.

The theory should be useful in all situations where the learning objective is of the kind we are discussing here. However, the problem is that the implications of the theory vary with the object of learning. Its meaning has to be interpreted for every particular case and for every specific object of learning. And the only way of doing so is by ensuring that the teachers themselves are engaged in the work of finding the necessary patterns of variation for the different objects of learning.

An approach similar to this can be seen in the Japanese 'lesson study' which Stiegler and Hiebert (1999) drew to international attention when they suggested it as a possible explanation for the uniquely high achievements of Japanese students in mathematics and science. 'Lesson study' is a traditional form of in-service training of teachers in Japan. A group of teachers, who teach the same subject and who work together, choose a specific object of learning (learning target) and try to find the best way to help the students to appropriate it. They design a lesson or a series of lessons for this purpose and produce collaborative lesson plans. A member of the group then carries out the lesson in his/her own class, while the others observe the lesson, analyse and discuss what has happened, before developing a new design and lesson plan, which another member of the group carries out, again observed by the others. After yet another analysis and discussion, they document their experiences in such a way that other teachers can profit from them. Even if 'experts' from the outside have been invited to join the group, the work with lesson study is rooted in teachers' own experiences, rather than in any theory. In addition, as a rule, there is no external systematic evaluation.

The idea of 'design experiments', introduced by Collins (1992) and Brown (1992), was based on the premise that you cannot use scientific experiments (varying one factor at the time, while keeping the other constant) to test conjectures about teaching, as factors in teaching cannot be disaggregated. There is a whole set of interacting factors within the design. We have then to look for the effects of such a design, through comparisons with other designs and through the accumulation of experience through a systematic series of adjustments to the teaching. A design experiment is theory-based and aimed at testing theoretical conjectures about the complex situations of pedagogical reality.

By combining the ideas of lesson study and design experiment, we have found a new way of developing pedagogical insights, namely *learning study* (Lo *et al.*, 2005). It is carried out by a group of teachers, preferably together with a researcher, with the aim of achieving a certain pedagogical goal or object of learning. The group tries to find a powerful way to achieve this aim through several cycles of improvement along the lines of the lesson study model but, in this case, the work is based on a specific theory. Moreover, the lesson is preceded by a test of what the students already know, followed by a test of what they have actually learned. All this is like a design experiment approach, except that here the teachers 'own' the study themselves; they choose the object of learning and the way to handle it, but are guided by the theory and supported by a researcher.

The different lessons are, of course, carried out in different ways. This variation in the enacted object of learning can then be related to the lived object of learning, that is to the students' results. In the end, a document is produced, which is useful both for teachers' practice and for continued research. Every study is a way of trying out the conjectures that originate from the theory on which the experiment was based.

'Learning study' is advantageous for all three groups involved: students achieve a better grasp of the object of learning, teachers understand how an object of learning can be handled and researchers find out how the theory works in concrete instances. Learning study is not defined in terms of a certain object of learning or a certain theory, but presumes *some* object and *some* theory. The advantage of the theory of variation is that it changes with the object of learning and if it can be formulated in a sufficiently clear and comprehensive way, it constitutes a powerful resource for the teachers (and for the researchers too) in handling the many varying objects of learning.

No research findings about learning study are yet available for higher education, but the idea of lesson study is currently being used as the main vehicle for the improvement of the quality of learning and teaching at the University of Wisconsin (see http://www.uwlax.edu/soft/lsp). There are, nevertheless, good reasons why lesson study – or even better, learning study – in higher education could have a marked impact on student learning. If the way in which the content is dealt with is the single most important factor that constrains the effectiveness of learning, then alerting university teachers to the idea of 'different ways of dealing with the content' must be beneficial. In addition, to recognize the importance of that idea they must be able to see the effects of variation in ways of dealing with the same content. When university teachers start looking at their colleagues' ways of dealing with the same content that they themselves have taught, and when ways of dealing with content become a topic of conversation for them, then an important step towards the improvement of university teaching and learning will have been taken. Lesson studies and learning studies are just two of the ways of making this happen.

The variation theory of learning

As stated at the beginning of this chapter, variation theory aims at making theoretical tools available for the teachers themselves. The theory is not seen so much as a set of eternally true statements about reality, but as an instrument for handling that reality for specific purposes and in more powerful ways than it can be done without using these tools, other things being equal. The aim is to make a form of learning possible, learning, which means that new and more powerful ways of seeing certain phenomena, or certain classes of situations, are developed. This form of learning is considered fundamental to how the meaning of different things develops and changes in people. However, are our examples actually about this form of learning?

To see something in a certain way depends on discerning certain critical features and bringing them together in awareness simultaneously. That awareness is not of the totality of the world we experience, but what is necessary and critical for our specific purposes in relation to an object of learning. It is the discernment of critical features which distinguishes one way of seeing something from another and – as a rule – provides a more powerful way of seeing the same thing. Unlike phenomenology, the theory neither aims at capturing the experienced world in all its richness nor seeks to describe the structure and workings of the human intellect, as cognitive psychology does. The theory is driven by an interest in pedagogical knowledge, the question of why someone learns what someone else fails to learn. The reasons can lie, in part, in genetic predispositions, prior knowledge, motives and so on, but variation theory describes the conditions which are needed for appropriating specific objects of learning. We do not want to argue that these conditions are the most important factor, but we do say that they are necessary and that to create them is, has been, and is going to be, central for teachers, whether in schools or higher education (cf. Carlgren & Marton, 2000).

Hence, in the end, variation theory is about differences in capabilities between, and within, human beings. And we argue that the differences in capabilities have to do with people's opportunities for discerning aspects of the world around them through experiencing variation, that is differences in these aspects. This is what Pang (2002) calls the 'two faces of variation'. He alludes to the fact that what we call the theory of variation describes how people experience variation in different aspects of the world around them and therefore experience that world in different ways. And it has sprung from the research programme of phenomenography, which also describes variation (i.e. differences) in people's ways of seeing and experiencing their world. The strictly descriptive research approach of phenomenography is thus being transformed into a theory, which explains the earlier descriptive results. This means, hopefully, that we have taken some steps towards the development of a *pedagogical* theory of learning, which should be valuable to both teachers and researchers, and which can be used to encourage collaboration between teaching colleagues in exploring the critical features of important concepts, and the variations in those features that need to be made explicit for students if the quality of their learning is to be improved.

Acknowledgements

The writing of this chapter was financially supported by the Swedish Research Council. Noel Entwistle, the Editor of this book, was extremely generous in trying to make this chapter more accessible to its readers for which I feel a deep sense of gratitude.

References

Bowden, J., & Marton, F. (1998). *The university of learning*. London: Routledge Falmer.

Brown, A. L. (1992). Design experiments: Theoretical and methodological challenges in creating complex interventions in classroom settings. *Journal of the Learning Sciences, 2,* 141–178.

Carlgren, I., & Marton, F. (2000). *Lärare av imorgon*. Stockholm: Lärarförbundet.

Chik, P. P. M., & Lo, M. L. (2004). Simultaneity and the enacted object of learning. In F. Marton & A. B. M. Tsui (Eds.), *Classroom discourse and the space of learning* (pp. 89–110). Mahwah, NJ: Lawrence Erlbaum.

Collins, A. (1992). Toward a design science of education. In E. Scandlon & T. O. Shea (Eds.), *New directions in educational technology* (pp. 15–22). Berlin: Springer.

Hatala, R. M., Brooks, L. R., & Norman, G. R. (2003). Practice makes perfect: The critical role of mixed practice in the acquisition of ECG interpretation skills. *Advances in Health Sciences Education, 8,* 17–26.

Holmqvist, M., Gustavsson, L., & Wernberg, A. (2005). *Learning patterns*. Paper presented at the 11th biennal Conference of the European Association for research on Learning and Instruction, Nicosia, Cyprus, August 23–27.

Lo, M. L., Pong, W. Y., & Chik, P. P. M. (Eds.). (2005). *For each and everyone: Catering for individual differences through learning studies*. Hong Kong: Hong Kong University Press.

Marton, F., & Booth, S. (1997). *Learning and awareness*. Mahwah, NJ: Lawrence Erlbaum.

Marton, F., & Pang, M. F. (2006). On some necessary conditions of learning. *Journal of the Learning Sciences, 15*, 193–220.

Marton, F. & Tsui, A. (Eds.). (2004). *Classroom discourse and the space of learning*. Mahwah, NJ: Lawrence Earlbaum.

Pang, M. F. (2002). Two faces of variation. *Scandinavian Journal of Educational Research, 47*, 145–156.

Rovio-Johansson, A. (1999). *Being good at teaching: Exploring different ways of handling the same subject in Higher Education*. Göteborg: Acta Universitatis Gothoburgensis.

Stiegler, J., & Hiebert, J. (1999). *The teaching gap: Best ideas from the world's teachers for improving education in the classroom*. New York: Free Press.

Student Learning and University Teaching, 31–48
BJEP Monograph Series II, 4
© 2007 David Perkins

The
British
Psychological
Society

www.bpsjournals.co.uk

3 – Theories of difficulty

David Perkins*

Harvard Graduate School of Education, USA

Both educational researchers and experienced teachers develop what might be called theories of difficulty. A strong theory of difficulty identifies learners' characteristic trouble spots for a particular area of instruction and includes some causal analysis of why they occur toward improved teaching and learning. The literature on learning and development offers numerous ways of understanding conceptual difficulties, as well as recognizing problems of ritualized knowledge, inert knowledge, knowledge too foreign for learners to engage it readily, and tacit knowledge, the partly unconscious nature of which poses learning challenges. In a number of studies, a strong theory of difficulty has led to improved learning. In everyday teaching, teachers' response to recurrent difficulties may fall short. One not uncommon reaction is to blame the learners' weaknesses and simply keep teaching in the same way. Another better reaction is to 'teach harder', lavishing more time and attention on characteristic difficulties without any causal analysis of what makes them problematic. Most effective is to 'teach smarter' based on a causal analysis refined through experience. The construction of informal theories of difficulty is an important part of the craft of teaching.

In theory there is no difference between theory and practice. In practice there is

Yogi Berra, baseball player, coach and manager

One of the most important questions educators can ask falls into just four words: What makes this hard? For example, consider understanding the nature of understanding itself. What makes that hard? For many years I have taught a graduate course on cognitive psychology and its implications for teaching and learning, with the nature of understanding an important theme. Many students initially think of coming to understand something – say, a concept in physics or philosophy – as a matter of 'getting it.' This reflects notions of understanding-as-possession and understanding-as-immediate-perception deeply entrenched in common parlance, as shown by usages like capturing or holding on to an idea, seeing the point, or seeing what someone means (Perkins, 1998). These notions misleadingly suggest that teaching for understanding is a matter of providing enough information and support to carry most learners past the threshold where things click. On the learner side of the

---

*Correspondence should be addressed to Professor David Perkins, Harvard Graduate School of Education, Appian Way, Cambridge MA 02138, USA (e-mail: david_perkins@gse.harvard.edu).

DOI:10.1348/000709906X162442

equation, many learners sustain a 'you either get it or you don't' mindset, which, when the conceptual going gets tough, leads them to give up or to settle for remembering key facts and routines' (Dweck, 2000).

This shallow but magnetic getting it conception of understanding makes it hard to develop a more sophisticated conception of understanding. Hence, I target the difficulty. I make explicit the contrast between the getting it model and a more incremental model where understanding develops through a series of active thinking-centred experiences (Perkins & Unger, 1999; Wiske, 1998). I give examples. I ask students to classify cases. Most importantly, I ask them to construct their own examples in the context of design tasks that put a premium on the richer conception of understanding.

There is absolutely nothing unusual about this story. Experienced teachers of physics know that students are likely to muddle up mass and weight or mass and density, and take special pains to pre-empt the confusions. Teachers of second languages know that the deeply habituated grammar of students' first language contaminates that of the second language, so they make moves to correct this. Teachers of history know that students are likely to view historical events through contemporary eyes rather than putting on the mindset of the past, a problem generally called presentism, so they teach in ways that build awareness of today's biases and prior worldviews.

In other words, as educators we formulate what might be called *theories of difficulty* about the content we teach: what parts are difficult and what causes the difficulty. From there, we organize our teaching to target the difficulties. This is a part of our role as active alert professionals, formative evaluators of our own pedagogy, diagnostic observers of our students' performance and enthusiastic gardeners in the fields of our craft.

Of course, theories of difficulty are not just the province of the educator in the classroom. Considerable educational research deals with what amount to technical theories of difficulty. For half a century, investigators have charted a range of misconceptions that plague the learning of science all the way through the university level, offered interpretations of why these misconceptions occur, and explored ways of teaching and learning that combat them. Developmental psychologists from Piaget on have proposed a variety of stage-like theories of the growth of the young mind, arguing that concepts of varying complexity become accessible in stages, as the learner develops mental schemata and sufficient mental bandwidth to code them and so on.

One way or another, theories of difficulty get a lot of attention, which suggests that they are at the same time both important and problematic. The importance is easy to see. A good theory of difficulty, whether the informal construction of a practitioner or the formal analysis of a psychologist, not only identifies what aspects of a content area are troublesome but reveals the underlying causes, pointing the way to more powerful instruction.

However, theories of difficulty are problematic as well. On the research side, the lively debate characteristic of scholarly inquiry certainly marks the research on science misconceptions, developmental trajectories and other areas alluded to above. On the frontlines of the classroom, theories of difficulty can simply misdiagnose the true natures of a difficulty or prove shallow, or get dismissed in favour of other causes, such as poorly prepared students.

All this means that as educators we ought to give theories of difficulty a careful look. What is a theory of difficulty more precisely? What sorts of theories of difficulty are there? Can theories of difficulty powerfully inform instruction? How can they prove problematic and what to do about the problems?

What is a theory of difficulty?

Theories of difficulty focus on the persistent difficulties of learning that nag us educators year after year. These come in a dismaying range of shapes and sizes. There are the examples given earlier, the inertia of familiarity (the getting it model of understanding), the conflation of neighbouring concepts (mass and weight), overextension (first language syntax contaminating second languages) and the assimilation of new information to old frameworks (the problem of presentism in teaching history). Then there is encapsulation (students learn the official story for the classroom, but that's not what they think things are really like), ritualization (students know the ritual of, say, long division or designing a certain standard electrical circuit, without more general understanding), resistance (as against foreign cultures or strange ideas) and so on.

However, a theory of difficulty is much more than just a list of trouble spots. It also includes some account of how those spots cause trouble, where the conflation or overextension or ritualization or resistance or whatever comes from. Sometimes the answer is pretty obvious. It's natural to muddle up close together concepts like weight and mass, natural to overextend the familiar, like the syntax of your first language. However sometimes, as we will see later, the causes of the difficulties run considerably deeper than that. Anyhow, without at least some sort of an informal causal model, one does not have much of a theory of difficulty.

One thing theories of difficulty are not, not quite, is theories of pedagogy. Ideas about the ideal shape of pedagogy make up an important part of any educator's repertoire. Such ideas concern how to organize the teaching–learning process for good results. They incorporate recommendations about the kinds of activities likely to foster learning, the nature and organization of information supportive of learning, matters of pace and sequence and so on.

A theory of difficulty contrasts with a full-scale theory of pedagogy in a very straightforward way: The two have different objects. A theory of pedagogy concerns the teaching–learning process itself, but a theory of difficulty concerns the hurdles of content. It foregrounds what parts or aspects of content persistently prove troublesome for learners and why. In itself, a theory of difficulty provides no blueprint for better learning, any more than ideas about gravity and friction and acceleration provide a blueprint for putting a satellite into orbit. However, a good theory of difficulty defines the design challenge, posing specific pedagogical problems we can then try to address.

A theory of difficulty relates to pedagogy in another way as well. It assumes that what might be called 'pretty good pedagogy' is already in operation. Pretty good pedagogy means good in a generic way, but not fine-tuned by a theory of difficulty for the specific troubles of the specific content.

The most important point about pretty good pedagogy is that, lamentably, it cannot be taken for granted. For some quick ideas about pretty good pedagogy, Perkins (1992) offered four basics of pedagogy under the name Theory One: clear information, thoughtful practice, informative feedback and intrinsic or extrinsic motivation. Perkins framed these as obvious conditions for learning, a first-order conception of pedagogical principles that deserved attention because it was in actual practice so often neglected. Perkins (1992) also sketches how beyond Theory One considerations lie more pretty good pedagogy in the form of various versions of constructivist pedagogy, which recommends engaging learners in ways that lead them to grapple with the ideas and information in play and to a degree make their own meanings.

Theories of difficulty make little sense without pretty good pedagogy. It is fruitless to ask what aspects of Fractions Arithmetic or Newtonian Physics or Greek Civilization or Macroeconomics bother students in the context of a fundamentally weak teaching and learning process. Naturally, learners will show many sorts of confusions and misunderstandings, with no way to tell which troubles reflect the knottiness of the content and which the naughtiness of slack instruction. Although it is all too easy to fool ourselves as practitioners that we are truly exercising pretty good pedagogy, nonetheless most fundamentally theories of difficulty concern the challenges of content left over when we are.

Theories of conceptual difficulty

People in many different roles have good reason to pay attention to theories of difficulty: researchers on learning and human development, researchers in disciplinary specialties, instructional designers, teachers in any discipline at any age and even students. With so many constituencies, it's hardly surprising that theories of difficulty range far and wide: some technical, some more for practical use, some spelled out, some informal; some interdisciplinary and some focused on particular disciplines. Here and in the next section, I will foreground a few of the more articulated theories of difficulty advanced by scholars and educators as they puzzle over what persistently make learning hard.

When we think of knowledge being difficult, perhaps we think first and foremost of knowledge that is conceptually difficult, confounding and evasive not just in a surface way, as when science co-opts terms from natural language and gives them a technical meaning, but in some fundamental manner.

Developmental theories of conceptual difficulty

Many notable theories of conceptual difficulty have what might be called a structural-developmental character. They find beneath the surface structural features of the content tied to characteristic patterns of child and adult development. The classic example of this comes from the work of Piaget *et al.* and Inhelder who pretty much founded the field of developmental psychology, as it is now understood (Inhelder & Piaget, 1958). They observed that learners of various ages encountered systematic difficulties with certain kinds of content. Their model traced the difficulties back to logical structures imbedded in the content, for instance the logical structure of being able to see and enumerate all possible combinations of something, or to examine independently the influence of multiple influences on something, generally called control of variables. They argued that in the course of time, through experience and development, learners acquired certain logical schemata that allowed encoding these aspects of content. Learners without the schematic repertoire simply were not equipped to understand the target content at a deep level.

As a theory of difficulty, the Piagetian tradition locates difficulty in the mismatch between the schematic repertoire of the learner and the often hidden structural presumptions of the content. Since the original work of Piaget and Inhelder, a number of scholars have challenged the specifics of their model. However, developmentalists, looking at both children and adults, have advanced models in the same general spirit, often questioning the original claim that the logical structures in question cut across domains and develop more or less at the same time (e.g. Case, 1992; Fischer, 1980; Kegan, 1994; Loevenger, 1976; Perry, 1970).

For example, Case (1992) proposes *central conceptual structures* in areas such as number and narrative. The conceptual structure for number includes the mapping from number labels to sets with that number of elements, the ideas of successor and predecessor as one more and one less and so on. According to Case, it is the construction of the central conceptual structures that equips learners to understand the more sophisticated aspects of the materials that they encountered. Although the details of the developmental model differ considerably from that of Piaget and Inhelder, the resultant theory of difficulty has much the same character: Learners encounter trouble when the content they face involves structures they are not yet equipped to encode.

For another example, William Perry (1970) focuses on development during the college years, proposing that students' attitudes towards knowledge vary widely, from a 'there's a right answer and I need to learn it' mindset through a view that knowledge is relative and highly contextual to a view that commitment is essential but always undergoing some reconstruction. How a student responds to the character of particular content as well as the style of instruction reflects the student's place in this sequence. Students early in their development are likely to approach knowledge framed as uncertain and under construction with an unproductive mindset, expecting the teacher to know and straightforward answers to be discovered eventually.

Epistemic theories of conceptual difficulty

While considerable work with a structural orientation has a developmental cast, other researchers have looked to the underlying logic of content without so much emphasis on the trajectory of a maturing child and more on the epistemology of the disciplines, their distinctive patterns of constructing concepts and theories, and conducting inquiry and offering evidence.

Generations of researchers on science learning have thrived in this area. Chi (1992), striving to understand the difficulties that even college students have with grasping fundamental concepts in science suggests that accommodating certain concepts requires what she terms an *ontological shift*, a shift in the fundamental kind of thing or stuff in play. For instance, students tend initially to understand electrical circuits through a substance conception, an electrical substance flowing into wires to fill them. A better understanding (although still incomplete) comes from a process conception that sees the entire electrical circuit as subject to a constraint system, Ohm's laws, with electricity in all parts of the circuit falling into the pattern specified by the constraints (Chi, 1992; Slotta & Chi, 1999).

Also puzzling over difficulties in science understanding, diSessa (1993) points to *phenomenological primitives* or *p-prims* for short, somewhat simplistic schemas very helpful as practical guides in many circumstances but also misleading, often standing in the way of more sophisticated insight. For example, diSessa characterizes one such p-prim as 'dying away', the sense people have that motion and some other phenomena naturally peter out, without needing any special causal explanation like friction for this behaviour. This p-prim interferes with understanding Newtonian principles of motion among other things.

Resnick (1994, 1996) examines the difficulties that learners encounter with phenomena where there is no central causal agent. For example, people tend to think that the queen bee rules the hive, whereas the complexity of hive behaviour is emergent, the collective consequence of relatively simple rule systems displayed by the worker and other bees that in interaction produce complex hive behaviour.

Feltovich, Spiro, and Coulson (1993) analyse what they term *advanced knowledge acquisition*, learning beyond facts and routines but short of true expertise. They focus on the case of medical learning, identifying a number of factors that rendered concepts and conceptual systems more challenging for learners. The authors propose eight dimensions of difficulty: concreteness/abstractness, discreteness/continuity, static/dynamic, sequentiality/simultaneity, mechanism/organicism, separability/interactive-ness, universality/conditionality and linearity/non-linearity. The more a misconception falls towards the simpler ends of these continua and the more a sophisticated conception falls towards the complex end, the greater the learning challenge.

Grotzer (2003) and Perkins and Grotzer (2000, 2005) offer an analysis of several types of complex causality. Their model emphasizes how students face challenging concepts in science expecting relatively simple one domino knocks over another patterns of causality with relatively visible agents. In contrast, many scientific models involve hidden mechanisms, complex rather than domino-like causal relationships, probabilistic rather than deterministic mechanisms and in the spirit of Resnick, distributed rather than centralized causality. The authors argue that problems with complex causality underlie many of the surface misconceptions that students from elementary school through university display around science concepts.

What can be said here of science learning can be said more generally. By and large, the trouble generated for science learning by ontological shifts, phenomenological primitives, emergent phenomena, complex causality and other factors show up also in, for instance, economics, engineering and history.

Threshold concepts as loci of difficulty

As a final example, Meyer and Land (2003) develop the idea of *threshold concepts*, concepts especially pivotal to a stage-like advance in understanding a discipline. Mastery of a threshold concept opens up a new world of understanding in the discipline to students. Examples mentioned by Meyer and Land for the university level include opportunity cost from economics, limits and complex numbers for mathematics, and signification within literary and cultural studies.

Threshold concepts are likely to seem foreign and conceptually difficult. They may be treated by students, or indeed teachers, in ritualized ways that avoid some of their challenges but also sacrifice their transformative potential. The idea of threshold concepts is an invitation to instructors to look deeply into their disciplines and into their teaching experience, identifying likely threshold concepts and investing special attention in helping students to master them.

Learners' response to conceptual difficulty

Besides recognizing the theories of conceptual difficulty themselves, it's worth examining the students' response to conceptual difficulty. Very often, their response takes the form of a coping strategy of oversimplification, flattening out the depth and the nuances and settling for a relatively routine and superficial version of the knowledge in play.

For example, Entwistle (2003) examines the alternative ways students approach the challenges of difficult material. Intrinsic interest, a priority placed on understanding, and ideas and evidence thoughtfully analysed towards building understanding all mark a deep approach to learning. The contrasting surface approach emphasizes memorization and procedural learning, provoked by fear of failure and wanting to look good. Entwistle also contrasts strategic study with its careful time management and eye on strong grades with more haphazard approaches.

Dweck (2000) looks to students' tacit theories of intelligence as a way of understanding the way they engage the content. Learners with an *entity theory* of intelligence see themselves as having a limited capacity to accommodate complexity, leading to a 'either you get it or you don't' mindset and early quitting or withdrawal to a surface approach when the learning gets difficult. Students with an *incremental theory* of intelligence, in contrast, see their capacity as subject to expansion and work away at challenges bit by bit.

Feltovich *et al.* (1993) note a number of dispositions in learners that lead to the loss of depth and nuance. Some examples include taking analogies too literally, treating a snapshot of a moment in a process as representing adequately the whole process, taking a particular principle as accounting for all of a phenomenon when it only accounts for part, and treating a very multidimensional phenomenon as reflecting only one or a few dimensions.

All these authors acknowledge some students' predilections towards simplifying and routinizing complexity, but they all also caution that instructional styles often open the door to students with such leanings and not uncommonly practically shove them through it through instructional practices that settle for facts and routines as 'good enough' and reinforce stereotypes such as 'math is the toughest subject' or 'girls are not good at math.'

Other theories of difficulty

The disciplines bring with them the abundant conceptual difficulties, but other sorts of difficulty as well. Perkins (2006; see also 1992, 1999 for earlier versions) offered a rough taxonomy of five types of persistently troublesome knowledge, examining their relationship to constructivist pedagogy: conceptually difficult knowledge, ritual knowledge, inert knowledge, foreign knowledge and tacit knowledge. Let us take a look at the last four here.

Ritual knowledge

The earmark of ritual knowledge is its meaningless and routine character. Ritual knowledge gets expressed in a mechanical way, by saying the right thing and doing the right thing, with limited understanding of the story underneath or the appropriate range of application outside the academic context. It's what we say and do to score the right answer. The names and dates of history are often little more than the ritual knowledge, although of course they can act as attachment points for important understandings. The algorithms of arithmetic, such as the notorious invert and multiply method of dividing fractions, typically have this ritual character.

Both for students and for teachers, ritual knowledge often functions as an adaptive strategy for avoiding the real conceptual difficulties of a topic as outlined in the previous section. An elegant example of this comes from science education researcher Marcia Linn (2002), who relates with relish a particular student's take on a Newtonian principle: 'Objects in motion remain in motion in the classroom, but come to rest on the playground.' We can see here diSessa's (1993) earlier mentioned p-prim of 'dying away' in full robust operation. Another example, this one for mathematics, illustrates how students can come to terms with the classroom environment in ways that evade deep learning.

> I know what to do by looking at the examples. If there are only two numbers I subtract. If there are lots of numbers I add. If there are just two numbers and one is smaller than the other it is a hard problem. I divide to see if it comes out even and if it doesn't I multiply. (Taba & Elzey, 1964)

These and many other students who resort to ritual knowledge deserve some credit for practical intelligence. Plainly they have figured out how to game the system and if that seems short-sighted on their part it's also worth remembering that the pattern of typical instruction is all too easy to game.

Inert knowledge

Another common problem of learning is *inert knowledge*, knowledge easily cued up by a direct question or a test item but not activated in general context of potential application (Bereiter & Scardamalia, 1985; Bransford, Franks, Vye, & Sherwood, 1989). For example, students may learn something about statistics and probability in classrooms, yet in everyday contexts rarely think about whether they really have enough of a sample for a conclusion or what the baseline probabilities are likely to be for one interpretation of a situation versus another. The patterns of learning characteristic of much of education – focusing on a particular text, doing the problems at the end of a chapter, paying little attention to applications outside the walls of the institution – are almost a recipe for inert knowledge.

Such a failure of connection-making is also often expressed as a problem of *transfer of learning*, learning theory's term for the way learning around one topic or skill in one context impacts on another, either positively or negatively (positive transfer vs. negative transfer). We educators routinely expect considerable positive transfer; what we teach and what our students learn will impact their lives in all sorts of ways. Students of history will become wiser in their interpretations of current events; students of economics will manage their finances better and so on. However, considerable research on transfer of learning warns that we get far less transfer than we want (e.g. Cormier & Hagman, 1987; Detterman & Sternberg, 1992; Salomon & Perkins, 1989).

Foreign knowledge

Difficulty with understanding new content often arises because current belief systems are comfortably familiar and sometimes deeply entrenched, making the new content appear bizarre or alien. An example mentioned earlier is the problem of presentism in teaching history. Students tend to view the past events through the lens of contemporary understandings, not easily putting on the mindsets of times and cultures past (Carretero & Voss, 1994). A practice or decision that through modern eyes might seem cruel or obtuse often takes on a very different meaning when understood contextually. For example, the historical Middle Eastern practice of punishing theft by cutting off the thief's hand may seem vicious today, but in a time where there were no jails and no reliable way to extract fines, what forms could punishment take? The more severe alternative was death, an action that also could easily trigger a clan feud. Thus situated, the practice becomes more reasonable (Charfi, 2005).

As this example hints, an even more acute version of foreign knowledge arises when people come up against contemporary frames of reference very different from their own. This is a common reaction when people discuss their views in contexts of conflict, with the hope of some kind of conflict resolution (Salomon, 2004). The barriers lie not in the logical complexity of the belief and value systems of the other culture, which are indeed no more intricate than one's own, but in the way those beliefs and values clash with the precious core of one's own identity.

Tacit knowledge

Recognizing the presence and the role of tacit knowledge is a fundamental challenge for educators. Polanyi (1958) and many later writers have underscored the importance of tacit knowledge in human thought and action. In normal practice, a great deal of the disciplinary 'game' of what counts is a good question, what inquiry looks like, what serves as evidence, and so on, is likely to be tacit. There are of course important efficiencies in relegating routine expectations and patterns of practice to the undercurrents, as Polanyi emphasizes. Moreover, the normally tacit operation of this game is not so much of a problem in apprenticeship situations, including the kinds of doctoral study where students participate in ongoing research. There, the rich social contexts can enculturate the young learner. However, in more formal settings, even at the university level, the tacit game of the discipline is likely to be much less in evidence and many students simply miss out on it.

Educators have found many ways of labelling the hidden demands of disciplinary understanding, towards surfacing them and sharing them with learners. McCune and Hounsell (2005) and many others refer to the *ways of thinking and practising* or *WTPs* that various disciplines require, emphasizing the challenge of not just remembering content and applying stepwise methods but embracing the logic and the spirit of discipline. Entwistle, Nisbet, and Bromage (2005) point to the *inner logic of the subject and its pedagogy* in examining electrical engineering, beginning with the WTPs characterizing the core demands of the discipline and connecting those with typical patterns of pedagogy addressing those demands.

In the same vein Schwab (1978) and Bruner (1973) discuss the *ways of knowing* and Perkins (1994, 1997) treats the *epistemic games* or *epistemes* of disciplines. For instance, mathematics looks to formal proof for evidence, science to experimental verification, literary studies to evidence from the text and context, history to artifacts and critically interpreted testimony. At a general level, these scholars make much the same point: It is all too easy to learn a fair measure of a discipline's facts and routines without really developing a sense of how the game is played. Without such a sense, the discipline will never truly be understood.

The difficulty of too many difficulties

There are other theories of difficulty as well, too many, one might say. What good is such a jungle of theories to educators on the front lines? Many of them are full of jargon, hard going for the disciplinary specialist who has no particular interest as such in epistemes or stages of cognitive development or ontological shifts. For another, with all these theories in view, which one is right?

The technical character of many of these theories of difficulty, especially those of a structural and epistemological character, is a very real challenge, but also is something of an artifact of what's written for what audiences. It's certainly possible to discuss any of this work in more commonsensical ways. Phrases like *inert knowledge, troublesome knowledge, ways of thinking and practising, the inner logic of the subject, complex causality* and *threshold concepts* by design as well as their track records user-friendly.

As to which theory is right, the answer is that the question itself is not quite right. These various theories of difficulty are not truly rivals in the sense of the face-off between the phlogiston and the oxygen theory of combustion. Instead, several theories of difficulty might apply at the same time. A common confusion in studying physics could reflect a mix of some broad stage-like phenomenon, and lack of familiarity with the sorts of causal models involved, and the tacit character of the epistemology of physics in much instruction, and a weak hold over an earlier threshold concept important to understanding the concept at hand.

If this seems to face educators and educational designers with a formidable problem of choice and judgment, it's worth remembering that essentially analogous problems of choice and judgment prove commonplace in professional and everyday life. When we make a medical decision or an investment decision or cast our vote, we routinely recognize that a number of factors weigh on one or another side, and we find ourselves in need to make contextual decisions about which factors count for the most. It's not so different with the theories of difficulty. The educators who are by far the worst off are those who have no well-formed theory of difficulty at all – one, remember, that gives a causal account of how the troubles arrive.

How theories of difficulty can inform instruction

In the world of Candide, where all is for the best, theories of difficulty would always lead to substantially better learning. However, it's not that simple and for two rather simple reasons. First off, you need not just a theory of difficulty but a good one. Your theory may say 'The butler did it' when in fact it was the chauffeur. Second, a theory of difficulty explains where persistent difficulties come from without writing a recipe for what to do about it. Not only does that require a further ingenious step, but also some theories of difficulty seem much more actionable than others. In other words, there is absolutely no reasons to view theories of difficulty as magic wands waved over the troubles of learning that make them go away.

With the hard realities acknowledged, it's important to reassure us that the theories of difficulty can serve the goals of education powerfully indeed. Four quick examples follow representing relatively diverse theories of difficulty.

Central conceptual structures

Mentioned earlier was Robbie Case's developmental model of central conceptual structures in areas like number and narrative. One offshoot of this work was an intervention called Rightstart (Griffin, Case, & Capodilupo, 1995). The intervention focused on kindergarten children the majority of who showed an understanding of number markedly below that of their peers.

Through a range of activities, Rightstart sought to build-up basic understandings of small numbers, for instance the mapping from number labels like 'three' to sets with three items, the notion that four was the successor of three and corresponded to a set with one more item and so on, all this of course pursued in everyday language with concrete hands-on materials. Comparison of control and treatment groups revealed that children participating in the Rightstart treatment performed much better on several transfer tasks involving number that varied markedly from the activities used in the instruction. Perhaps the most removed of these was simple sight-reading in music, which involved the subtask of counting to find the right note.

Complex causality

Also mentioned earlier was a model of complex causality, mapping how students' difficulties in understanding science and other concepts reflected the way those concepts often involved in hidden mechanisms, interactive rather than domino-like causal relationships, probabilistic rather than deterministic influences and distributed rather than centralized causality (Grotzer, 2003; Perkins & Grotzer, 2000, 2005).

Grotzer *et al.* constructed a number of interventions based on this model and conducted formal experiments examining whether elementary school students benefited from them. The comparison groups received carefully designed active learning experiences with hands-on experimentation – pretty good pedagogy! – without introducing ideas about complex causality. In contrast, the treatment group instructors introduced ideas about complex causality pertinent to the target concepts in question, not didactically but in interactive inquiry-oriented ways.

Across a series of experiments on various science topics, the students under the complex causality conditions displayed considerably greater understanding of the target concepts (e.g. Basca & Grotzer, 2001; Grotzer, 2004; Grotzer & Basca, 2003; Grotzer & Sudbury, 2000; some studies are summarized in Perkins & Grotzer, 2005). For instance, in a study of the understanding of electrical circuits involving fourth graders, most students experiencing a combination of activities and discussion designed to foster relevant concepts of complex causality achieved the most sophisticated rating of understanding on post-interviews, whereas in control groups few did (Grotzer & Sudbury, 2000; Perkins & Grotzer, 2005).

Dodging entrenchment

Another, rather different challenge of learning is entrenchment, as when learners hold fast to a belief system with strong personal and cultural roots. Here the suggestion sometimes arises that learning can be more effective when it does not directly address the cases closest to learners' homes and hearts.

A striking experiment in this direction occurred when researchers arranged for some Israeli 12th grade students to study the Northern Ireland conflict in a four-month programme (Lustig, 2002 as cited in Salomon, 2004). The programme foregrounded the different perspectives on the two sides of the Northern Ireland conflict, but the Israeli–Palestinian conflict was never mentioned. At the end of the programme, the students were asked to write two essays: one describing an Israeli–Zionist position and the other a Palestinian position. Results were compared with a non-treatment control group of Israeli students. The students who had studied Northern Ireland proved much more able to write fully developed essays expressing the Palestinian viewpoint, used the first person more in doing so, and included more terms related to the potentials of conflict resolution.

Teaching for transfer

As noted earlier, transfer of learning is a common challenge for the teaching–learning process, particularly for transfer, where the context of application differs considerably from the context of learning. Some authors have gone so far as to suggest that significant for transfer simply does not occur very much. It is not in the nature of the human mind to make such connections with any facility.

Salomon and Perkins (1989) questioned this conclusion through an analysis of a number of studies testing for transfer of learning. Although there were many findings of non-significant transfer, there were also some clear instances of substantial transfer. Why did transfer occur on some occasions and not on others? Salomon and Perkins pointed out that the differences could be explained by examining the conditions of teaching and learning. As a broad trend, transfer of learning appeared when the conditions of learning supported it directly with such elements as: thorough learning of the ideas or skills in the first place, prompts for deliberate connection making, practice in diverse contexts, encouragement of metacognition and so on. Transfer failed when the teaching–learning scenario included few elements to support it, assuming that somehow it would 'just happen' because the potential connections were there to be made.

These glimpses of theories of difficulty in action tell a consistent story about how they can help the practical business of education. Such theories of difficulty explain their various difficulties in ways that point to what teachers might do about them. Central conceptual structures not in place? Introduce activities that build them up. Understandings of core science concepts elusive? Engage learners in learning about the underlying causal models they presume. Entrenchment a problem? Get at the topic through cases far from home, less likely to trigger defences. Transfer not occurring? Include elements in the instruction that calculatedly foster the connection-making learners are not so likely to make if left entirely to their own devices.

Yes, theories of difficulty can be powerful indeed. However, they also have difficulties of their own.

How theories of difficulty are problematic

When I teach my course on cognitive psychology and teaching and learning, I routinely ask students to construct theories of difficulty for their individually chosen design projects. Like any teacher, I don't always get what I want. The idea of theories of difficulty has its own difficulties! I can count on a number of students offering for a first pass remarkably thin accounts of the difficulties inherent in the topics they've chosen to address for their design projects, accounts like 'The children have problems because the ideas are so complex', or 'The subject in itself isn't motivating.'

The problem is that complexity and tediousness are just not very diagnostic conceptions. Hence, I nudge them towards something more diagnostic: 'You need a theory of difficulty for your topic that really belongs to it and digs into its particularities, rather than a theory of difficulty that would sound pretty much the same for a thousand other topics.' And yes, it helps.

'It's complex' is a shallow theory of difficulty and not the only kind of shallowness one can find in the turbulent swim of educational practice. Here is a little list.

- *Overgeneral:* Like our 'it's complex' example.
- *Topic instead of cause:* We notice within the sweep of the subject matter particular consistent trouble spots – in mathematics at various levels ratios or word problems or factoring or integration by parts. On that basis, we strive to teach harder by

spending more time, but not in a very targeted way for lack of a causal theory about what makes them difficult.

- *Symptom instead of cause:* This comes a little closer to causes without quite getting there. Recalling the list of symptoms mentioned earlier, it's certainly useful to pinpoint just what sorts of difficulty students display: failure of transfer, conflation of key concepts, resistance to new frameworks and so on. With that in mind, again we can teach harder to try to correct the symptoms. However, the lack of a causal theory puts a limit on what can be done.
- *Formulaic fix:* The craft of teaching offers plenty of formulas for fixing particular problems. 'Well, when my students show that kind of problem, here's what I do.' Routines of this sort can be very useful, but again they have limited flexibility in place of a more general causal understanding of what's going on.

All of these fall short of a full-fledged theory of difficulty, but they do lend a certain focus to the teaching–learning process. Far more removed from a good theory of difficulty is blaming something outside the content altogether. Perhaps the all-time favourite here is to blame the students. 'Kids today spend too much time watching television.' 'College today is all about beer and dates.' 'Nothing in their backgrounds prepares them for this.' 'The previous teacher should have laid a better foundation.'

Two other common targets of blame are time and resources. 'If only I had more time, with so much to cover.' 'If only we had a really good text.' 'If only we had more computers.'

What's tricky about such attributions of difficulty is their, sometimes, truth: Many students do have weak backgrounds, available time is certainly a major influence on learning, some texts are much better than others and the artful use of technology can be an important resource. However, projecting the difficulty on the students or the conditions often provides an escape route from the specific difficulties of the content, looking to something one can't change rather than to something that one can.

All that is a view from practice about what makes theories of difficulty challenging. However, the troubles don't stop there. Researchers and educational designers face plenty of vexations of their own. First of all, when you want a theory of difficulty, you want the right one of course, but figuring out which one is right can be just as troublesome here as in any discipline.

The so-called reading wars about how best to teach reading give us a classic case in point. In the public arena of education, those wars played out as a polarized rivalry between phonics and whole language instruction, an emphasis on helping youngsters crack the code of phonetic spelling vs. an emphasis on the holistic act of reading. Snow and Juel (2005) recount how behind this politicized debate lies a long history of technical research into the nature of reading development, with serious scholars articulating theories and advancing evidence on both sides of the case. Today it has become clear that some version of phonics usually needs to play a serious role in the early development of reading, although the richness of whole-language kinds of instruction appears to be tremendously important for the maturation of reading skills and positive reading attitudes. The point is that it's taken a long time and considerable serious scholarship to sort out what might appear to be a simple question.

Thus yes, researchers and educators can struggle mightily to resolve the right theory of difficulty between direct rivals. However, as warned earlier, the landscape is generally messier than that anyway. Alternative theories of difficulty very often are not direct rivals at all. They point to potential contributing causes, with maybe the one or the other but often some complicated mix doing the mischief.

Another conundrum for researchers is that the deepest theories of difficulty are not necessarily the most helpful. Theories of difficulty have a double job to do, on one hand to explain how the difficulties arise but on the other hand to suggest in practical terms how to address them. Technically refined theories of difficulty that allude to deep psychological mechanisms may serve the first goal well while the second suffers. Ideally, theories of difficulty need to strike the tricky balance between deep explanation and straightforward functional implications.

Nevertheless, a theory of difficulty will not simply write a recipe for the intervention to go with it. Designers and teachers need to bridge from a theory of difficulty to an intervention, which inevitably involves all sorts of paraphernalia beyond the theory of difficulty itself: activities, materials, pacing and so on. With that comes another bother for the ardent theorist: The success of an intervention is at best a weak test of the validity of the underlying theory of difficul. . An intervention can fail for all sorts of reasons that have nothing to do with the underlying theory, problems of execution, poorly prepared materials, a test population with other problems that trump the target problem and so on. Likewise, an intervention can succeed to a degree for reasons that have little to do with the underlying theory: more focus on the target problem, more time, invigorating student interest and so on.

All in all, the pursuit of good theories of difficulty is a challenging mission, suspended vexingly between the ideal quests of theoretical psychology and sociology and the pragmatic workaday craft of practitioners. Aiming to serve them both, this pursuit gets caught up in the web of sometimes-conflicting demands they both generate.

Bridging to insight

Theories of difficulty play a conspicuous role and a powerful one in the search for better education. They point to a two-level vision of the teaching–learning process. The foundation is what we've called pretty good pedagogy. However, the trouble with pretty good pedagogy is that it is never quite good enough. It always leaves a residue of persistent trouble spots: conflations, omissions, overgeneralizations, failures of transfer and so on.

This residue demands the refinement of the second level. For *really* good pedagogy, we need to add a theory of difficulty that identifies the trouble spots in that particular content, strives to explain them and points towards adjustments in the teaching–learning process to help with them. Thus, theories of difficulty become a natural part of the teaching experience for any discipline at any age, a natural front for teachers learning about their students and their own craft, and a natural part of considerable research on teaching–learning and human development.

This second level involves a learning loop for educators themselves, one traversed in sophisticated or non-sophisticated ways. Figure 1 shows us the options. Indicated in the diagram by 'blame', the least helpful response to trouble spots locates them outside the content and the teaching–learning process itself, blaming the students and blaming the conditions. Therefore, the teacher continues to teach in the same way and the students to learn in the same way, and both suffer the consequences of a loop that generates plenty of frustration but no adaptation. Indicated by 'focus', a

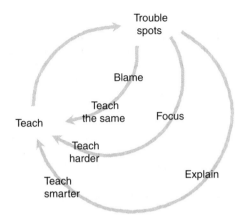

Figure 1. Three responses to troublesome knowledge.

range of responses to the trouble spots prove not so strong on explanation but at least zoom in on the difficulties with more time and attention. And that certainly helps. At least we can teach harder. Finally, indicated by 'explain' a fully developed theory of difficulty looks under the surface to trace the trouble spots to their causes, leading to a fundamentally more powerful teaching–learning process.

What does this mean for the dedicated educator? It's not hard to list a few general heuristics for pursuing this adaptive loop well, along the following lines.

(1) Don't blame the learner or the conditions.
(2) Don't settle for a formulaic fix.
(3) Get beyond the topics to the symptoms.
(4) Get beyond the symptoms to the causes.
(5) For help fathoming the causes, bear in mind ways of constructing typical theories of difficulty (e.g. the underlying epistemic games or inner logic of the discipline and its pedagogy, looking for threshold concepts, ways of thinking and practising) and typical theories of difficulty (e.g. complex causality, entrenchment, tacit knowledge and so on).
(6) Base a pedagogical strategy on your explanation.
(7) Treat it all as an informal hypothesis as you continue to teach and learn.

It may even be that theories of difficulty are a better meeting place for educational researchers and practitioners than pretty good pedagogy. After all, as teachers we already tend to think that we're exercising generally good pedagogy, whether we are or not. However, we all know that there are few problems left over, which prepares us to take a step further. In fact, the line between generally good pedagogy and theories of difficulty is not so sharp, thus attention to theories of difficulty could be something of a Trojan horse for not only attending to difficulties but getting back to some aspects of generally good pedagogy.

One thing for sure, an exploration of theories of difficulty provides abundant justification for the opening quote from Yogi Berra, 'In theory there is no difference between theory and practice. In practice there is.' Yes, there is. However, as the best theories of difficulty show, we can aspire to build a stronger bridge between them.

References

Basca, B. B., & Grotzer, T. A. (2001, April). *Teaching about the nature of causality in a unit on pressure: How does it impact student understanding?* Paper presented at the Annual Conference of the National Association for Research in Science Teaching, Seattle.

Bereiter, C., & Scardamalia, M. (1985). Cognitive coping strategies and the problem of inert knowledge. In S. S. Chipman, J. W. Segal, & R. Glaser (Eds.), *Thinking and learning skills: Current research and open questions* (Vol. 2, pp. 65-80). Hillsdale, NJ: Erlbaum.

Bransford, J. D., Franks, J. J., Vye, N. J., & Sherwood, R. D. (1989). New approaches to instruction: Because wisdom can't be told. In S. Vosniadou & A. Ortony (Eds.), *Similarity and analogical reasoning* (pp. 470-497). New York: Cambridge University Press.

Bruner, J. (1973). The growth of mind. In J. Anglin (Ed.), *Beyond the information given* (pp. 437-451). New York: Norton.

Carretero, M., & Voss, J. F. (Eds.). (1994). *Cognitive and instructional processes in history and the social sciences*. Hillsdale, NJ: Erlbaum.

Case, R. (1992). *The mind's staircase: Exploring the conceptual underpinnings of children's thought and knowledge*. Hillsdale, NJ: Lawrence Erlbaum Associates.

Charfi, M. (2005). *Islam and liberty: The historical misunderstanding*. London: Zed Books Ltd.

Chi, M. T. H. (1992). Conceptual change within and across ontological categories: Examples from learning and discovery in science. In R. Giere (Ed.), *Cognitive models of science: Minnesota studies in the philosophy of science* (pp. 129-186). Minneapolis, MN: University of Minnesota Press.

Cormier, S. M., & Hagman, J. D. (Eds.). (1987). *Transfer of learning: Contemporary research and applications*. New York: Academic Press.

Detterman, D., & Sternberg, R. (Eds.). (1992). *Transfer on trial*. Norwood, NJ: Ablex.

diSessa, A. (1993). Toward an epistemology of physics. *Cognition and Instruction*, *10*(2 & 3), 105-226.

Dweck, C. S. (2000). *Self-theories: Their role in motivation, personality, and development*. Philadelphia, PA: Psychology Press.

Entwistle, N. J. (2003). Enhancing teaching-learning environments to encourage deep learning. In E. De Corte (Ed.), *Excellence in higher education* (pp. 83-96). London: Portland Press.

Entwistle, N. J., Nisbet, J. B., & Bromage, A. (2005). *ETL project subject area report for electronic engineering*, www.ed.ac.uk/etl/publications.html.

Feltovich, P. J., Spiro, R. J., & Coulson, R. L. (1993). Learning, teaching, and testing for complex conceptual understanding. In N. Frederiksen & I. Bejar (Eds.), *Test theory for a new generation of tests* (pp. 181-217). Hillsdale, NJ: Erlbaum.

Fischer, K. W. (1980). A theory of cognitive development: The control and construction of hierarchies of skills. *Psychological Review*, *87*(6), 477-531.

Griffin, S. A., Case, R., & Capodilupo, S. (1995). Teaching for understanding: The importance of central conceptual structures in the elementary school mathematics curriculum. In A. McKeough, J. Lupart, & A. Marini (Eds.), *Teaching for transfer: Fostering generalization in learning*. Hillsdale, NJ: Erlbaum.

Grotzer, T. A. (2003). Learning to understand the forms of causality implicit in scientific explanations. *Studies in Science Education*, *39*, 1-74.

Grotzer T. A. (2004). *The understandings of consequence project report #5: Technical paper*. Unpublished paper, Harvard University, Cambridge.

Grotzer, T. A., & Basca, B. B. (2003). Helping students to grasp the underlying causal structures when learning about ecosystems: How does it impact understanding? *Journal of Biological Education*, *38*(1), 16-29.

Grotzer, T. A., & Sudbury M. (2000, April). *Moving beyond underlying linear causal models of electrical circuits*. Paper presented at the Annual Conference of the National Association for Research in Science Teaching, New Orleans.

Inhelder, B., & Piaget, J. (1958). *The growth of logical thinking from childhood to adolescence*. New York: Basic Books.

Kegan, R. (1994). *In over our heads: The mental demands of modern life*. Cambridge: Harvard University Press.

Linn, M. (2002). *The role of customization of innovative science curricula: Implications for design, practice, and professional development*. Symposium at the annual meeting of the National Association for Research in Science Teaching, New Orleans, LA.

Loevenger, J. (1976). *Ego development: Conceptions and theories*. San Francisco: Jossey-Bass.

Lustig, I. (2002) *The effects of studying distal conflicts on the perception of a proximal one*. Unpublished masters thesis: University of Haifa.

McCune, V. S., & Hounsell, D. J. (2005). The development of students' ways of thinking and practising in three final-year biology courses. *Higher Education, 49*, 255-289.

Meyer, J. H. F., & Land, R. (2003). Threshold concepts and troublesome knowledge (1): Linkages to ways of thinking and practising within the disciplines. In C. Rust (Ed.), *Improving student learning: Improving student learning theory and practice*. Oxford: Oxford Centre for Staff and Learning Development.

Perkins, D. N. (1992). *Smart schools: From training memories to educating minds*. New York: The Free Press.

Perkins, D. N. (1994). The hidden order of open-ended thinking. In J. Edwards (Ed.), *Thinking: Interdisciplinary perspectives*. Victoria, Australia: Hawker Brownlow Education.

Perkins, D. N. (1997). Epistemic games. *International Journal of Educational Research, 27*(1), 49-61.

Perkins, D. N. (1998). What is understanding? In M. S. Wiske (Ed.), *Teaching for understanding: Linking research with practice* (pp. 39-57). San Francisco, CA: Jossey-Bass.

Perkins, D. N. (1999). The many faces of constructivism. *Educational Leadership, 57*(3), 6-11.

Perkins, D. N. (2006). Constructivism and troublesome knowledge. In J. H. F. Meyer & R. Land (Eds.), *Overcoming barriers to student understanding: Threshold concepts and troublesome knowledge* (pp. 33-47). London: Routledge.

Perkins, D. N., & Grotzer, T. A. (2000, April). *Models and moves: Focusing on dimensions of causal complexity to achieve deeper scientific understanding*. Paper presented at the annual conference of the American Educational Research Association, New Orleans.

Perkins, D. N., & Grotzer, T. A. (2005). Dimensions of causal understanding: The role of complex causal models in students' understanding of science. *Studies in Science Education, 41*, 117-166.

Perkins, D. N., & Unger, C. (1999). Teaching and learning for understanding. In C. Reigeluth (Ed.), *Instructional design theories and models* (Vol. II, pp. 91-114). Hillsdale, NJ: Erlbaum.

Perry, W. (1970). *Forms of intellectual and ethical development in the college years*. New York: Holt Rinehart and Winston.

Polanyi, M. (1958). *Personal knowledge: Toward a post-critical philosophy*. Chicago: The University of Chicago Press.

Resnick, M. (1994). *Turtles, termites, and traffic jams: Explorations in massively parallel microworlds*. Cambridge, MA: MIT Press.

Resnick, M. (1996). Beyond the centralized mindset. *Journal of the Learning Sciences, 5*(1), 1-22.

Salomon, G. (2004). Does peace education make a difference? *Peace and Conflict: Journal of Peace Psychology, 10*, 257-274.

Salomon, G., & Perkins, D. N. (1989). Rocky roads to transfer: Rethinking mechanisms of a neglected phenomenon. *Educational Psychologist, 24*(2), 113-142.

Schwab, J. J. (1978). Education and the structure of the disciplines. In I Westbury & N. J. Wilkof (Eds.), *Science, curriculum, and liberal education* (pp. 229-272). Chicago: Rand McNally.

Slotta, J. D., & Chi, M. T. H., (1999, March). *Overcoming robust misconceptions through ontology training*. Paper presented at the Annual Conference of the American Educational Research Association, Montreal.

Snow, C., & Juel, C. (2005). Teaching children to read: What do we know about how to do it? In M. J. Snowling & C. Hulme (Eds.), *The science of reading: A handbook* (pp. 501–520). Oxford: Blackwell.

Taba, H., & Elzey, F. (1964). Teaching strategies and thought processes. *Teachers College Record, 65*, 524–534.

Wiske, M. S. (Ed.). (1998). *Teaching for understanding: Linking research with practice*. San Francisco, CA: Jossey-Bass.

Student Learning and University Teaching, 49–59
BJEP Monograph Series II, 4
© 2007 The British Psychological Society

The
British
Psychological
Society

www.bpsjournals.co.uk

4 – Academics' experiences of teaching and of their subject matter understanding

Michael Prosser[1]*, Elaine Martin[2] and Keith Trigwell[3]
[1]Higher Education Academy, UK
[2]Victoria University, Australia
[3]University of Sydney, Australia

In this paper, we describe the phenomenographic approach to researching teaching and learning, and highlight how it differs conceptually from two other approaches to researching teaching and learning. We illustrate the implications of this approach with an example from a recently completed study of variation in the ways in which university academics' experience the understanding of their subject matter and how this relates to their teaching of the subject matter (Prosser, Martin, Trigwell, & Ramsden, 2005).

Over the last 20 years or so, we have been trying to understand:

- the structural variation in, and relationships between, the ways university students and their teachers experience their teaching and learning in higher education, and, more recently and
- how the teachers' experiences of teaching relate to other aspects of their academic experiences.

Research from the student learning perspective began with the work of Noel Entwistle and his group in Lancaster, England, Ference Marton and his group in Gothenburg, Sweden, and John Biggs in Newcastle, Australia. The key point of departure of this work was, and still is, that it is not the way teachers teach and design their courses, but the way students experience that teaching and the courses offered that is the key determinant of the quality of student learning.

Our research into teachers' experiences of teaching and learning has been supported continuously for the last 15 years by the Australian Research Council (see Appendix A for a list of projects and Appendix B for a selection of the publications from this work). In conducting this research, we have used a variety of approaches – qualitative (phenomenographic analysis and analyses of metaphors) and quantitative

*Correspondence should be addressed to Professor Michael Prosser, The Higher Education Academy, Innovation Way, York Science Park, Heslington, York YO10 5BR, UK (e-mail: mike.prosser@heacademy.ac.uk).

DOI:10.1348/000709906X162073

(factor and cluster analyses and structural equation modelling). In this paper, we focus on the phenomenographic work, outlining how we see this work in relation to other approaches to research that come from a student learning perspective We characterize what we see as the key aspects of a phenomenographic approach and describe the results of some of our latest work as a way of illustrating this approach and discuss implications of the approach for research and practice.

Contrasting models of teaching and learning from a student learning perspective

Research on teaching and learning in higher education, from the student learning perspective, has been conceptualized in three different ways: first, as a causal model (Richardson, in press, and Chapter 5 in this monograph), second, as a systems model (Biggs, 2003) and finally, as a relational model (Marton & Booth, 1997). These three types of models have all been used to help structure research and interpret the results of it, in the differing ways we shall now show.

Causal models define variables relating to teaching and learning independent of each other, and then study the causal relationships between the variables through, for example, path analyses. The constructs represented by the variables are considered to be relatively stable. Figure 1 (from Richardson, 2006) shows such a model with student learning outcomes seen as causally determined by students' perceptions of the academic environment, their study behaviour and their demographic backgrounds.

In a systems view of student learning, the variables representing the constructs are seen as being in continuous interaction with each other, as shown in Figure 2, where the arrows are used to highlight this continuous interaction between learning-focused activities, student factors and teaching context. The relationships are not seen as unidirectional: if students do not understand the material, their lack of understanding may encourage surface approaches to study, but surface approaches may also result in them not understanding the subject matter. The variables of activity and outcome are thus in continuous interaction, and simple cause and effect relationships cannot be determined.

In both the above examples, the variables representing the constructs are defined and measured independent of the others. Any teaching context variable, such as the workload required of students, is defined independent of a variable describing, say, a surface approach to learning. Experience is constituted in terms of a number of interacting and relating, but still independent, parts coming together to form a whole.

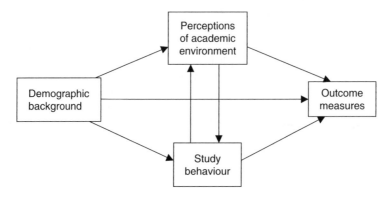

Figure 1. Causal model of influences on student learning.

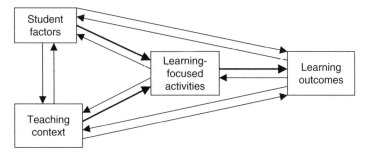

Figure 2. Model of influences on student learning showing continuous interactions.

A relational perspective, in contrast, does not conceive of experience as being made up of a number of separate independent parts causally relating or continuously interacting, but as an indivisible whole. Experience, from this perspective, can be separated into various components, but only for analytic purposes, with parts used only to help us to develop an understanding of the experience. Figure 3 (from Prosser & Trigwell, 1999) shows a model of a relational view of student learning.

From this perspective, student experience is conceived as being composed of a number of aspects which are not necessarily defined independent of each other. Experience is seen, not as a relatively stable entity in cognitive structure, but as a dynamic entity relating the individual to the context in which he or she is situated. At one moment, learning outcomes may be in the foreground of students' awareness, while at another, it may be the way in which they are approaching their studies or it may be their lack of prior knowledge and understanding that is in the foreground. In this view, student experience is thus dynamic and ever changing. If we accept the more complex view of experience outlined by the relational model, how can we then study and come to an understanding of experience in ways that can help to improve it?

A phenomenographic perspective

Phenomenography has developed as a way of understanding the structure of the experience, not at an individual level, but at a collective level. It attempts to identify and map the key differences in the way something is experienced. It does not attempt to describe an individual experience, but the underlying structure of that experience. It neither provides rich, thick, grounded descriptions of individual experiences, nor

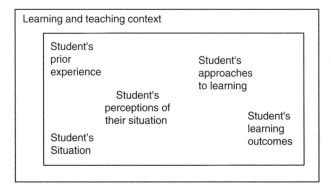

Figure 3. A relational view of student learning.

measures how much something is experienced; however, it maps the qualitative variation in the ways something is experienced, becoming the study of the structure of the variation in those ways of experiencing.

Phenomenography analyses and describes the key differences in the way something is experienced and the logical relationship between those key ways, but it does not describe the variation in *individual* experience but the variation in the experience of individuals at a *collective* level.

The outcomes of a phenomenographic study are:

- a set of *categories of description* (usually in the form of brief descriptions) and
- an *outcome space* describing the structural relationship between the categories (usually in the form of brief descriptions of key aspects of the experience and two-dimensional tables).

The structure is usually, but not necessarily, hierarchical through inclusion of less complex categories within the higher level ones. Experience can be seen as being relational, linking the subject (experiencer) to the object (that being experienced) or, in our own work, involving the relationship between the analyst and what is being analysed – usually a set of transcripts of interviews, indicating that the categories are neither subjective nor objective. While the categories are constituted and given meaning within context (e.g. teachers talking about a real example of teaching), the analysis results in a decontextualized set of categories of description in which are included only the key aspects of the differences in ways of experiencing.

In most of our studies, we have taken a step further than a pure phenomenographic study. We have attempted to locate the individual transcript in the outcome space. Although outcome space is not meant to represent individual variation, we have found it useful to classify individual transcripts within such a space. In addition, because outcome spaces have generally proved to be hierarchically inclusive in terms of increasing complexity, our approach has been to classify the transcript in terms of the most complex experience represented there.

This phenomenographic perspective can now be illustrated through our most recent study.

Relating the experience of understanding subject matter and the experience of teaching

Background to the present study

The present study, part of which is reported here, built on a substantial body of research relating to university teaching and student learning to look at the relationship between the experience of research and teaching as it is mediated by the experience of understanding subject matter. Previous work had found, in essence, that university teachers who used information transfer and teacher-focused approaches to teaching had students with a greater tendency to adopt surface approaches to learning, and reached learning outcomes of less quality, whereas those who used conceptual change and student-focused approaches to teaching had students who were more likely to have deeper approaches to learning with higher quality learning outcomes (Prosser & Trigwell, 1999; Trigwell, Prosser, & Waterhouse, 1999).

In our most recently completed research, we have shown how qualitative variation in the way academics experience their understanding of their subject matter is related to their experiences of teaching (Prosser *et al.*, 2005). We found that student-focused perspectives on teaching are associated with more complex and research-based understandings of subject matter.

Method

In the present study, a total of 37 teachers who were active in research were chosen from major disciplinary areas (Business, Law, Health Sciences, Humanities, Social Sciences, Science and Technology) and were interviewed about their experience of understanding of their subject matter, teaching and their research. The focus of the interviews was upon the subject matter selected by the interviewee and considered by the interviewee to be related to an aspect of their research and to one of their areas of teaching. Here we report on the results of the analysis of their experiences of teaching and understanding their subject matter.

Each teacher was interviewed, in depth, and the interviews were transcribed and analysed rigorously using analytical procedures developed previously for similar phenomenographic studies (Marton, 1981). The analysis was conducted in two stages and the results of the first stage are reported here. The aim of the first stage was to identify the qualitative variation in the experiences of the teaching and understanding of subject matter, as described in these transcripts, using the previously reported categories of description in these areas as a guide. In the second stage, the focus was on the new phenomenon of the experience of research (Prosser *et al.*, 2006).

The categories were then used to classify all the transcripts, with some subsequent adjustment to the categories and their structure to ensure that they captured the full variation represented there. The empirical relationship between the experience of understanding subject matter and the experience of teaching was then examined using a cross-tabs analysis.

Results from the present study

The categories of description of the experience of teaching constituted from our analyses of the 37 interview transcripts are shown below.

The act of teaching is experienced as:

Category A: Teacher-focused with the intention of transferring information to the students: subject matter is concrete, taken for granted and seen as being independent *parts* or topics.

Category B: Teacher-focused student activity with the intention of transferring information to students: subject matter is concrete, taken for granted and seen as a series of related topics or as *parts that are related to other parts*.

Category C: Teacher-focused student activity with the intention of enabling students to acquire the concepts of the discipline: subject matter is a concrete and connected structure of topics with *parts that are related to other parts*.

Category D: Teacher-focused student activity with the intention of enabling students to acquire the concepts of the discipline: subject matter is a concrete and connected structure within a discipline or field, with *parts being related to a whole* (field).

Category E: Student-focused student activity with the intention of enabling students to develop their conceptions: subject matter is relational with the relationship between teachers' understanding and students' experience seen in terms of a *whole made up of constituent parts*.

Category F: Student-focused student activity with the intention of enabling students to change their conceptions: subject matter is relational with the relationship between teachers' world-views and students' world-views seen as open to change and with subject matter seen in terms of *wholes related to other wholes*.

Structurally, the key difference between these experiences of teaching is that Categories A to D either focus on parts relating to other parts or parts relating to wholes. Only in Categories E and F is the focus on wholes (either constituted in terms of parts or relating to greater or other wholes). The outcome space is shown in Table 1.

Table 1. Outcome space for the experience of teaching

	Strategy		
	Teacher-focused		Student-focused
Intention	Teacher activity	Student activity	Student activity
Information transmission	A	B	
Concept acquisition		C, D	
Conceptual development			E
Conceptual change			F

The understanding of subject matter is experienced as:

Category A: A series of facts and/or techniques with an awareness that the subject matter sits within one or more fields of study, and with the focus being on the individual internal facts and processes pertaining to the subject matter.

Category B: A series of individual concepts or topics with an awareness that the subject matter sits within one or more fields of study, and with the focus being on the individual internal concepts and issues pertaining to the subject matter.

Category C: A series of concepts, issues or procedures, linked and integrated to form a whole with a coherent structure and meaning, with an awareness that the subject matter sits within one or more fields of study, and with the focus being on the internal structure of the subject matter.

Category D: A series of concepts, issues or procedures, integral to the formation of a whole and with a coherent structure and meaning, with an awareness that the subject matter is structured according to one or more organizing principles within a field (or fields) of study. The focus is on the internal structure of the subject matter and the way the concepts or procedures are related.

Category E: A coherent whole, supported by organizing theories within one or more broader fields of study, with an awareness that the subject matter comprises themes or issues which are problematic, such as a series of debates. The focus is on the ways in which the whole is generalized to a high level of abstraction.

Structurally, the key difference between these categories is that Categories A, B and C focus on parts, while Categories D and E focus on wholes. The outcome space is shown in Table 2.

Table 2. Outcome space for the experience of understanding the subject matter

			Structural		
	Internal structure of subject matter		Relationship between the subject matter and the field of study		
Referential	Atomistic	Linked relational	Integral relational	Extended abstract
Facts and techniques	A			
Concepts, issues and procedures	B	C	D	
Underpinning theories and conceptions				E

This whole-part structural relationship suggests a logical structure common to the sets of categories of description, which is summarized in Table 3.

Table 3. Structural relationship between the three sets of categories of description

		Structure			
	Focus on parts			Focus on wholes	
Categories	Parts	Parts to prts	Parts to whls	Whls to parts	Whls to whls
Experience of understanding subject matter	A	B	C	D	E
Experience of teaching	A	B, C	D	E	F

Based upon this logical relationship between the categories of description, we hypothesized that this relationship would be manifested in the empirical relationship between the categories, with the major shift being a move from a focus on parts to a focus on wholes. Table 4 shows that, after classification of each transcript in terms of the categories of description, a moderately strong relationship is found between categories describing the experience of understanding subject matter and those describing teaching (Somers' d = 0.672); the pattern in this relationship can be seen more clearly in Table 5. In all but one case in Table 4, the structure of the experience of understanding subject matter is of a higher order than the structure of the experience of teaching.

Discussion and conclusion

In this paper, we have highlighted the previously little-researched area of how academic staff understand their subject matter and the relationship of this to the way they teach that subject matter. We have focused on a group of 37 staff active in research. The relationship between teaching, subject matter and research, for this group, is discussed in a forthcoming paper (Prosser *et al.*, 2006).

What we see clearly in the results presented in this paper is a moderately strong relationship between the ways in which teachers understand their subject and the way

Table 4. Relationship between experience of teaching and experience of understanding subject matter

Experience of teaching	A (Parts)	B (Parts to parts)	C (Parts to wholes)	C/D	D (Wholes to parts)	E (Wholes to wholes)	Total
A (Parts)							0
A/B	2						2
B (Parts to parts)		4	1				5
C (Parts to parts)			1				1
C/D			4	2			6
D (Parts to wholes)		2	3		1	1	7
D/E			1				1
E (Wholes to parts)					6	3	9
E/F				1		1	2
F (Wholes to wholes)			1			3	4
Total	2	6	11	3	7	8	37

Somers' $d = 0.672$, $p < .001$

Table 5. Pattern of relationships between experience of teaching and experience of understanding subject matter

Experience of teaching	A Parts/Parts to parts	B	C Parts to wholes	C/D	D Wholes to parts & wholes	E	Totals
Parts/parts to parts A, A/B, B, C	6		2		0		8
Parts to wholes C/D, D, D/E	2		10		2		14
Wholes to parts/ wholes to wholes E, E/F, F	0		2		13		15
Totals	8		14		15		37

they teach that subject. At one extreme, the subject is seen as a series of topics or issues with little or no attention being paid to the whole discipline. When the subject is seen in this way, lecturers tend to talk about 'delivering' discreet 'packages' of information to students (Martin & Lueckenhausen, 2005). In such a scenario, there is little opportunity for students to see how they might integrate what they learn into a larger field of knowledge; what they know is likely to remain a series of isolated facts. At the other extreme, when the subject matter is seen by an academic as a coherent whole, students are more likely to be helped into a relationship with the field as a whole and to experience, and develop, a personal understanding of that whole. The focus on cohesive wholes, as opposed to unrelated parts, has been shown by our previous work to be associated with higher quality learning outcomes (Trigwell *et al.*, 1999). Therefore, put simply, we argue that how university teachers understand their subject will affect the ways in which they will represent that subject to their students and, ultimately, how effectively their students will learn that subject.

To conclude, we link this study back to the phenomenographic method discussed at the beginning of the paper. From a phenomenographic perspective, the task of that supporting teacher development is, first, to be alerted to the variation in the ways academic staff talk about teaching and learning and, second, to encourage reflection on, and discussion of, these variations. In the study discussed above, this means supporting academic staff to reflect upon, and see the variation in, the ways in which they experience their subject matter.

Such reflection and analysis is at the heart of the phenomenographic 'variation theory' (Marton & Booth, 1997 and Chapter 2 in this monograph). The idea that underlies this theory is that without variation we are unable to discern one thing from another. Variation is the tool for discerning what is known from what is new, for discerning what is similar from what is different. However, for this variation to be useful as a development tool, the attention of academic staff has to be focused onto a specific phenomenon. How they experience that phenomenon must be highlighted. The structured 'outcome space' that maps the variation in a phenomenographic study brings together what is experienced or what is known (the epistemology) and how it is experienced (the ontology). On the basis of the research highlighted in this study, for instance, academic staff would need to be helped to focus on what they know in terms of their understanding of subject matter and how they know it. Overall, the aim of this approach is to raise awareness of teachers' understanding of their own teaching and their students' learning.

Perhaps, one of the reasons why phenomenographic 'variation theory' has had significant success as a development tool is that it challenges the common sense notion of teaching as giving information and learning as receiving that information. Once there is engagement with knowledge, then we are talking about 'being' a university teacher or learner, not just having knowledge or skills. Increasing awareness of 'being' allows us to help teaching academics to explore the ways in which they and their colleagues approach their teaching tasks and the ways in which their students likewise, approach their learning tasks.

At the heart of phenomenography is the assumption that some types of teaching or learning are better than others. Those teachers and learners who engage with a particular task or phenomenon and who unite their being with their knowing (or, in phenomenographic terms, connect the 'what' with the 'how') will become more aware of the richness and the complexity of the task they face and more open to seeing variation in the understanding of that phenomenon. This openness to being engaged with the knowledge is what Ference Marton, in his early work (Marton & Säljö, 1976), called a 'deep' approach and he contrasted this with a 'surface' approach. As it has often been pointed out elsewhere, reducing teaching and learning to knowledge, skills or competencies ignores this essential engagement (Barnett, 2004; Dall'Alba & Sandberg, 1996). University students become professionals: doctors, engineers, lawyers, as they engage with professional knowledge, not as they take on more information. University teachers become strong facilitators of learning when they engage with the task of helping students to learn. Likewise, developers of university teachers become facilitators of teaching and learning when they engage with the task of helping academic staff to reflect on their teaching and their students learning and to see variations in that teaching and learning. This chapter has sought to illustrate how an understanding of findings from the phenomenographic approach explored above, and using the approach itself as a development activity, can help university teaching staff to see teaching and learning in an importantly new light.

Acknowledgements

The study described in this paper was funded by the Australian Research Council. The support is gratefully acknowledged, as are the contributions by Paul Ramsden and Heather Middleton to, respectively, the conceptualization and the conduct of the study.

References

Barnett, R. (2004). Learning for an unknown future. *Higher Education Research and Development, 23*, 247–260.

Biggs, J. (2003). *Teaching for quality learning at university.* Buckingham: Open University Press.

Dall'Alba, G., & Sandberg, J. (1996). Educating for competence in professional practice. *Instructional Science, 24*, 411–437.

Martin, E., & Lueckenhausen, G. (2005). How university teaching changes teachers: Affective as well as cognitive challenges. *Higher Education, 49*, 389–412.

Marton, F. (1981). Phenomenography: Describing conceptions of the world around us. *Instructional Science, 10*, 177–200.

Marton, F., & Booth, S. (1997). *Learning and awareness.* New Jersey: Lawrence Erlbaum and Associates.

Marton, F., & Säljö, R. (1976). On qualitative differences in learning: I. Outcome and process. *British Journal of Educational Psychology, 46*, 4–11.

Prosser, M., Martin, E., Trigwell, K., & Ramsden, P. (2005). Academics' experiences of understanding of their subject matter and the relationship of this to their experiences of teaching and learning. *Instructional Science, 33*, 137–157.

Prosser, M., Martin, E., Trigwell, K., Ramsden, P., & Middleton, H. (2006). *University academics' experiences of research and its relationship to their experience of teaching.* Manuscript submitted for publication.

Prosser, M., & Trigwell, K. (1999). *Understanding learning and teaching: The experience in higher education.* Buckingham: Open University Press.

Richardson, J. T. E. (2006). Investigating the relationship between variations in students' perceptions of their academic environment and variations in study behaviour in distance education, *British Journal of Educational Psychology, 76*, 867–893.

Trigwell, K., Prosser, M., & Waterhouse, F. (1999). Relations between teachers' approaches to teaching and students' approaches to learning. *Higher Education, 37*, 57–70.

Appendix A: Australian research council funded projects

2005-2007: Learning through online and co-present discussion in higher education: expectations, experiences and outcomes; Goodyear, P., Ellis, R., & Prosser, M.

2002-2004: Relations between academics' understanding of their subject matter and their experiences of research and teaching; Prosser, M., Ramsden, P., Martin, E., & Trigwell, K.

1998-2000: University teachers' understanding of their subject matter and its relationship to how and what they teach; Prosser, M., Martin, E., Trigwell, K., Ramsden, P., & Entwistle, N.

1994-1996: Academic departments and the quality of teaching and learning; Ramsden, P., Martin, E., Prosser, M., & Trigwell, K.

1990-1991: Academics' experiences in teaching first year science courses; Prosser, M., & Trigwell, K.

Appendix B: Selected publications from projects

Books and chapters in books

Martin, E. (1999). *Changing academic work*. Buckingham: Open University Press.

Martin, E., Prosser, M., Trigwell, K., Ramsden, P., & Benjamin, J. (2001). What university teachers teach and how do they teach it? In N. Hativa & P. Goodyear (Eds.), *Teacher thinking, beliefs and knowledge in higher education* (pp. 103-126). Dordtrecht: Kluwer. (Reprint of paper 45 in *Articles in Refereed Journals*.)

Prosser, M., & Trigwell, K. (1998). Teaching in higher education. In B. Dartt & G. Boulton-Lewis (Eds.), *Teaching and Learning in Higher Education* (pp. 250-267). Melbourne: Australian Council for Educational Research.

Prosser, M., & Trigwell, K. (1999). *Understanding learning and teaching: The experience in higher education*. Buckingham: Open University Press.

Ramsden, P. (1992 & 2004). *Learning to teach in higher education*. London: Routledge.

Trigwell, K., & Prosser, M. (2003). Qualitative differences in university teaching. In M. Tight (Ed.), *Access and Exclusion* (pp. 185-216). Oxford: JAI Elsevier.

Journal articles (Phenomenographic)

Martin, E., Prosser, M., Trigwell, K., Ramsden, P., & Benjamin, J. (2000). What university teachers teach and how they teach it. *Instructional Science, 28*, 387-412.

Martin, E., Trigwell, K., Prosser, M., & Ramsden, P. (2003). Variation in the experience of leadership of teaching in higher education. *Studies in Higher Education, 28*(3), 247-260.

Prosser, M., Martin, E., Trigwell, K., Ramsden, P., & Lueckenhausen, G. (2005). Academics' experiences of understanding of their subject matter and the relationship to their experiences of teaching and learning. *Instructional Science, 33*, 137-157.

Prosser, M., & Trigwell, K. (1999). Relational perspectives on higher education teaching and learning in the sciences. *Studies in Science Education, 33*, 31-60.

Prosser, M., Trigwell, K., & Taylor, P. (1994). A phenomenographic study of academics' conceptions of science teaching and learning. *Learning and Instruction, 4*, 217-231.

Trigwell, K., & Prosser, M. (1996). Changing approaches to teaching: A relational perspective. *Studies in Higher Education, 21*, 275-284.

Trigwell, K., & Prosser, M. (1997). Towards an understanding of individual acts of teaching and learning. *Higher Education Research and Development, 16*, 241-252.

Trigwell, K., Prosser, M., Martin, E., & Ramsden, P. (In Press). University teachers' experiences of change in their understanding of the subject matter they have taught. *Teaching in Higher Education, 10*.

Trigwell, K., Prosser, M., & Taylor, P. (1994). Qualitative differences in approaches to teaching first year university science courses. *Higher Education, 27*, 74-84.

Student Learning and University Teaching, 61–71
BJEP Monograph Series II, 4
© 2007 The British Psychological Society

The
British
Psychological
Society

www.bpsjournals.co.uk

5 – Variations in student learning and perceptions of academic quality

John T. E. Richardson*
The Open University, UK

It is commonly assumed that there is a link between students' approaches to studying in higher education and their perceptions of their academic environment. However, initial attempts to demonstrate this link were not convincing. I describe the results of five studies in which students were asked to complete an inventory on approaches to studying as well as the Course Experience Questionnaire. All five studies showed an intimate relationship between students' approaches to studying and their perceptions of the academic quality of their courses. Nevertheless, strictly speaking, these results are purely correlational in nature, and they tell one nothing about the existence or the direction of any causal relationship between students' perceptions of academic quality and their approaches to studying. The application of path analysis to the results from two of the five studies suggests that the relationship is in fact a bi-directional one.

Approaches to learning and perceptions of academic quality

Interview-based research carried out in Britain and Sweden during the 1970s indicated that students in higher education may adopt three different approaches to studying:

- a 'deep' approach based on understanding the meaning of the course materials;
- a 'strategic' approach based on achieving the highest possible marks or grades; and
- a 'surface' approach based on memorizing the course materials for the purposes of assessment.

The choice of one approach to studying rather than another seemed to depend on the content, the context, and the demands of particular learning tasks (see Laurillard, 1979; Marton, 1976; Ramsden, 1979). Subsequent quantitative studies showed that the same students may exhibit different approaches, depending upon the demands of different course units, the quality of the teaching, and the nature of the assessment (Eley, 1992; Scouller, 1998; Vermetten, Lodewijks, & Vermunt, 1999).

* Correspondence should be addressed to Professor John Richardson, Institute of Educational Technology, The Open University, Walton Hall, Milton Keynes MK7 6AA, UK (e-mail: j.t.e.richardson@open.ac.uk).

DOI:10.1348/000709906X162082

These findings suggest that changes in the design and the delivery of specific courses will affect how students tackle those courses. In particular, they tend to imply that the use of appropriate course design, teaching methods, and modes of assessment will induce desirable approaches to studying. Unfortunately, the evidence that the use of specific interventions will bring about desirable approaches to studying is scarce (Gibbs, 1992; Hambleton, Foster, & Richardson, 1998; Kember, Charlesworth, Davies, McKay, & Stott, 1997). One explanation for this is that the impact of contextual factors is mediated by students' perceptions of their academic environment. It follows that teaching interventions will be ineffective unless they serve to modify the students' perceptions. However, this account assumes that there is a direct association between approaches to learning and perceptions of the academic environment.

Previous research into the relationship between approaches and perceptions

Initial attempts to evaluate this idea used two instruments developed by Ramsden and Entwistle (1981). The Approaches to Studying Inventory (ASI) was used to obtain students' self-reports on 16 aspects of studying, subsumed under a meaning orientation, a reproducing orientation, an achieving orientation, and a non-academic orientation; and the Course Perceptions Questionnaire (CPQ) was used to obtain their self-reports on eight aspects of their academic environment. Ramsden and Entwistle gave the ASI and the CPQ to 2,208 students at 54 institutions of higher education. The results revealed several relationships:

- Perceptions of a heavy workload were linked with high scores on the ASI scales that defined a reproducing orientation.
- Perceptions of clear goals and standards were linked with high scores on the ASI scales that defined an achieving orientation.
- High scores on the ASI scales concerned with intrinsic motivation and the use of evidence were associated with a positive evaluation of teaching.

Nevertheless, Ramsden and Entwistle acknowledged that there was 'not a great deal of overlap' between the two sets of measures (p. 375; see also Entwistle & Ramsden, 1983, p. 184). Parsons (1988) administered the ASI and the CPQ to both English- and Afrikaans-speaking students at one institution of higher education in South Africa. Once again, perceptions of a heavy workload were associated with high scores on the ASI scales that defined a reproducing orientation. However, the results confirmed that there were few associations between the major orientations to studying and scores on the CPQ, and that even those associations which did attain statistical significance were weak and unlikely to be of much practical importance.

Entwistle (1989) and Ramsden (1989) both argued that any association between perceptions and study behaviour would be less apparent at the individual (student) level than at the aggregate (course or department) level, because different students in the same course or department would be likely to experience their academic environment in a similar manner. In fact, the latter idea turns out to be entirely mistaken. The studies mentioned earlier by Eley (1992), Scouller (1998), and Vermetten *et al.* (1999) all found considerable variations in how different students experienced the same courses.

Another possibility is that there were problems with both instruments. For instance, some of the ASI's scales are not very robust, particularly those measuring an achieving orientation and a non-academic orientation (see Richardson, 2000, pp. 90–96, 101–105 for a review). Richardson (1990) argued that it was more appropriate to abbreviate the ASI to the eight scales which had been most consistently identified with a meaning orientation and a reproducing orientation in the original study carried out by Ramsden and Entwistle (see also Entwistle & Ramsden, 1983, p. 52). This yields a shortened instrument containing 32 items.

Questions were also raised about the adequacy of the CPQ. Ramsden (1991) devised a new instrument, the Course Experience Questionnaire (CEQ). This contains 30 items in five scales relating to different aspects of effective instruction: Good Teaching, Clear Goals and Standards, Appropriate Workload, Appropriate Assessment, and Emphasis on Independence. Since 1993, an adapted version of the CEQ (containing only 17 of the 30 original items) has been administered annually to all new graduates from Australian universities. This version includes a sixth scale concerned with the fostering of generic skills. For research purposes, Wilson, Lizzio, and Ramsden (1997) proposed that the original 30-item version of the CEQ should be augmented with the Generic Skills scale to yield a 36-item questionnaire.

The CEQ and the short version of the ASI appear to be psychometrically superior to the CPQ and the original ASI. They might therefore be expected to provide clearer evidence of the relationship between students' approaches to studying and their perceptions of their academic environment. Students' scores on the different scales of the CEQ are correlated with one another, and they seem to define a single dimension of perceived academic quality. For the purposes of this article, I shall simply refer to students' overall scores on the CEQ, calculated as the average of their scores across its constituent scales.

Empirical studies to test the nature of the relationship

Study 1

Sadlo (1997) was interested in the impact of problem-based learning on students' approaches to studying and their perceptions of the academic environment. She gave the short version of the ASI and the original (30-item) version of the CEQ to 225 students at six different schools of occupational therapy. The curricula were classified as being problem-based, subject-based, or hybrid. She found that students following problem-based curricula tended to produce more positive ratings of their courses on the CEQ. Subsequent analyses showed that these students also obtained lower scores on the scales of the ASI that defined a reproducing orientation and higher scores on the scale measuring a deep approach (Sadlo & Richardson, 2003).

In addition, students who produced more positive ratings of their courses on the CEQ tended to obtain lower scores on the scales of the ASI that defined a reproducing orientation but higher scores on the scales of the ASI that defined a meaning orientation. This is evident in the bar graph shown in Figure 1. Sadlo and Richardson used a multivariate analysis of variance in order to quantify the degree of overlap between the students' CEQ scores and ASI scores using the complement of Wilks' lambda. This estimated the amount of variance shared between the two sets of scores as 56.3%.

Study 2

Lawless and Richardson (2002) administered the 32-item version of the ASI and the 36-item version of the CEQ to students taking six different courses by distance

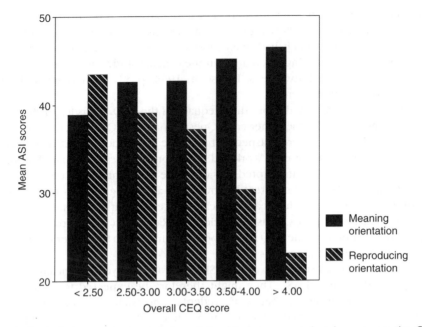

Figure 1. Study 1: bar graph showing the relationship between students' scores on the Course Experience Questionnaire (CEQ) and their scores on meaning orientation and on reproducing orientation from the short version of the Approaches to Studying Inventory (ASI). The overall score on the CEQ is the *mean* score across 5 scales from 1 to 5. The scores on the ASI are the *total* scores across 16 items from 0 to 64. The bar graph shows the mean scores on the ASI for students categorized into five groups according to their scores on the CEQ. Source: unpublished data from Sadlo and Richardson (2003).

learning with the Open University. The original wording of some of the items in these instruments is not suitable for students in distance education; in particular, items referring to 'lecturers' or 'teaching staff' are inappropriate when the curriculum is delivered by means of specially written materials. However, most distance-learning institutions use various kinds of personal support (such as face-to-face tutorials or teleconferencing) to try to narrow what Moore (1980) called the 'transactional distance' with their students. This means that 'teachers' in distance education have more specific roles either as the writers of course materials or as tutors.

Lawless and Richardson modified both instruments by removing any references to 'lecturers' or 'teaching staff' so that the items referred to either tutors or teaching materials. They administered the ASI and the CEQ in a single survey and obtained usable data on both instruments from 1,198 students. Both the ASI and the CEQ functioned well in this situation, except that the CEQ scale concerned with good teaching split into two separate scales that were concerned with good materials and good tutoring, and the CEQ scale concerned with emphasis on independence proved to be concerned more with student choice than autonomy. Further analyses showed that students who produced positive ratings of their courses on the CEQ again tended to obtain lower scores on the scales of the ASI that defined a reproducing orientation and higher scores on the scales of the ASI that defined a meaning orientation. The overlap in variance between the scores on the CEQ and the scores on the ASI was 47.1%.

Study 3

There is, of course, an increasing use of information technology both in campus-based higher education and in distance education. Richardson and Price (2003) therefore studied students' perceptions of academic quality and their approaches to studying on electronically delivered courses. The survey was identical to that used by Lawless and Richardson (2002), but it was administered to students taking two different postgraduate courses in computing at the Open University supported by electronically provided materials and on-line tuition. Usable data on both the CEQ and the ASI were obtained from 233 students. Students who produced positive ratings of their courses on the CEQ again tended to obtain lower scores on the scales of the ASI that defined a reproducing orientation and higher scores on the scales of the ASI that defined a meaning orientation. The overlap in variance between the scores on the CEQ and the scores on the ASI was 64.3%.

Study 4

Even the short version of the ASI has proved not to be entirely satisfactory from a research perspective (see Richardson, 2000, pp. 113–119). Since 1992, Entwistle and his colleagues have been developing a new questionnaire, the Revised Approaches to Studying Inventory (RASI; Entwistle, Tait, & McCune, 2000). In its latest version, this contains 52 items in 13 scales which measure various aspects of a deep approach, a strategic approach and a surface approach (now interpreted as major constructs rather than as individual scales).

Richardson (2003) administered the RASI together with the 36-item version of the CEQ to students who were taking a 12-week introductory web-based course in computing with the Open University. Usable data on both instruments were obtained from 173 students. Both the CEQ and the RASI seemed to function reasonably well in this highly distinctive context. Students who produced more positive ratings of their courses on the CEQ tended to obtain lower scores on the scales of the RASI that defined a surface approach but also higher scores on the scales of the RASI that defined a deep approach and a strategic approach. The overlap in variance between the scores on the CEQ and the scores on the RASI was 82.6%.

Study 5

In order to provide a more extensive evaluation of the CEQ and the RASI in the context of distance education, Richardson (2005) administered both instruments to students who were taking seven courses with the Open University. These were all traditional distance-learning courses supported by paper-based materials and face-to-face tuition. Usable data on both the CEQ and the RASI were obtained from 2,137 students. Both instruments seemed remarkably robust in the context of distance education. Once again, students who produced more positive ratings of their courses on the CEQ tended to obtain lower scores on the scales of the RASI that defined a surface approach but also higher scores on the scales of the RASI that defined a deep approach and a strategic approach (see Figure 2). The overlap in variance between the scores on the CEQ and the scores on the RASI was 61.2%.

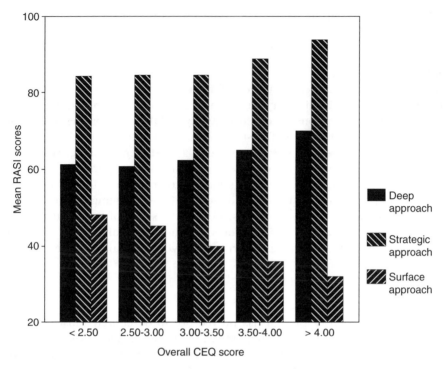

Figure 2. Study 5: bar graph showing the relationship between students' scores on the Course Experience Questionnaire (CEQ) and their scores on deep approach, strategic approach, and surface approach from the Revised Approaches to Studying Inventory (RASI). The overall score on the CEQ is the mean score across 7 scales from 1 to 5. The scores on deep and surface approach are the total scores across 16 items from 16 to 80; the scores on strategic approach are the total scores across 20 items from 20 to 100. The bar graph shows the mean scores on the RASI for students categorized into five groups according to their scores on the CEQ. Source: unpublished data from Richardson (2005).

Models of the relationship between perceptions and approaches

The results of all the five studies are consistent with those obtained by Ramsden and Entwistle (1981) and Parsons (1988) in demonstrating a link between students' approaches to studying in higher education and their perceptions of the academic environment. The latter researchers compared responses given to the ASI and the CPQ, and the overlap in variance between these two instruments was far from impressive. On the face of it, this could be taken to indicate that students' perceptions of their academic environment were not an important determinant of their approaches to studying.

In contrast, the findings of our studies using the short ASI or the new RASI together with the CEQ are striking in view of the overlap in variance between students' approaches to studying and their perceptions of their academic environment. This was estimated at between 47.1 and 82.6%, with a mean across the five studies weighted by the sample size of 57.6%. In a bivariate relationship, this would correspond to a correlation coefficient of 0.76, and thus these findings imply that there exists an intimate relationship between students' approaches to studying and their perceptions of the academic quality of their courses. This is consistent with the idea that approaches to studying depend on the perceived content, context and demands of particular learning tasks.

Nevertheless, the finding of an overlap between students' scores on the CEQ and their scores on the ASI or the RASI is only correlational in nature. Strictly speaking, it says nothing at all about either the existence or the direction of any causal relationship between approaches to studying and perceptions of the academic environment. Many researchers have inferred from the results of the early interview-based studies that variations in students' perceptions of their academic environment give rise to variations in their study behaviour (e.g. Lizzio, Wilson, & Simons, 2002; Prosser & Sendlak, 1994; Prosser, Trigwell, Hazel, & Gallagher, 1994; Ramsden, 1988; Trigwell & Prosser, 1991). There are, however, other possibilities.

In principle, it is possible that variations in students' approaches to studying give rise to variations in their perceptions of the learning context. Marsh (1987) suggested that students might rate their courses more highly if they received better grades. In the same way, students might judge their courses more favourably if they find that they have adopted more congenial approaches to studying (Richardson, 2005). Another possibility is that the causal link between perceptions of the academic environment and approaches to studying is bidirectional, so that variations in perceptions give rise to variations in approaches to studying and vice versa. This was envisaged in Biggs' (1993) 'cognitive systems approach' to student learning.

Finally, some researchers have proposed that there is an 'internal' or intrinsic relation between different aspects of a student's awareness of learning (Marton & Svensson, 1979). In particular, Trigwell and Prosser (1997) proposed that there was an 'internal relationship' between students' perceptions of their academic environment and their self-reports of their approaches to studying, so that these 'are not independently constituted but are considered to be simultaneously present in the students' awareness' (p. 243; see also Prosser & Trigwell, 1999a, 1999b, p. 13). In other words, students' perceptions and approaches to studying are not distinct ontological categories but are merely different aspects of a single category.

A path analysis of the relationship between perceptions and approaches

Richardson (2006) endeavoured to discriminate among these different theoretical accounts by embedding the possible causal links between students' perceptions and their approaches to studying within a general model that also included the students' demographic background and measures of outcome (see Figure 3). He applied the

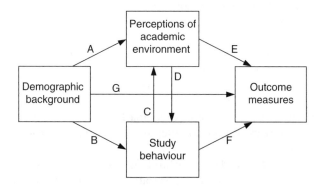

Figure 3. A general theoretical model of the relationship between students' perceptions of their academic environment and their reported study behaviour. From Richardson (2006, p. 869).

techniques of multiple regression to data from Studies 2 and 5 and concluded that in both cases, there was evidence for the causal efficacy of all the paths shown in the figure.

By the way of illustration, consider the relationship between study behaviour and outcome measures. In examining the results of Study 5, Richardson noted that the students' scores on the RASI predicted their overall marks. In particular, students who obtained high scores on three of the four subscales measuring a surface approach tended to obtain lower marks. The causal model in Figure 3 identifies three different ways in which this might have arisen:

- One is that variations in students' demographic background are simply the common cause of variations in study behaviour (Path B) and variations in measures of outcome (Path G). In other words, there is no genuine relationship between study behaviour and measures of outcome at all. If so, the magnitude of the relationship between students' RASI scores and their marks should be reduced or eliminated when the effects of background variables are statistically controlled, but Richardson found this was not the case.
- Another possibility is that variations in study behaviour give rise to variations in students' perceptions (Path C) and that variations in students' perceptions give rise to variations in measures of outcome (Path E). In other words, the relationship between study behaviour and measures of outcome is mediated by the students' perceptions. If so, the relationship between RASI scores and marks should be attenuated when the effects of CEQ scores are statistically controlled. Richardson found that in some respects this was indeed the case, and he interpreted this as evidence for the causal efficacy of Paths C and E.
- The third possibility is that there is just a direct relationship between the variations in study behaviour and variations in measures of outcome (Path F). If so, then there should be a significant residual relationship between RASI scores and marks even when the effects of *both* background variables *and* CEQ scores are statistically controlled. Richardson found that this, too, was the case, and he took this as evidence for the causal efficacy of Path F.

Now consider the relationship between students' perceptions and outcome measures. In examining the results of Study 5, Richardson noted that the students' scores on the CEQ also predicted their overall marks. In particular, students who produced high ratings of their courses on four of the seven subscales tended to obtain higher marks. Once again, the causal model in Figure 3 identifies three different ways in which this might have arisen:

- One is that variations in students' demographic background are simply the common cause of variations in perceptions (Path A) and variations in measures of outcome (Path G). In other words, there is no genuine relationship between students' perceptions behaviour and measures of outcome at all. If so, the relationship between students' CEQ scores and their marks should be reduced or eliminated when the effects of background variables are statistically controlled, but Richardson found this was not the case.
- Another possibility is that variations in students' perceptions give rise to variations in their study behaviour (Path D) and that variations in their study behaviour give rise to variations in measures of outcome (Path F). In other words, the relationship between students' perceptions and measures of outcome is mediated by their study

behaviour. If so, the relationship between CEQ scores and marks should be attenuated when the effects of RASI scores are statistically controlled. Richardson found that in some respects this was the case, and he interpreted this as evidence for the causal efficacy of Paths D and F.

• The third possibility is that there is just a direct relationship between variations in perceptions and variations in measures of outcome (Path E). If so, then there should be a significant residual relationship between CEQ scores and marks even when the effects of *both* background variables *and* RASI scores are statistically controlled. Richardson found that this, too, was the case, and he took this as evidence for the causal efficacy of Path E.

Of the four theoretical accounts mentioned earlier, the first proposed that variations in students' perceptions give rise to variations in their study behaviour, but not vice versa. This seems inconsistent with these findings insofar as there was evidence for a causal relationship between variations in study behaviour and variations in students' perceptions. The second account proposed that variations in study behaviour give rise to variations in perceptions, but not vice versa. This seems inconsistent with these findings insofar as there was evidence for a causal relationship between variations in perceptions and variations in study behaviour. The third account proposed that there were causal links in both directions between perceptions and study behaviour, and this is supported by the results of Richardson's path analysis.

Prosser and Trigwell (1999b) talked about their idea of an internal relationship between perceptions and study behaviour as a 'perspective' (pp. 14–15), suggesting that it was only intended as a framework and not as a testable theory. Even so, the results of the path analysis show that variations in students' perceptions have direct effects on measures of outcome, even when variations in their study behaviour are controlled, and that variations in study behaviour have direct effects on measures of outcome, even when variations in students' perceptions are controlled. According to Richardson (2006), these results indicate that students' perceptions and their study behaviour are distinct ontological categories and are not simply aspects of the same underlying phenomenon, as posited by Prosser and Trigwell.

In short, approaches to studying in higher education are driven in part by students' perceptions of their academic environment, and yet students' perceptions of their academic environment are equally driven in part by the extent to which they are able to adopt congenial approaches to studying. Consequently, attempts to enhance the quality of student learning in higher education need to address both students' perceptions of their academic context and their study behaviour within that context. In general, as Richardson concluded, researchers and practitioners should think more flexibly and creatively when trying to conceptualize the ways in which various aspects of the student experience are manifested in learning outcomes.

References

Biggs, J. B. (1993). From theory to practice: A cognitive systems approach. *Higher Education Research and Development, 12*, 73–85.

Eley, M. G. (1992). Differential adoption of study approaches within individual students. *Higher Education, 23*, 231–254.

Entwistle, N. (1989). Approaches to studying and course perceptions: The case of the disappearing relationship. *Studies in Higher Education, 14*, 155–156.

Entwistle, N., Tait, H., & McCune, V. (2000). Patterns of response to an approaches to studying inventory across contrasting groups and contexts. *European Journal of Psychology of Education, 15*, 33-48.

Entwistle, N. J., & Ramsden, P. (1983). *Understanding student learning*. London: Croom Helm.

Gibbs, G. (1992). *Improving the quality of student learning*. Bristol: Technical & Educational Services.

Hambleton, I. R., Foster, W. H., & Richardson, J. T. E. (1998). Improving student learning using the personalised system of instruction. *Higher Education, 35*, 187-203.

Kember, D., Charlesworth, M., Davies, H., McKay, J., & Stott, V. (1997). Evaluating the effectiveness of educational innovations: Using the Study Process Questionnaire to show that meaningful learning occurs. *Studies in Educational Evaluation, 23*, 141-157.

Laurillard, D. (1979). The processes of student learning. *Higher Education, 8*, 395-409.

Lawless, C. J., & Richardson, J. T. E. (2002). Approaches to studying and perceptions of academic quality in distance education. *Higher Education, 44*, 257-282.

Lizzio, A., Wilson, K., & Simons, R. (2002). University students' perceptions of the learning environment and academic outcomes: Implications for theory and practice. *Studies in Higher Education, 27*, 27-52.

Marsh, H. W. (1987). Students' evaluations of university teaching: Research findings, methodological issues, and directions for future research. *International Journal of Educational Research, 11*, 253-388.

Marton, F. (1976). What does it take to learn? Some implications of an alternative view of learning. In N. Entwistle (Ed.), *Strategies for research and development in higher education* (pp. 32-42). Amsterdam: Swets & Zeitlinger.

Marton, F., & Svensson, L. (1979). Conceptions of research in student learning. *Higher Education, 8*, 471-486.

Moore, M. G. (1980). Independent study. In R. D. Boyd, J. W. Apps, & Associates, *Redefining the discipline of adult education* (pp. 16-31). San Francisco: Jossey-Bass.

Parsons, P. G. (1988). The Lancaster Approaches to Studying Inventory and Course Perceptions Questionnaire: A replicated study at the Cape Technikon. *South African Journal of Higher Education, 2*, 103-111.

Prosser, M., & Sendlak, I. (1994). Student Evaluation of Teaching Questionnaire. *Research and Development in Higher Education, 16*, 551-555.

Prosser, M., & Trigwell, K. (1999a). Relational perspectives on higher education teaching and learning in the sciences. *Studies in Science Education, 33*, 31-60.

Prosser, M., & Trigwell, K. (1999b). *Understanding learning and teaching: The experience in higher education*. Buckingham: SRHE & Open University Press.

Prosser, M., Trigwell, K., Hazel, E., & Gallagher, P. (1994). Students' experiences of teaching and learning at the topic level. *Research and Development in Higher Education, 16*, 305-310.

Ramsden, P. (1979). Student learning and perceptions of the academic environment. *Higher Education, 8*, 411-427.

Ramsden, P. (1988). Context and strategy: Situational influences on learning. In R. R. Schmeck (Ed.), *Learning strategies and learning styles* (pp. 159-184). New York: Plenum Press.

Ramsden, P. (1989). Perceptions of courses and approaches to studying: An encounter between paradigms. *Studies in Higher Education, 14*, 157-158.

Ramsden, P. (1991). A performance indicator of teaching quality in higher education: The Course Experience Questionnaire. *Studies in Higher Education, 16*, 129-150.

Ramsden, P., & Entwistle, N. J. (1981). Effects of academic departments on students' approaches to studying. *British Journal of Educational Psychology, 51*, 368-383.

Richardson, J. T. E. (1990). Reliability and replicability of the approaches to studying questionnaire. *Studies in Higher Education, 15*, 155-168.

Richardson, J. T. E. (2000). *Researching student learning: Approaches to studying in campus-based and distance education*. Buckingham: SRHE & Open University Press.

Richardson, J. T. E. (2003). Approaches to studying and perceptions of academic quality in a short web-based course. *British Journal of Educational Technology, 34*, 433–442.

Richardson, J. T. E. (2005). Students' perceptions of academic quality and approaches to studying in distance education. *British Educational Research Journal, 31*, 7–27.

Richardson, J. T. E. (2006). Investigating the relationship between variations in students' perceptions of their academic environment and variations in study behaviour in distance education. *British Journal of Educational Psychology, 76*, 867–893.

Richardson, J. T. E., & Price, L. (2003). Approaches to studying and perceptions of academic quality in electronically delivered courses. *British Journal of Educational Technology, 34*, 45–56.

Sadlo, G. (1997). Problem-based learning enhances the educational experiences of occupational therapy students. *Education for Health, 10*, 101–114.

Sadlo, G., & Richardson, J. T. E. (2003). Approaches to studying and perceptions of the academic environment in students following problem-based and subject-based curricula. *Higher Education Research and Development, 22*, 253–274.

Scouller, K. (1998). The influence of assessment method on students' learning approaches: Multiple choice question examination versus assignment essay. *Higher Education, 35*, 453–472.

Trigwell, K., & Prosser, M. (1991). Improving the quality of student learning: The influence of learning context and student approaches to learning on learning outcomes. *Higher Education, 22*, 251–266.

Trigwell, K., & Prosser, M. (1997). Towards an understanding of individual acts of teaching and learning. *Higher Education Research and Development, 16*, 241–252.

Vermetten, Y. J., Lodewijks, H. G., & Vermunt, J. D. (1999). Consistency and variability of learning strategies in different university courses. *Higher Education, 37*, 1–21.

Wilson, K. L., Lizzio, A., & Ramsden, P. (1997). The development, validation and application of the Course Experience Questionnaire. *Studies in Higher Education, 22*, 33–53.

Student Learning and University Teaching, 73–90
BJEP Monograph Series II, 4
© 2007 The British Psychological Society

The
British
Psychological
Society

www.bpsjournals.co.uk

6 – The power of teaching-learning environments to influence student learning

Jan D. Vermunt*
Utrecht University, The Netherlands

This paper focuses on the power of learning environments in relation to the quality of student learning. In the first part, recent developments in research on student learning will be presented. These pertain to dimensions of student learning, consistency and variability in students' use of learning strategies, developments in learning patterns during the educational career, dissonance in students' regulation of learning processes and relationships between student learning patterns and personal, contextual and performance variables. In the second part, a number of learning environments, all widely used in higher education, will be examined with regard to the degree of self-regulation, and the initiative and responsibility they foster in students: traditional teaching, assignment-based teaching, problem-based learning, project-centred learning, self-directed specialization learning, competency-based teaching, dual learning and autodidactic learning. In the third part, the implications for teaching and curriculum design will be discussed.

The main issue is how the quality of student learning may be fostered throughout a curriculum. It will be argued that the ultimate goal of higher education is to prepare students for lifelong self-regulated, cooperative and work-based learning. Key features of powerful teaching-learning environments from this perspective are that: they prepare students for lifelong learning; they foster high-quality student learning; the teaching methods change in response to students' increasing metacognitive, self-regulatory skills; and the complexity of the real-life problems used as an impetus for learning gradually and systematically increases along six dimensions. Finally, learning implications for the teachers teaching in those curricula will be discussed.

Some recent developments in research on student learning
Dimensions of student learning
During the last few decades, research on student learning has flourished. In the 1980s, that research mainly pertained to the depth with which students process subject matter and to their study motivation. For example, Marton and Säljö (1984) speak of a deep and surface

*Correspondence should be addressed to Professor Jan Vermunt, IVLOS Institute of Education, Utrecht University, PO Box 80127, 3508 TC Utrecht, The Netherlands (e-mail: j.d.vermunt@ivlos.uu.nl).

DOI:10.1348/000709906X162406

approach to learning, and Biggs (1987) makes a distinction between three types of learning strategies (deep, surface and achieving) and three types of study motivation (intrinsic, extrinsic and achievement). Later on, the research expanded to the way students regulate their learning processes (metacognitive regulation; Brown, 1987) and to their knowledge and beliefs about learning and themselves as learners (metacognitive knowledge and beliefs; Flavell, 1987). Research of Brown, Flavell and others showed that metacognitive knowledge and self-regulation processes are important predictors of learning outcomes.

In recent theories, often four domains or components of student learning are discerned (see e.g. Entwistle & McCune, 2004; Lonka, Olkinuora, & Mäkinen, 2004; Pintrich, 2004; Richardson, 2000; Vermunt & Vermetten, 2004): cognitive processing strategies, metacognitive regulation strategies, conceptions of learning and learning orientations. Cognitive processing strategies are those learning strategies that students use to process the subject matter. They directly lead to learning outcomes in terms of knowledge, understanding, skills, etc. Metacognitive regulation strategies are those learning strategies that students use to regulate and steer their learning processes and lead therefore indirectly to learning outcomes. Conceptions of learning are the beliefs and views people have about learning and associated phenomena: how different learning tasks can be tackled, who is responsible for what in learning, what good teaching looks like, etc. Learning orientations refer to the whole domain of personal goals, motives, expectations, attitudes, worries and doubts students have with regard to learning and studying (Gibbs, Morgan, & Taylor, 1984). Vermunt (1996, 1998) uses the term 'learning style' as an encompassing concept in which the cognitive processing of subject matter, the metacognitive regulation of learning, conceptions of learning and learning orientations are united. Later on, because the term 'learning style' is often associated with invariant personality characteristics, he and his colleagues changed to using the more neutral term 'learning pattern' to denote this united phenomenon (Vermunt, 2005; Vermunt & Vermetten, 2004). In a series of studies with university students, he consistently found four such patterns: undirected, reproduction-directed, meaning-directed and application-directed learning (see Table 1).

Table 1. Patterns in student learning: various components

| Component | Learning pattern | | | |
	Undirected	Reproduction-d	Meaning-d	Application-directed
Processing strategy	Hardly any	Stepwise (memorizing and analysing)	Deep (relating and critical processing)	Concrete (concretizing and applying)
Regulation strategy	Lack of regulation	Externally regulated	Self-regulated	Both self- and externally regulated
Conception of learning	Learning as being stimulated by others	Learning as taking in knowledge	Learning as constructing knowledge	Learning as using knowledge
Learning orientation	Ambivalent	Certificate and self-test oriented	Personally interested	Vocation oriented

Students with an *undirected learning* pattern hardly get to the processing of the subject matter, mainly because they have a lot of trouble with the learning activity 'selecting', discerning more and less important parts of the subject matter: they find everything equally important. Because they are not able to reduce the large amount of study materials, it is almost impossible for them to cope with it. They experience a lack of regulation in their study behaviour, notice that they have problems with the regulation of their learning, but at the same time, they do not know well how to do it differently and better. Often they continued their way of learning from secondary education to their current approach. In their conceptions of learning, they attach much value to being stimulated by teachers and other educational agents and to cooperation with fellow students, hoping that others can alleviate the study problems they experience. They are ambivalent in their study orientation: they ask themselves whether their studies are not too hard for them, whether they have chosen the right subject area, whether they have not aimed too high, etc.

The undirected learning pattern is nicely illustrated in the following interview fragment with a student of natural sciences of the Open University. This student has extended her approach to learning from secondary school directly to her new studies, but finds that she gets stuck when doing so.

> S: It is very difficult to select. When you are in class, you can ask: 'Do you have to know this, or is this not so important?'. But when you are on your own that is very difficult. You never know well what they want you to know.

> I: But do the learning objectives indicate what is important?

> S: Yes, but these are also very general. That you can explain something in broad outlines, for example, how the earth is built up. But then you still do not know how much they want you to know about that. No example is given about how much you should know about it. I don't find them so clear. (. . .) Some people know it as soon as they have read it, but that is not the case with me. I really have to write down everything, if necessary three times. Before the exam I just will write down everything another time. That is the way it really goes in. (. . .) I cannot learn in another way.

Students with a *reproduction-directed learning* pattern go through the subject matter in a stepwise way, study the material thoroughly, analytically, in detail, and learn a lot by heart. Contrary to the previous pattern, they often do succeed to discern the more and less important parts of the subject matter, and in this way, reduce the subject matter to an amount that can be remembered. In the regulation of their learning, they let themselves be strongly directed by external sources: teachers, directions in the study materials, fellow students, etc. They view 'learning' as a process in which the knowledge that is externally present, in the heads of experts, in books, on the internet, etc., should be transferred to their own head, so that it can be reproduced at a later time. In their learning orientation, they are very directed at testing their own capabilities and gaining certificates, credits and so on.

The following interview fragment originates from an adult student exhibiting this reproduction-directed pattern and shows a very quantitative approach.

> S: There are no parts of which I think: 'Oh, I know those already'. There are parts that look familiar to me, but for me that is no reason to say: 'I just do that a bit faster, because I know that'. No, I read everything very precisely! (. . .) Then I read it all over again. The second time I not only read, but I also mark. With a marker pen I indicate what text I should definitely know by heart. Between 40 and 50% is yellow then, so very much. And central concepts and words I should have in my head I mark red. When the exams are coming

closer, I start reading everything for the third time. (. . .) In my view there is only one way: I have to make sure that a mass of those concepts gets into my brains. So it is: rehearse, rehearse, rehearse. If I do it four times I know it better than after three times, and after five times I know it better than after four times.

The third pattern is *meaning-directed learning*. Students who approach their studies in this way use deep processing strategies: they look for relationships between parts of the subject matter, try to bring structure into these and are critical towards what they read and hear; they think about the logic of arguments, check whether the conclusions of authors follow logically from the facts on which they are based, etc. They self-regulate their learning to a high degree: they set their own goals, monitor their progress well, diagnose the causes of their misunderstandings and consult other sources about the subjects that are dealt with in addition to the prescribed literature. They view 'learning' more as constructing their own knowledge and insights and believe that they are themselves mainly responsible for the success of their own learning. Often they study out of personal interest in the topics of their studies.

In the following interview fragment, a student describes how she uses a deep processing strategy, as a component of a meaning-directed learning pattern.

S: My way of studying is that I always try to see relationships and to get an overview over the subject matter. There is a certain line in a chapter, a story, and I try to follow that. For example, there are different theories about a topic. Then I summarize the core of each theory and also the pro's and contra's, and which theory is a reaction to which theory. (. . .) My summary is very important to me, because I get an overview over the subject matter, I see the main lines and connections that get lost when I only read from page to page.

Whereas, in the meaning-directed learning pattern, students' attention is primarily focused on relationships within the subject matter, students who learn according to an *application-directed learning* pattern mainly pay attention to relationships between the subject matter and the surrounding world. Students process the subject matter mainly in a concrete way: they try to form concrete images with abstract material and think about how the subject matter can be applied in practice. In this pattern, both more self-regulated and externally regulated strategies occur. Students with this learning pattern attach importance to learning to use the knowledge they acquire: if knowledge cannot be used, it is useless and does not have to be learned. The underlying learning orientation is often vocational: students want to prepare themselves for a future profession or they want to improve themselves in their current profession.

The application-directed learning pattern is easily recognizable in the following two interview fragments. The first originates from an Open University law student and the second from a psychology student in a regular university.

I: Are there parts in the courses that you find more important than other parts?

S: The practical things are often much more important for yourself. The things you hear when you listen to the debates in the Parliament, the things from daily life. (. . .) If you read in the newspaper that a minister is in trouble, then you already think: what would happen with this and that when a Member of Parliament proposes to change that law? Then you bring your knowledge into practice.

I: What do you try to gain from your studies?

S: You try to apply it in practice. I think you get knowledge by studying, and of course it is very useful that you can also apply these things when you find a job in the future. Maybe also just applying them in practice for yourself, so looking around in your own environment what happens there, and comparing that to what you have learned and done.

Consistency and variability in students' use of learning strategies

Vermetten, Lodewijks, and Vermunt (1999) studied the degree of consistency and variability in students' use of learning strategies. They asked law students from two subsequent cohorts about their learning strategies in four different courses. Analyses of variance showed variation in students' use of learning strategies for the different courses. However, intra-individual correlations showed that students were also consistent to a certain degree in their strategy use over different courses. Their results point to both a context-specific and a person-bound component in the use of learning strategies, both explaining roughly the same amount of variance in strategy use. In another study, Vermetten, Vermunt, and Lodewijks (1999) administered the Inventory of Learning Styles to first- and second-year university students on two different occasions with an interval of about 6 months. For learning strategies, the test–retest correlations varied between 0.51 and 0.72. Learning orientations showed correlations between 0.58 and 0.71 and conceptions of learning between 0.54 and 0.64.

Developments in learning patterns during the educational career

Several studies investigated the way students of different age groups learn. Although these were not longitudinal studies in which people are followed for years, tentative insights can be derived from these studies about possible developments in student learning patterns during the educational career. For example, Klatter (1995) studied the way first year secondary school pupils learned (12 years old on average) and her results deviated significantly from those found among higher education students. These pupils were less able to distinguish different learning strategies, conceptions of learning and learning orientations than were higher education students, suggesting a clear lack of differentiation within the various learning components at that age. Boekaerts, Otten, and Simons (1997) found comparable results in their study with pupils from the first-, second- and third-year of secondary education (aged 12–14 years). This points to a possibly interesting developmental phenomenon. Maybe someone's development as a learner proceeds along this line of increasing differentiation within learning components.

Another possible developmental line concerns the increasing interrelations between the learning strategies people employ and their learning conceptions and orientations (Vermunt & Verloop, 2000). For adult students, there are often strong associations between these learning components, while for students in the first years of secondary education, these associations are almost absent (Boekaerts *et al.*, 1997; Klatter, 1995). This second developmental line could mean that as people's age and/or educational experience progresses, their learning behaviour is coming ever more under the control of their learning views and motives.

A third interesting difference between the various age cohorts concerns the application-directed learning pattern. This pattern seems to come into existence as a separate dimension in learning only rather late and is first visible with students in higher education. Before that, the application-directed learning elements are still completely interwoven with the meaning-directed elements and these two patterns coincide. Only with young adults (from about 18 years onward) are they beginning to be distinguished. Therefore, a third possible developmental line could be the emergence of meaning- and application-directed learning as two separate, distinguishable dimensions in learning. The strong application directedness that often characterizes the learning of adults also points in this direction. The gap between theory and practice that adults so often experience in their learning seems to exist to a much lesser degree in the learning of younger students. Thus, it seems to be the case that the distinction between meaning-directed and reproduction-directed learning is found first in the conceptual development of young people as learners, while application-directed learning only emerges later on, out of and distinct from meaning-directed learning.

Dissonance in students' regulation of learning processes

Meyer (2000) found that, for some groups of students, the expected linkages between learning conceptions, motives and processes did not occur, a phenomenon he named 'dissonance'. Vermunt and Verloop (2000) were able to identify five forms of dissonance:

(1) Lack of differentiation within learning strategies, conceptions or orientations;
(2) Lack of integration between learning strategies, conceptions and orientations;
(3) Incompatibility of learning strategies, conceptions and orientations;
(4) Lack of application-directed learning and
(5) Elements missing from the learning patterns.

A lack of differentiation within learning strategies, conceptions and orientations (phenomenon 1) means that students do not see the difference between different ways of processing the subject matter, various ways of regulating one's own learning processes, different conceptions of learning and diverse learning motives. Possibly, they lack the metacognitive knowledge and concepts that represent different forms of learning and that make it possible to perceive their own learning in a differentiated way. Lack of integration between learning strategies, conceptions and orientations (phenomenon 2) means that the learning activities that students undertake are not in line with their views on learning and/or their learning motives. Views, motives and actions are not congruent (compare Vermunt & Verloop, 1999). As was noticed earlier, an increasing differentiation within learning components and an increasing integration between learning components form two important lines along which a learner can develop. This may mean that low-achieving pupils and students may lag behind in their development as a learner.

Incompatibility of learning components (phenomenon 3) may mean that opposing forces are working within students in their adaptation to the teaching-learning environment. A study of Beishuizen, Stoutjesdijk, and Van Putten (1994), for example, showed that students who combined a deep approach with self-regulation, and those who combined a stepwise (surface) approach with external regulation, achieved well on a certain task. Those are the combinations of processing and regulation strategies that occur most often empirically and that are also theoretically 'sound'. On the other hand, students who combined external regulation with a deep approach, and especially those who combined self-regulation with a surface approach, achieved much worse. This points to the possibility that some students use different, even incompatible learning strategies and that this incompatibility is associated with low achievements.

The lack of a clear, distinct application-directed learning pattern (phenomenon 4) is a phenomenon that is often observed. It seems to be the case that this pattern develops relatively late, since this pattern forms a distinct dimensions only with groups of advanced or adult students. The study of Lindblom-Ylänne and Lonka (2000) shows clearly that application directedness is an important dimension of individual differences among advanced medical students.

The phenomenon of missing elements of learning patterns (phenomenon 5) means that some students learn according to a 'bare' version of a learning pattern. They leave out essential elements from it, as for example when some students leave out the analytical elements from a reproduction-directed learning pattern.

Relationships between student learning patterns and personal and contextual factors

Busato, Prins, Elshout, and Hamaker (1999) studied the relationship between learning pattern and the 'big five' personality factors among psychology students. In general, these relationships were modest. The strongest positive relationships were between meaning-directed learning and 'intellectual openness' and between reproduction-directed learning and both 'conscientiousness' and 'agreeableness'. A study of Vermetten, Lodewijks, and Vermunt (2001) pointed in the same direction.

Severiens and Ten Dam (1997) studied relationships between learning patterns, gender and gender identity of students in adult secondary education. With regard to gender, they found that men, compared with women, scored higher on undirected learning and lower on reproduction-directed learning. In the other learning patterns (meaning-directed and application-directed learning), there were no gender differences.

Wierstra, Kanselaar, Van der Linden, Lodewijks, and Vermunt (2003) developed an instrument to assess students' perceptions of their study environment and administered this, together with the Inventory of Learning Styles, to a large group of international exchange students. The results showed that meaning-directed learning was associated with a study environment perceived as emphasizing connections between study elements and as student oriented in nature, within a more democratic teaching-learning relationship. Reproduction-directed learning was associated with a study environment perceived as emphasizing remembering facts and not encouraging active participation in the course, within a more authoritarian relationship between teachers and students.

An unexpected finding from this study was that educational cultures in Europe, at least in the perception of exchange students, can be grouped into two types. The first type is characterized by more authoritarian relationships between students and teachers, and mainly traditional teaching aimed at knowledge transmission. The second type has more democratic relationships between students and teachers, and more small group teaching aimed at activating students' knowledge construction. The first type predominated in many southern European countries, while the second was more frequently present in northern European countries, like Scandinavia, the UK, etc. Remarkably, the border between the educational cultures turned out to run exactly between the Netherlands and Belgium! This may even explain why several trans-national cooperation projects between Dutch and Belgian educational institutes did not succeed as well as were hoped for.

Rozendaal, De Brabander, and Minnaert (2001) investigated the relationships between students' learning patterns and their epistemological beliefs. They found that meaning-directed learning was associated with a more relativistic view of knowledge. Students with a more absolutistic view of knowledge were more likely to report aspects of a reproduction-directed learning pattern.

Relationships between learning patterns and learning outcomes

In various studies, relationships have been investigated between the way students learn and the learning outcomes they achieve. With exam results, the following general picture emerges (Busato *et al.*, 1999; Lindblom-Ylänne & Lonka, 1999; Vermunt, 2005). Undirected learning is consistently and negatively associated with the exam achievements that students realize. Meaning-directed learning mostly shows a positive relationship with study success. Reproduction-directed learning shows no or a negative association with study achievements and application-directed learning generally shows no relationship at all with exam results. Lonka, Heikkilä, Lindblom-Ylänne, and Maury (1997) correlated student learning patterns with portfolio scores in an innovative course. They found a significant positive correlation with meaning-directed learning and a significant negative correlation with reproduction-directed learning.

Student-teacher learning

Research into student learning has generally focused on how students learn at university (academic learning), but during the last decade, there has been an increasing use of dual forms of teaching-learning methods, especially in professionally oriented trajectories. Preparing for a profession is more effective when students learn not only from books, but also from their own practical experiences.

One type of education for which this is certainly true is teacher education. Most teacher education programmes have a significant practice component and so student-teachers have several sources to learn from: the subject matter, the theory from the institute, their own experiences during practice teaching and the practical knowledge of the, mostly experienced, cooperating teacher at the practice school. The issue of whether, and if so how, student-teachers combine these knowledge sources has been central in some recent studies.

Oosterheert and Vermunt (2001) interviewed student-teachers extensively about their learning activities, the way in which they combined theory and practice, their worries, doubts and how they dealt with emotions during learning. Based on these interviews, they could identify different patterns in these student-teachers' learning. They developed an instrument to be able to assess these patterns on a larger scale. All students turned out to be application directed in their learning, but in different ways. 'Survival-oriented' students thought that a lot of teaching leads automatically to learning the profession. 'Reproductive' students tried to develop a way of teaching by trying out teaching strategies pragmatically. They try to remember what works and to forget what does not work, and are strongly 'doing oriented'. Meaning-directed students think that learning to teach mainly coincides with the development of their frame of reference. Some of them need much external support, while others actively combine information from different sources for themselves to construct an integrated knowledge base.

A deep approach in student-teacher learning manifests itself differently than in academic student learning. According to Zanting, Verloop, and Vermunt (2001), a deep approach in the context of learning to teach means that students: (a) explicate their own beliefs based on their practical experience, elicit their mentor's practical knowledge and study the 'theory'; (b) compare these three information sources and (c) draw conclusions for their own actions and/or a personal theory. They developed a method to foster this kind of deep approach with student-teachers. Mansvelder-Longayroux, Beijaard, and Verloop (2002) studied both the deep approach and the self-regulation in student-teachers' learning. They analysed portfolio fragments of student-teachers on the presence of six types of learning activities: remembering, evaluating, analysing, critical processing, diagnosing and reflecting. Of the 1778 learning activities that were identified in this way in 39 portfolios, 93% turned out to refer to remembering and evaluating. 'Remembering' in this case meant that an event is described that happened in the past (e.g. something that happened during a lesson), 'evaluating' that a value judgment is attached to that event (e.g. 'that went well, bad, wrong, cool', etc.). Only 7% of the learning activities referred to deep approach and self-regulation: analysing, diagnosing, critical processing, reflecting on/of those events (i.e. meaning directed). Their study thus did not support the idea that the introduction of a portfolio automatically leads to more meaning-directed learning.

Main teaching-learning environments in higher education and the quality of student learning

In the last 20 years, students' learning processes have been given an increasingly central place in thinking about the quality of teaching (see e.g. Entwistle, McCune, & Hounsell, 2003). Previously, 'good teaching' was conceived of as 'explaining the subject matter well'. Whether students had also understood the subject matter well was primarily seen as their own responsibility. Today we speak of 'good teaching' only when the teacher has brought about good learning in the student. But what is 'good learning'?

Over the last decade, our research group has done a series of studies on the way students learn and the factors that influence that way of learning. As we have seen, four qualitatively different ways of learning repeatedly show up: undirected, reproduction-directed, meaning-directed and application-directed learning. Discussions with teachers often show that meaning- and application-directed learning are considered to be 'good' in higher education and undirected learning to be undesirable. Often the discussions get heated when the value of reproduction-directed learning is discussed: some consider it a necessity, others reprehensible.

What ways of learning students practise in their studies turns out to be associated with their views on learning and teaching (their learning conceptions) and their study attitude and motivation (their learning orientation). This may explain why Vermetten *et al.* (1999) found that the way of learning is rather stable over time and different courses, but certainly not unchangeable: the way of teaching also matters.

Another dimension on which learning processes may be described is the degree of independence with which they are conducted. All kinds of learning and regulation activities may be employed, to a greater or lesser extent, by the students themselves or by the teaching-learning environment, such as teachers, tutors, computers, etc. One may speak of self-regulated learning when students mainly conduct those learning and regulation activities themselves. Cooperative learning means that students work together on learning tasks. Teaching can be more or less directive in this, and the degree of self-regulation that is expected from groups of cooperating students can vary accordingly. Learning alone is therefore the opposite of cooperative learning and is certainly not the same as self-regulated learning.

We thus have a variety of contrasting teaching approaches which differ in the extent to which external regulation or self-regulation dominates. Although these generic types vary considerably in the ways in which they are implemented in practice, it is still instructive to look at some of the differences that can be discerned among them.

Traditional teaching

This type of teaching represents what was dominant in most universities throughout the previous century. The subject matter was determined completely by the teacher, often not in the form of cases, problems or tasks, but as books or chapters of which the content had to be learned. In lectures, the teachers explained and clarified the subject matter. Sometimes, smaller working groups were used to help to deepen the knowledge being acquired, to clarify problems and to provide feedback on assignments. At the end of a semester, or of a whole academic year, there was an exam period in which all subjects of the past period were assessed. The subject matter, learning objectives, study resources, criteria for the learning outcomes, assessment and feedback were all completely in the hands of the teacher. Students had freedom only in the choice of their learning activities and their approaches to studying.

Assignment-based teaching

In assignment-based teaching, guided self-study is the main learning concept. Compared to traditional teaching, there are fewer lectures, more assignments for self-study and more time spent working in small groups. The number of teaching hours is reduced to about a third of the total study time, thereby offering students more time for individual study. Students conduct their self-study guided by precise instructions in the assignments. In working groups, students' results of their assignments are discussed and their learning is adjusted by the teaching team. In this way, students actively and independently process the study materials in which they are intensively supervised by the course team. The regulation of students' learning processes is mainly in the hands of the teachers: they decide the subject matter, learning objectives, criteria for learning outcomes, assessment and feedback. In choosing the learning activities and study resources, students have more freedom and responsibility.

Problem-based learning

In problem-based learning (PBL), students work in small groups of about 10 (the tutorial group) trying to understand, explain and solve problems. The starting-point for the learning process is a problem; a short description of a phenomenon about which students should acquire knowledge. The problem-based way of working is system-atically structured generally into seven steps, the 'seven-jump': (1) clarifying terms and concepts not readily understood; (2) defining the problem; (3) analysing the problem; (4) summarizing the various explanations of the problem into a coherent model; (5) formulating learning objectives; (6) individual study activities outside the group and (7) report and synthesize the newly acquired information.

In the tutorial group, students analyse the problem and formulate learning objectives: questions to which they should find answers through individual study. After a period of individual study, the students meet again and report what they have learned about the problem. Then, matters which are still unclear are clarified and the acquired knowledge is discussed, critically evaluated and integrated. During their work in the tutorial group, the students are guided by a tutor, whose main task is to facilitate the learning and group processes. The tutorial group generally meets twice a week for sessions of some 2 hours. During the first hour of such a meeting, students try to understand and explain the problem discussed previously and report what they have found studying the literature (step 7). During the second hour, students discuss a new problem and formulate learning objectives for individual study with regard to this new problem (steps 1-5). As well as these tutorial groups, students also have practical work, skills training and a few lectures. At the end of a block period that typically lasts between 5 and 8 weeks, the block test is administered, after which a new block period starts with another theme.

Project-centred learning

The starting-point for project-centred learning is a project assignment or problem. This concerns authentic, real-life assignments that are often directly derived from professional practice. Sometimes, students can choose from a number of assignments or problems to work on; they work at the project assignment independently in small groups (mostly 4-5 students). Prior to, or parallel with, the actual project work, often a phase of knowledge acquisition is designed through other working methods, like PBL or lectures. Students then have to apply this knowledge to the project assignment. Often, once a week, a meeting takes place under the guidance of a teacher, in which progress is discussed, difficulties are solved and the next project phase is previewed. The project proceeds in phases that are finished with an assessment of process and product. The project results in a group product, for example, a design, an advice, a plan, a proposition and the like. At the end of a project block, the products or other outcomes are often presented to the whole group of students in the presence of the teachers and sometimes also the customers. The product is assessed along criteria that are made in advance. Often, also the project presentation is assessed in terms of content and form. Sometimes, the knowledge acquisition is assessed separately and individually. Sometimes, also individual portfolios are used to be able to assess the individual learning achievements and the contribution of the individual students to the group process and product.

Self-directed learning of specialized subjects

In the later years of studies in higher education, forms of self-directed learning of specialized subjects are often applied that are individually supervised. A well-known example is the Master Thesis in the form of a report of empirical or theoretical research. By then, students have acquired the essential common knowledge base of the discipline and specialize in certain aspects of it, in which they are most interested. Sometimes, two or three students may work together on such a project, when there are common interests. Typically, projects like these have a somewhat longer duration (3-6 months) and part of the project often involves knowledge acquisition about the specific subject. One or two staff members function as supervisors. Students write a research proposal in which the research problem, goals, activities, resources to be used, the project's outcomes aimed at and the way of supervision are described. In essence, this comes down to a study task or project assignment that the students formulate for themselves. This proposal is discussed with the supervisors, and based on their comments, students revise the proposal before starting their actual work. Further supervision is often tailor-made, depending for example on the research phase the student is in, the difficulty level of the project and the need for supervision or the degree of self-regulation a student is capable of. After finishing the research, the report and the research process are evaluated, based on criteria that were formulated beforehand.

Competency-based teaching

A competency is an integrated whole of knowledge, insights, skills and attitudes. Competency-based teaching makes extensive use of realistic, complex tasks derived from professional practice. Often, it is demand driven and students are encouraged to self-regulate their learning processes. At the start of their studies, students perform an intake assessment, meant to give them insight into their individual starting competencies in relation to the competency profile expected of them at the end of their training. Based on a self-evaluation after a couple of months, they make a personal development plan (PDP), in which they indicate what competencies they will seek to acquire, and in what way that will happen, during the remainder of their academic training. Often this results in a learning or study contract, in which student and educational institute lay down the learning route and mutual effort obligations. Sometimes, this is done in terms of choices from the educational programme provided, and sometimes students design learning tasks themselves to attain certain competencies. In their portfolio, students collect evidence of their growth in the various competencies, and they reflect on their development as a whole. In between, they may do various progress assessments with which they may evaluate their learning progress and that may lead to adjustments in their personal development plan. When students think they have collected enough evidential material in their portfolio, they can have them evaluated and receive credit points. Sometimes, during such an assessment they have to show certain competencies *in vivo* to the assessors. Towards the end of their training, students do a final assessment to evaluate the extent to which they have reached their target learning goals. A 'study career coach' plays a major role in the coaching and supporting of students in all choices and phases of their learning routes.

Work-based learning

In work-based learning, often used in vocational programmes, students combine studying at the university with learning from practice. For example, in university-based teacher education programmes, student-teachers do teaching practice at a secondary school for a substantial proportion of their study time. There, they observe lessons from experienced teachers, conduct lessons themselves, do practice research, supervise pupils, consult their mentor teachers and form part of the school organization as a whole. The other half of their study programme consists of the theoretical part of their studies at the university. In this way, students have three important sources to learn from: their own practical experiences, the practical knowledge of the mentor teacher and the other teachers in the school, and the 'theory' of learning, teaching and pedagogy offered and discussed at the university. Other examples can be found in medical education, law school and so on.

The crucial question in such types of training programs is how the different kinds of knowledge students acquire can be brought together into an integrated knowledge base. This requires a different way of thinking than in wholly university-based programmes. The sequence in which the subject matter should be dealt with is, for example, no longer mainly based on the logic of the subject, but much more on the concerns and learning needs that students develop during their practice work. When an inappropriate educational model is used, students develop three separate knowledge bases that are tightly interconnected. When the theoretical part of the programme is designed according to principles of problem-based learning, students bring cases or problems into the tutorial group that they have experienced in practice, as a starting-point for a problem-based learning cycle. Evaluation of learning progress may involve using portfolios.

Autodidactic learning

In autodidactic learning, learners themselves decide all aspects of their learning processes: the problems addressed, the learning objectives, the learning activities, the resources to be consulted, the learning outcomes aimed at, and assessment and feedback. Learners become their own teachers. Of course, people can choose to share some aspects of this learning with colleagues or others and give each other feedback. In education, at least in the formal curriculum, fully autodidactic learning will hardly ever appear, if only because students' learning achievements ultimately have to be evaluated by the institution that guarantees the quality of the diplomas that are delivered. It does however occur often after students have graduated from higher education and need to keep their knowledge and skills up to date through 'lifelong' learning.

Table 2 summarizes the main differences in regulation identified in our description of the typical ways in which these differing approaches are implemented. The numbers in the table refer to the eight contrasted methods described earlier, as indicated in the footnote.

Table 2. Regulation of students' learning processes in the eight[1] teaching-learning environments on a dimension from teacher-regulated to student-regulated

Learning process	Teacher-regulated	Shared regulation			Student-regulated
Problems/tasks/ cases/assignments	1 2 3	4 5	6	7	8
Learning objectives	1 2	3 4	5 6	7	8
Learning activities	1	2 3	4 5	6 7	8
Study (re)sources	1	2 3	4	5 6 7	8
Criteria learning outcomes	1 2 3	4	5 6	7	8
Assessment and feedback	1 2 3	4 5	6 7		8

[1]: 1, traditional teaching; 2, assignment-based teaching; 3, problem-based learning; 4, project-centred learning; 5, self-directed specialized learning; 6, competency-based teaching; 7, work-based learning; 8, autodidactic learning.

All the last seven teaching-learning methods foster active learning through assignments, problems or cases, but they increase in the extent of self-regulation that is expected from students, and in the size and complexity of the problems they work on. They also vary in the degree of cooperation that is expected from students. It can be seen that learning activities are the first to be handed over to students, while assessment and feedback are the last. This analysis draws attention to the need to describe approaches to teaching in higher education in a more nuanced manner than by simple dichotomies, such as teacher-focused versus student-focused (Trigwell & Prosser, 2004). Such categories tend to imply homogeneous approaches, whereas the examples provided above indicate important variations in the extent and way in which the balance between external- and self-regulation is achieved.

Implications for teaching and curriculum design

From this analysis, it is suggested that there are key features in what can be seen as 'powerful' teaching and learning environments:

- They prepare students for lifelong, self-regulated, cooperative and work-based learning;
- They foster high-quality student learning;
- The teaching methods change in response to students' increasing metacognitive and self-regulatory skills and
- The complexity of the problems dealt with increases gradually and systematically.

Education that is aimed at teaching students to learn and think in an increasingly self-regulated way is characterized by a gradual shift in the task division in the learning process from educational 'agents' (e.g. teacher, tutor, book or computer) to students (Vermunt & Verschaffel, 2000). Initially, explicit external regulation is offered to students. Subsequently, that support is gradually withdrawn. At the same time, students are taught how to exert control over their learning processes themselves. Learning to learn and think independently means a gradual transfer of learning functions from the teachers to the students, a gradual shift from external to internal regulation of learning (see Figure 1). The method of teaching typically changes to allow increasing self-regulation in students' learning. As a result, students are continuously challenged to try a next step in their self-regulated learning and thinking. The ultimate goal is to help students become lifelong learners by the time they graduate, willing and able to keep on developing in their professional area after the termination of their educational career and never to stop learning.

In practice, however, in current degree programmes, teaching-learning methods do *not* change much over time to encourage greater self-regulation by students. Even in problem-based learning, for example, the procedure described earlier stays much the same from year to year. This way of working is generally challenging for first-year students, as they are not expected to regulate their learning to the same extent in

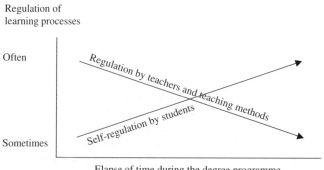

Figure 1. Decrease of teacher regulation and increase in student regulation over time.

secondary education. During the first year of study, however, students do tend to acquire the self-regulation skills required in PBL. Nevertheless, there is little change in the standard PBL procedure thereafter and so the way of working for students becomes a routine and the challenge ceases to exist (see Figure 2). And this tendency is found not only in PBL; most teaching-learning methods are implemented in similar ways throughout the degree programme.

If we consider it important that students learn to learn and think in an ever more self-regulated way, the teaching-learning methods need to change to provide a progressive increase in self-regulation year by year. This would then lead to a curriculum that is typified by gradual, systematically decreasing external regulation from teachers and an increasing self-regulation by students (transfer of regulation). That might lead to a pattern of teaching-learning methods that succeed each other: for example, assignment-based teaching could be the starting-point followed by PBL, project-centred learning, self-directed specialization learning, competency-based teaching and work-based learning. This principle would have to be applied flexibly, however. For example, getting acquainted with professional practice in the early study years will be very useful in some studies (e.g. the medical curriculum), while PBL or assignment-based learning may be the best teaching method for difficult subject matter in the third year.

Following this pattern, the development of self-regulation in student learning is fostered in two ways. Progressing through the degree course, first, students are confronted with ever larger and more complex tasks, problems or assignments in which they have to call upon an increasingly varied set of acquired skills (e.g. Ten Cate, Snell, Mann, & Vermunt, 2004). Then, the external regulation in tasks and teaching methods decreases, so that students are given an ever increasing role in determining the problems that they work on, the learning goals that direct learning, the choice of learning activities, the search for suitable sources, the determination of the criteria the learning outcomes should meet, the monitoring of learning progress and the evaluation of learning outcomes.

Elsewhere, we named this view of teaching *process-oriented teaching,* because it is targeted at the processes of knowledge construction and utilization (see Simons, 1997; Vermunt & Verschaffel, 2000; Volet, McGill, & Pears, 1995). It is based on an analysis of the interplay that can occur between teaching methods and the way students approach their studies (Vermunt & Verloop, 1999). It is characterized by a gradual diminution of the external regulation of learning processes through teaching agents and calls

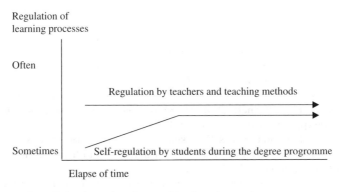

Figure 2. Pattern of regulation in unchanging teaching-learning environments.

increasingly on self-regulation of learning processes by students, individually and in small groups.

New teachers' roles and skills

The roles that teachers are expected to fulfil in the teaching-learning methods we have discussed vary considerably. In traditional teaching, teachers have primarily to be able to explain the subject matter well, to regulate the learning of their students and to motivate them to learn. In assignment-based teaching, skills involve designing good assignments, giving feedback, coaching and setting students to work actively. In PBL, the teacher fulfils roles like tutor, skills trainer and assessor, problem designer and block coordinator. Project-centred teaching presupposes that a teacher can supervise and guide project groups, coach the cooperation within groups and deal with the individualistic behaviour of students. In competency-based teaching, the teachers have to become study career advisors, competency assessors, professional growth consultants and the like, while work-based learning calls for teacher roles like mentor, portfolio advisor, authentic test designer and being able to clarify and guide student concerns. In all student-oriented forms of teaching, teachers should be able to fulfil roles as diagnostician, challenger, model, activator, monitor, reflector and evaluator of students' learning processes. In addition to all these, teachers may have still more roles as, for example, acting as educational developers or consultants on e-learning.

Just as first-year students find it difficult to adjust to the self-regulation required in PBL courses, so university staff find it equally difficult to adopt the very different roles that educational developers are expecting of them. The transitions are not simply of learning new skills, but fundamentally changing a mindset that previously involved regulating the study programme and controlling student activities working independently, to one which accepts an increasing level of student autonomy and collaborative learning. To call this change 'demanding' is to understate what is being expected; any such change will take many years to accomplish, but such changes are essential if we are to help students to become self-regulated and self-motivated learners by the time they leave university.

References

Beishuizen, J., Stoutjesdijk, E., & Van Putten, K. (1994). Studying textbooks: Effects of learning styles, study task, and instruction. *Learning and Instruction, 4*, 151–174.

Biggs, J. (1987). *Student approaches to learning and studying*. Melbourne: Australian Council for Educational Research.

Boekaerts, M., Otten, R., & Simons, R. (1997). Leerstijl in de onderbouw van het voortgezet onderwijs - Een onderzoek naar de bruikbaarheid van de ILS [Learning style in the first years of secondary education - A study on the usability of the ILS]. *Tijdschrift voor Onderwijsresearch [Dutch Journal of Educational Research], 22*, 15–36.

Brown, A. L. (1987). Metacognition, executive control, self-regulation and other more mysterious mechanisms. In F. E. Weinert & R. H. Kluwe (Eds.), *Metacognition, motivation and understanding* (pp. 65–116). Hillsdale, NJ: Erlbaum.

Busato, V. V., Prins, F. J., Elshout, J. J., & Hamaker, C. (1999). The relation between learning styles, the Big Five personality traits and achievement motivation in higher education. *Personality and Individual Differences, 26*, 129–140.

Entwistle, N., & McCune, V. (2004). The conceptual bases of study strategy inventories. *Educational Psychology Review, 16*, 325–345.

Entwistle, N., McCune, V., & Hounsell, J. (2003). Investigating ways of enhancing university teaching-learning environments: Measuring students' approaches to studying and perceptions of teaching. In E. de Corte, L. Verschaffel, N. Entwistle, & J. van Merriënboer (Eds.), *Powerful learning environments: Unravelling basic components and dimensions* (pp. 89-107). Pergamon: Oxford.

Flavell, J. H. (1987). Speculations about the nature and development of metacognition. In F. E. Weinert & R. H. Kluwe (Eds.), *Metacognition, motivation and understanding* (pp. 21-29). Hillsdale, NJ: Erlbaum.

Gibbs, G., Morgan, A., & Taylor, E. (1984). The world of the learner. In F. Marton, D. Hounsell, & N. Entwistle (Eds.), *The experience of learning* (pp. 165-188). Edinburgh: Scottish Academic Press.

Klatter, E. (1995). Leerstijlen in de brugklas – een onderzoek naar een vakspecifieke leerstijl [Learning styles in the first year of secondary education – a study on a subject specific learning style]. In H. C. Schouwenburg & J. T. Groenewoud (Eds.), *Studievaardigheid en leerstijlen [Study skill and learning style]* (pp. 169-191). Groningen: Wolters-Noordhoff.

Lindblom-Ylänne, S., & Lonka, K. (1999). Individual ways of interacting with the learning environment: Are they related to study success? *Learning and Instruction, 9*, 1-18.

Lindblom-Ylänne, S., & Lonka, K. (2000). Dissonant study orchestrations of high-achieving university students. *European Journal of Psychology of Education, 15*, 19-32.

Lonka, K., Heikkilä, A., Lindblom-Ylänne, S., & Maury, S. (1997, August). *Are epistemologies related to study activities in an innovative course?* Paper presented at the 7th Conference of the European Association for Research on Leaning and Instruction, Athens, Greece.

Lonka, K., Olkinuora, E., & Mäkinen, J. (2004). Aspects and prospects of measuring studying and learning in higher education. *Educational Psychology Review, 16*, 301-323.

Mansvelder-Longayroux, D., Beijaard, D., & Verloop, N. (2002). Het portfolio als reflectie-instrument voor docenten-in-opleiding [The portfolio as a reflection instrument for student teachers]. *Pedagogische Studiën, 79*, 269-286.

Marton, F., & Säljö, R. (1984). Approaches to learning. In F. Marton, D. Hounsell, & N. Entwistle (Eds.), *The experience of learning* (pp. 36-55). Edinburgh: Scottish Academic Press.

Meyer, J. H. F. (2000). The modeling of 'dissonant' study orchestration in higher education. *European Journal of Psychology of Education, 15*, 5-18.

Oosterheert, I. E., & Vermunt, J. D. (2001). Individual differences in learning to teach: Relating cognition, regulation and affect. *Learning and Instruction, 11*, 133-156.

Pintrich, P. (2004). A conceptual framework for assessing motivation and self-regulated learning in college students. *Educational Psychology Review, 16*, 385-408.

Richardson, J. T. E. (2000). *Researching student learning*. Buckingham: SRHE and Open University Press.

Rozendaal, J. S., De Brabander, C. J., & Minnaert, A. (2001, August). *Boundaries and dimensionality of epistemological beliefs*. Paper presented at the 9th Conference of the European Association for Research on Leaning and Instruction, Fribourg, Switzerland.

Severiens, S. E., & Ten Dam, G. T. M. (1997). Gender and gender identity differences in learning styles. *Educational Psychology, 17*, 79-93.

Simons, P. R. J. (1997). From romanticism to practice in learning. *Lifelong learning in Europe, 1*, 8-15.

Ten Cate, O., Snell, L., Mann, K., & Vermunt, J. (2004). Orienting teaching towards the learning process. *Academic Medicine, 79*(3), 219-228.

Trigwell, K., & Prosser, M. (2004). Development and use of the approaches to teaching inventory. *Educational Psychology Review, 16*, 409-424.

Vermetten, Y. J., Lodewijks, H. G., & Vermunt, J. D. (1999). Consistency and variability of learning strategies in different university courses. *Higher Education, 37*, 1-21.

Vermetten, Y. J., Lodewijks, H. G., & Vermunt, J. D. (2001). The role of personality traits and goal orientations in strategy use. *Contemporary Educational Psychology, 26*, 149-170.

Vermetten, Y. J., Vermunt, J. D., & Lodewijks, H. G. (1999). A longitudinal perspective on learning strategies in higher education: Different viewpoints towards development. *British Journal of Educational Psychology, 69*, 221-242.

Vermunt, J. D. (1996). Metacognitive, cognitive and affective aspects of learning styles and strategies: A phenomenographic analysis. *Higher Education, 31*, 25-50.

Vermunt, J. D. (1998). The regulation of constructive learning processes. *British Journal of Educational Psychology, 68*, 149-171.

Vermunt, J. D. (2005). Relations between student learning patterns and personal and contextual factors and academic performance. *Higher Education, 49*, 205-234.

Vermunt, J. D., & Verloop, N. (1999). Congruence and friction between learning and teaching. *Learning and Instruction, 9*, 257-280.

Vermunt, J. D., & Verloop, N. (2000). Dissonance in students' regulation of learning processes. *European Journal of Psychology of Education, 15*, 75-89.

Vermunt, J. D., & Vermetten, Y. J. (2004). Patterns in student learning: Relationships between learning strategies, conceptions of learning, and learning orientations. *Educational Psychology Review, 16*, 359-384.

Vermunt, J. D., & Verschaffel, L. (2000). Process-oriented teaching. In R. J. Simons, J. van der Linden, & T. Duffy (Eds.), *New learning* (pp. 209-225). Dordrecht, Boston: Kluwer Academic Publishers.

Volet, S., McGill, T., & Pears, H. (1995). Implementing process-based instruction in regular university teaching: Conceptual, methodological and practical issues. *European Journal of Psychology of Education, 10*, 385-400.

Wierstra, R. F., Kanselaar, G., Van der Linden, J. L., Lodewijks, H. G., & Vermunt, J. D. (2003). The impact of the university context on European students' learning approaches and learning environment preferences. *Higher Education, 45*, 503-523.

Zanting, A., Verloop, N., & Vermunt, J. D. (2001). Student teachers eliciting mentors' practical knowledge and comparing it to their own beliefs. *Teaching and Teacher Education, 17*, 725-740.

British Journal of Educational Psychology, 91–111
BJEP Monograph Series II, 4
© 2007 The British Psychological Society

The
British
Psychological
Society

www.bpsjournals.co.uk

7 – Teaching–learning environments in contemporary mass higher education

Dai Hounsell* and Jenny Hounsell
Moray House School of Education, University of Edinburgh, UK

The concern of this chapter is with research into undergraduate course settings as teaching-learning environments, in which how and what students learn may be subject to a range of direct and indirect influences. The chapter discusses findings from a large-scale ESRC-funded project concerned with the investigation and enhancement of teaching-learning environments in undergraduate courses in contrasting subject areas. The findings presented in this chapter are focused on student and staff experiences and perceptions of first- and final-year course units in three bioscience departments, and draw on both questionnaire and semi-structured interview data. The outcomes of the research are distinctive in two principal respects. First, the concept of *ways of thinking and practising in a subject* is introduced as a promising means of encapsulating key facets of high-quality learning, particularly in the later years of study. These are not confined to knowledge and understanding but also include subject-specific skills, an evolving familiarity with the values and conventions of scholarly communication within a discipline and an understanding of how new knowledge is generated within the field. Secondly, building on Biggs' model of *constructive alignment*, the concept of *congruence* is introduced as a broader framework for investigating and analysing aspects of teaching-learning environments that reflects contemporary mass higher education. Four dimensions of congruence are highlighted in this chapter: teaching-learning activities, assessment and the provision of feedback to students, students' backgrounds and aspirations, and course organization and management.

Background and introduction

The coming of mass higher education

The second half of the twentieth century saw a remarkable expansion in student enrolments in higher education, in the UK and in the more developed economies generally. Two very visible consequences of this expansion were that the proportion of 18- to 21-year-olds pursuing first degrees in British universities and colleges tripled between the 1960s and the early 2000s, while by 2002–03 there were over two million

*Correspondence should be addressed to Professor Dai Hounsell, Higher and Community Education, School of Education, University of Edinburgh, Paterson's Land, Holyrood Road, Edinburgh EH8 8AQ, UK (e-mail: Dai.Hounsell@ed.ac.uk).

DOI:10.1348/000709906X170975

students studying at higher education institutions, of which over one million were undergraduates studying for a first degree. A third consequence has been increasing student diversity. While there has been disappointingly little change in the percentages of students from lower social class groupings entering higher education in recent years, the proportion of those from ethnic minorities is currently higher than for the population as a whole and the proportion of mature entrants – those aged 21 or over at the start of their first degrees – grew to one in five students by 2002/03 (HEFCE, 2005; SFC, 2004).

As the sociologist Martin Trow had famously predicted in 1973, growth on this scale would not simply represent quantitative change: it would also entail a qualitative transformation of universities that would constitute a shift from elite to mass forms of higher education. The shift, Trow suggested, would bring changes on many fronts, including the extent of student homogeneity, the size of institutions, the forms of instruction and the relationships between students and faculty (Trow, 1973).

The concern of the present chapter is with some key characteristics of learning and teaching in the age of mass higher education which typifies the opening decade of the twenty-first century. It examines contemporary undergraduate courses as *teaching–learning environments*, i.e. taking account not just of the organization and provision of teaching but of a wider array of influences, direct and indirect, intentional and unintended, on the learning and studying experiences of the students concerned (Hounsell, 1997). The focus is chiefly on the psychosocial 'learning milieu' (Parlett, 1977) of the academic department, and the most immediate and significant influences on how and what students learn in a given course unit in the form of, for example, curriculum design, teaching–learning provision, assessment requirements and the backgrounds and circumstances of the students and staff associated with the unit (Entwistle, McCune, & Hounsell, 2003). Central though these 'inner' environmental influences are, however, the focus is not exclusively at this level, as will become evident, for account has also to be taken of the evolving impact on this inner environment of the advent of mass higher education.

To this end, the chapter draws on findings from an empirical study of a sample of first-year and final-year course units in the biosciences in three contrasting university settings (Hounsell, McCune, Hounsell, & Litjens, 2006). The study formed part of a much larger research project which sought to investigate and enhance teaching and learning across a range of subject areas that comprised economics (Reimann, Land, & Meyer, 2006) electronic engineering (Entwistle, Nisbet, & Bromage, 2005) and history (Anderson & Day, 2005) as well as the biosciences. The project was funded by the Economic and Social Research Council within its Teaching and Learning Research Programme.

Research on teaching–learning environments

Contextual perspectives on student learning

The roots of contemporary research perspectives on contextual influences on learning can be traced back nearly half a century, and were in the first instance predominantly sociological. Becker's groundbreaking ethnographic study of students' social and academic experiences of university life, *Making the Grade* (Becker, Geer, & Hughes, 1968), brought to light the extent to which assessment marks or grades functioned as a campus currency, informing and shaping the relative value that students placed on particular learning–teaching activities and in turn determining their study priorities. Thus what Snyder (1973) later dubbed 'the hidden curriculum' – the ground rules for academic survival learned by students, as they became more campus-wise – could act to distort and subvert the espoused goals of the formal curriculum as set out in syllabuses, course handbooks and institutional policies and procedures. Learning the art of 'selective negligence' (i.e. what aspects of the curriculum were crucial and which could safely be ignored) seemed to be a key student skill in the face of syllabuses that could seem unmanageably large or with boundaries that were only loosely demarcated. Similarly, in a smaller scale study, Miller and Parlett (1974) showed how students' academic achievement could be related to the extent to which they were contextually 'cue-conscious' – that is, alert to tacit as well as more overt hints and clues by lecturers about what it was most important to learn in order to get high grades. Those students who actively sought out cues to what lecturers prized were more likely to do well in assessments than those who were deaf to such cues.

A more psychologically informed approach to contextual influences subsequently emerged in large-scale research by Entwistle and Ramsden on the effects of academic departments on students' approaches to studying (Entwistle & Ramsden, 1983; Ramsden & Entwistle, 1981). Interview data complemented by questionnaire findings on over two thousand students across 66 departments showed a clear association between, on the one hand, a reproductive orientation to learning (the consistent deployment of surface approaches) and students' perceptions of their courses as calling for a high formally assigned workload and a lack of choice over content and method of study. However, the links were not always to the detriment of high quality learning, for consistency in the use of deep approaches – a meaning orientation – was found to be related to courses where staff were seen by students as committed to good teaching (and particularly in providing help with studying) and where students felt they had greater freedom to choose how and what they learned. Equally significantly, these two sets of relationships held up across the six contrasting subject areas surveyed. In a subsequent review of these and other findings on the context of learning, Ramsden (1984/1997) observed:

> The single most important message to emerge from these research findings is that intense effort must be made in course planning and in the setting of assessment questions, to avoid presenting a learning context which is perceived by students to require, or reward, surface approaches. It is not enough to assume that course materials or assessment methods will encourage students to think deeply about the subject matter, however carefully they have been designed: it is necessary to consider the students' perspective on what is required. It is useless, for example, simply to tell students that verbatim reproduction of information in an examination is wrong, to expect this warning to discourage surface approaches, and to blame the students when it does not. If students feel that there is insufficient time to study the examined topics properly (perhaps because of the demands of other courses), or if they have experienced inadequate teaching, or if they are given high marks for reproducing lecture notes, or if their previous knowledge within the area is insufficiently developed, then they will feel constrained to use surface approaches. Only by studying the internal relationships between how students perceive course demands and how they approach studying can the complexity, and apparent paradoxes, in student learning be understood. (Ramsden, 1984/1997)

This body of work, and the findings which emerged from it, set a pattern for how contextual influences on student learning could subsequently be investigated and conceptualized. Indeed, the research could be considered to mark a conceptual and methodological watershed. First, its paramount concern was with teaching–learning environments as they are perceived and experienced by the students concerned. This perspective – what Marton (1981) has called a second-order perspective – should be seen as a *sine qua non* rather than a limitation or shortcoming, acknowledging that teaching–learning environments are first and foremost subjective realities that need to be investigated through the eye-views of those participating in them. Put another way, the lived experience of a curriculum may be very different from the curriculum-as-planned or indeed the curriculum-as-implemented, if the latter is mediated only from the vantage point of the teaching and support staff. Second, it adopted a mixed-method research design that sought to capitalize on the complementary strengths and limitations of questionnaires and semi-structured interviews, rather than relying solely or mainly on interview evidence, as did the majority of the subsequent phenomenographic studies of students' experiences of learning (see for example Bruce & Gerber, 1997; Marton & Booth, 1997). Third, the research design did not simply proceed from a presumption of what makes for effectiveness in a teaching-learning environment, but took the processes and outcomes of learning exhibited by students as a reference-point and criterion of impact. Finally, it was acknowledged that differences between disciplines and subject areas could extend beyond epistemology and methodology to contextual characteristics of course and departmental settings.

Course settings as teaching–learning environments

In subsequent studies of environmental influences on student learning, a prominent and recurring theme has been that of the pervasive 'backwash effect' of assessment (Biggs, 2003; Watkins, Dahlin, & Ekholm, 2005), notably in studies which have explored students' approaches to assessment tasks which are perceived to differ in the learning outcomes sought and ostensibly rewarded (Scouller, 1998; Thomas & Bain, 1984; Tynjälä, 1998). However, what is also evident from surveying the burgeoning literature on teaching–learning environments is the sheer breadth of potentially relevant contextual factors, embracing not only departmental, subject and institutional influences but also wider social, cultural and political ones. Even an attempt at a conceptual map of the former and more immediate influences – the 'inner' teaching-learning environment – yields the rich array of possibilities depicted in Figure 1 (Entwistle *et al.*, 2003). Therefore, there has been a growing need for a more parsimonious conceptual framework or model that interrelates learning processes and outcomes with contextual influences, and the most noteworthy recent example is to be found in Biggs' *constructive alignment* (Biggs, 2003, 1996). In Biggs' model – a fusion of research on students' experiences of learning, constructivist theories of pedagogy and objectives-based approaches to curriculum design – a university course is viewed as a teaching-learning system which functions optimally when learning outcomes are of an appropriately high-quality and are harmoniously matched to or 'aligned' with teaching and assessment:

> In aligned teaching, there is maximum consistency throughout the system. The curriculum is stated in the form of clear objectives, which state the level of understanding required rather than simply a list of topics to be covered. The teaching methods are chosen that are likely to realize those objectives; you get students to do the things that the objectives nominate. Finally, the assessment tasks address the objectives, so that you can test to see if

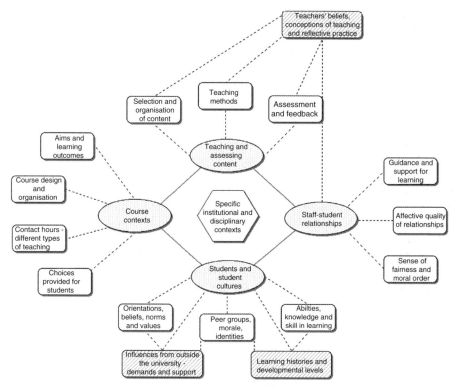

Figure 1. The 'inner' teaching–learning environment.

> the students have learned what the objectives state they should be learning. All components
> in the system address the same agenda and support each other. (Biggs, 2003)

Promising though it may be, however, constructive alignment has yet to undergo systematic empirical validation, and the large-scale study from which the present chapter is drawn has sought to close that gap by using it as a guiding concept in the study of undergraduate course settings as teaching–learning environments. However, as will be also apparent in the analysis which follows below, the concept of constructive alignment has been widened beyond teaching–learning and assessment activities, and in a form which seeks to acknowledge the variety of resource and other everyday constraints on the freedom of action of teaching staff in contemporary higher education (McCune & Hounsell, 2005). Given these modifications, the term 'congruence' has been adopted as a means of capturing the interrelationships between high-quality learning outcomes and the strategies deployed to pursue these outcomes.

Settings, samples and key findings on TLEs

The main phase of the biosciences component of the ETL project was carried out in collaboration with three bioscience departments of varying size and drawn from contrasting university settings. All three were actively committed to research and to teaching in the biosciences, while also valuing their links with the wider professional bioscience community. Department B1 was located in a post-1992 university with a strong commitment to promoting wider access to higher education and vocationally relevant degree programmes. B2 was a large cluster of bioscience departments that formed a faculty within an equally large and diverse 'ancient' university with a high research profile. B3 was a thriving department in a university which had been founded in the late 1960s with a leaning towards science and engineering. In each of the three universities, a first and a final-year course unit were the focus of the investigation.

All three first-year modules were second-semester foundation modules, taught through a combination of lectures and opportunities for laboratory-based practical work and small-group activities. B2F had an intake of over 600 students, while the other two units had intakes of around 100. Admission requirements varied with respect to the background qualifications of the incoming students, with the grades typically sought being higher for English 3-year degrees than those for 4-year Scottish degrees. B3F tended to have fewer mature students but a higher proportion than the others of students with an international baccalaureate. The size and scope of their staffing varied greatly, with B2F having a course team of 12 lecturers and associate lecturers plus 14 postgraduate tutors, B3F having a team of nine lecturers and some post-doctoral laboratory demonstrators, while B1F had a smaller team of three lecturers and a teaching assistant. The units also varied in the types of learning support offered, with course handbooks and websites containing varied amounts of information and the capacity to offer support varying from assigned tutors to drop-in tutorials. Assessment also varied greatly, both in terms of the percentage assessed by examination (80% in B3F but 20% in B1F) and in the types of coursework set, whether multiple-choice tests, lab reports or group posters and presentations.

The three final-year units investigated were specialized, honours-level modules with a combined enrolment of a little over 80 students. The three course units differed markedly in their approaches to teaching and learning and in their patterns of assessment. B1L was taught through lectures and tutorials and assessed by an examination and two essays. In B2L guest experts gave lectures and then provided data for a group problem-solving exercise for the students. This unit was assessed solely by examination. Each session of B3L consisted of a presentation by a pair of the students, followed by discussion. The presentations were assessed, and the students also completed two essays. The students taking B1L and B3L, and in some cases B2L, had spent at least one semester on placement in industry or academic research environments.

Data were gathered from students in two forms: the *Learning and Studying Questionnaire* (LSQ) was completed by students at the start of the semester and the *Experiences of Teaching and Learning Questionnaire* (ETLQ) and group interviews towards the end of the unit. One-to-one interviews were also conducted with key members of the course teams concerned.

The LSQ asked students about their orientations to learning, their reasons for taking the course unit and their general approaches to studying. The items in the ETLQ asked students about their approaches to studying on the particular course unit and about their experiences of the teaching–learning environment on the module as well as how demanding they found it. For each item, students responded on a scale of one to five, indicating how strongly they agreed with that item. The items were combined into scales, including ones for deep and surface approaches along with organized effort, and for students' perceptions of aspects of their environments such as clarity and goodness-of-fit of course aims and teaching, the feedback given on assignments, and staff and student support (Entwistle *et al.*, 2003; Table 1).

Table 1. Students' perceptions of their teaching–learning environments (ETLQ scales)

Clarity	Clear aims and curricular congruence
Choice	Choice in how and what to study
Teaching	Teaching which encourages understanding
Feedback	Clear and supportive guidance and feedback on set work
Assessment	Assessing understanding and critical thinking
Staff	Staff enthusiasm and support
Students	Student support
Interest	Interest and enjoyment

The analyses which follow are drawn from a total of 906 LSQs and 844 ETLQs completed by the students, together with interviews with 113 students and 31 staff (Hounsell *et al.*, 2006).

Key findings

Approaches to learning and ways of thinking and practising

The questionnaire data open up one valuable window on the learning processes of the students concerned. The data from the LSQ show that the biosciences students were more likely to be taking a deep approach than a surface approach to their studying by setting out to understand the meaning of what was being taught, by relating ideas to their own experience, by looking at evidence and following arguments and by monitoring their studying to improve their learning. Their responses also indicated that they were likely to be organizing their studying and managing their time, and to be putting in effort and concentrating on their studying. These tendencies were stronger for final-year students than for first-year students. As far as differences between course units was concerned, there was little evident difference between students in the three first-year course units, but in the final-year units, students in the post-1992 university were more likely than those in the late 1990s university to score highly on the 'organized effort' scale (B1L Mean 3.83, *SD* .83; B3L Mean 3.29, *SD* .79) (Figure 2).

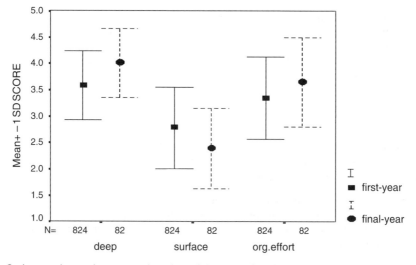

Figure 2. Approaches to learning and studying (Mean ± 1 Standard Deviation).

The interview analyses, especially of the final-year students, offer a further and novel vantage point, and one which is of particular value since the potential of the construct of deep approach to capture the most salient features of high-quality learning in a given discipline tends to lessen as students progress further in their academic studies (Hounsell & Anderson, 2005). What emerged from these analyses was that the students were learning distinctive *ways of thinking and practising* characteristic of, and particular to, the biosciences. These were not confined to knowledge and understanding but also included subject-specific skills, an evolving familiarity with the values and conventions of scholarly communication within a discipline and an understanding of how new knowledge was generated within the field.

The development of ways of thinking and practising in the biosciences could most noticeably be seen in the three final-year course units, with respect to two prominent areas of activity: the students' interactions with the primary literature in the discipline and with experimental data, and their efforts to communicate within the subject what they had learned (McCune & Hounsell, 2005). These two areas of activity were prevalent in all three-course units, despite the strong differences in how the three groups of students were taught and assessed. Opportunities to engage with experimental data could be found in lectures, in group problem-solving or in the individual preparation of coursework assignments. In addition, it was the assignments – whether written or oral – that offered the opportunity for students to gain expertise in communicating what they had come to know and understand, and by what means. Placements in industry or academic bioscience research institutes undertaken by many of the students also provided opportunities for practice in gathering and interpreting data, and in presenting their emerging findings to peers.

Students were expected both to be able to find and use appropriately up-to-date sources of information and to evaluate the evidence for particular interpretations of knowledge which could be contested by experts.

> If you're going to become a scientist, you need to quote papers; you need to have proper up-to-date references. That's one thing they're really pushing you to do this year, they're trying to turn you into real scientists. Hence, if you write essays, you're not going to get a good mark – even in exams – if you don't use references.
>
> --
>
> S1: You have to find various papers and understand them by reading them and then you have to summarize what they're saying, obviously whether you agreed with that or not. And [. . .] there's lot of disagreement, you know they're not all saying the same thing or coming from the same line of thought. So they have different opinions.
>
> S2: Yeah. So long as you've got evidence to back up your ideas with. As I say, it's not what it is just because it is; you've got to give evidence.

Final-year students were also learning the ground rules for communicating within the subject. One challenge was learning the differences between genres (oral presentations, experimental reports, analytical essays) while another was discovering the forms of language expected in different situations and by different groups of people (student peers, lecturers and tutors, colleagues on work placements).

> And for me, okay, the hardest part is going to be we cannot use any laboratory slang. So, we cannot say, 'Well, we put to the proteins to centrifuge', we have to say, like 'we pelleted the protein', but I mean for everything.[. . .] So, it's really technical, and it's really a good command of the language.
>
> --

> For the group meetings [on placement], we would just be sitting around the table having a chat, it wouldn't be a formal presentation or 'polished' results. You would just say, 'This is the preliminary result I got from such and such an experiment, what do you think of this, is there something I could improve in my experiment?'. Just a general chat. Whereas, if you move up to sort of department meetings it would be 'polished' data that you're presenting in a formal manner, so you would have to sort of be able to say, 'These are the experiments that were done and these are my results.... You would have to give them a lot more background information than necessarily you would with people who work on the same thing as you'.

The interviews with staff showed them to be concerned to foster various key facets of ways of thinking and practising in the biosciences. What students learned by way of subject matter could be considered less important than the wider expertise they were gaining as potential scientists.

> There's nothing [in the module] which would be key knowledge for someone who wants to be a molecular and cellular biologist, because there are various options. What we're trying to do is make them get to grips with a specific topic and analyse the problems associated with that topic, and be able to have a grasp of what's going on, what the research problems are, how you approach finding out more about that topic. [. . .] I just think it's a way of learning to think in particular ways, I suppose, developing their own skills in analysis in that area.
>
> --
>
> These seminar units reflect the interests of staff members at supposedly the highest level of non-experimental work that is available to undergraduates. The encouragement is to go out and look at the original literature. Hence, it leads an undergraduate into the type of scholarship that they will have to do if they go into science as a career.... The necessity, absolute necessity to consult the scientific literature outside of mainstream textbooks. The second but just as important is the ability to present these results to their peers.

Unsurprisingly, indications of the learning of ways of thinking and practising in the biosciences were much less evident in the three first-year course units, where the predominant goal was to provide students with a secure initial grounding of the subject on which to build subsequently a richer understanding. Moreover, many of these students differed from their final-year counterparts in not having yet made a firm commitment to studying the subject beyond their first or second-year. And course units with relatively large and diverse enrolments (in the case of these three units, ranging from a little under one hundred to over 600), teaching–learning activities tended to follow the well-established pattern of a combination of lectures, laboratory-based practical work and small-group activities.

Within such constraints, however, it was nonetheless possible for staff to begin sowing seeds for the development of ways of thinking and practising:

> I think the concept that nobody knows what's right in everything is definitely what we're trying to put across. The idea that we don't have all the solutions yet, to challenge things, to question things, 'Can both these people be right?'. I think that's very important at an early stage, a good healthy dose of cynicism I think will make you a better scientist [. . .] In the end of the day it's you and your data, and you make up your mind what you think, keep your mind very open in case new data comes in [. . .] Not that we're training them all to be research scientists, but I think that's good training for being a human being.

And despite large class sizes, opportunities to nudge students in this direction could be found in lectures or, as in the two following examples, in practicals and other group-based activities:

> L1:   I guess, in the 'Animal Behaviour' lab, the maggots don't always behave in the way that you would want them to. So I guess that's a kind of biological thing, you know, the students predict what's going to happen, and the maggots will either do it or not do it. And you say, 'Well, try to think why they do it, you know, do you always do what you're expected to do? . . . No'. That kind of thing, the unpredictability of biology, maybe comes out in the Animal Behaviour lab.
>
> L2:   They realize that there quite often aren't answers, direct answers.
>
> --
>
> We give them information, they have a relatively short period of time in which to assimilate the relevant facts, and somebody in that group has to present it to a larger group . . . And I think it combines skills of combining information, something that they're not familiar with, they probably haven't seen before, and discussing various aspects of an issue – something like cloning a sheep. They looked at it from the scientific side, how it was actually done, [and] from the ethical side, the problems associated with it.

However, there were also many indications in the student interviews that this was not merely an aspiration on the part of staff. As the following comments make manifest, the students saw themselves as beginning to adopt a more questioning and active approach to their learning of the subject:

> They do quite often remind you that, you know, you are a biologist or you are a scientist, you are researching this, you are looking into this. So they are always reminding you of that fact which, you do get into that frame of mind, and when you're sitting doing these experiments or investigations, it is quite good. You do think of yourself as researching it or doing it scientifically as opposed to just sitting there doing it as schoolwork or classwork.
>
> --
>
> Well the laboratory we had today, we were kind of expecting certain results. We were expecting to go a certain way, but towards the end the [lab supervisor] explained that it may not necessarily have been because of what we were perceiving it to be. Which makes you think, well, if that's the case everything could be a bit like that – there could be more than one answer for everything. [. . .] So yeah, I think they're trying to make us think more about what we're doing, and I think that's probably the most important thing that they're trying to get us to do, is to make us investigate, think for ourselves, don't take things at face value.
>
> --
>
> [My tutor] seems very interested in getting us to think a certain way, so the assignments that he sets are more about researching and learning how to read scientific papers, things that really are quite useful skills.

The six course settings as teaching–learning environments

The overall picture of the six course settings as teaching–learning environments which emerged from the questionnaire and interview data was a broadly favourable one. However, it was also apparent that the contextual influences upon the students' learning that could be identified were not confined to, or chiefly concentrated within, the provision of teaching–learning and assessment activities, as Biggs' model would imply, but ranged much more widely. Furthermore, and no less crucially, the contextual differences between first- and final-year course settings were such as to suggest that it would be inappropriate to treat such differences as negligible or incidental: on the contrary, they had the effect of determining whether or not particular dimensions of the perceived teaching–learning environment were to the fore, most obviously in the interview data.

Figure 3 indicates how congruence was operationalized in the data-analyses. Four dimensions of congruence can be picked out for closer scrutiny in these analyses:

- congruence of teaching–learning activities;
- congruence of assessment and feedback;
- congruence with students' backgrounds and aspirations;
- congruence of course organization and management.

The first two of these relate to all six-course settings. The third and fourth dimensions apply largely to the first-year courses.

Congruence of teaching–learning activities

As the questionnaire data indicate (Figure 4), the final-year course units were seen as offering well-organized, supportive learning and teaching climates in which teaching staff were enthusiastic and approachable, and in which interaction between students was encouraged. Indeed, the students' perceptions were positive across all three settings, despite the very marked differences already noted between these settings in the teaching–learning strategies pursued, as was also readily apparent in interview comments:

> S1: It is a really good module [. . .]. It all interlinks.
> S2: Yeah, with the lectures you're able to see it coming together . . . because of the relevance regarding how the science is applied, and how the basis of the science can be used to understand new concepts, so that helps bring that sort of process together.
> S3: Same here.
> --
> What I enjoyed most about it is that we've had a lecturer for each different topic [. . .] so it's been someone who's really keen on the topic and who really knows everything about it and

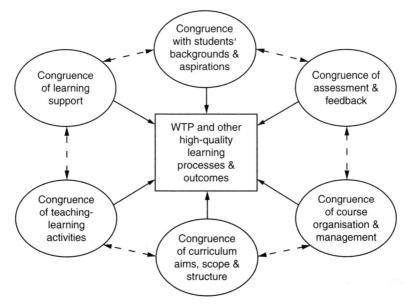

Figure 3. Congruence within teaching–learning environments.

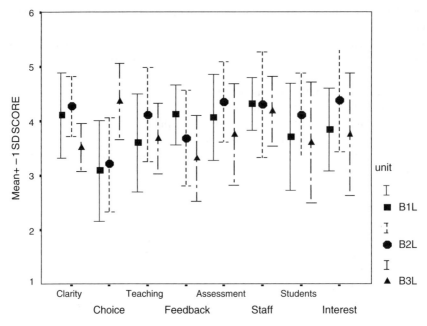

Figure 4. Final-year students' perceptions of their teaching–learning environments.

> is working on it [. . .] Because we get the half-hour break or twenty-minutes' break between each section, we always find ourselves just sitting and talking over the problems, because we get them beforehand [. . .] So we are just looking at them and just kind of talking through the stuff that we've learned in the first half, so that you learn it a lot better if you discuss it with other people.
>
> --
>
> I think it's actually quite useful too, that you're given a topic which you don't know anything about usually, and you have to actually research it. And also when other people present it, it's quite nice because it's different to lectures and you learn about the usefulness of certain applications or techniques.

In the three first-year course units, where teaching–learning strategies were outwardly much more similar, the students' perceptions were also positive across all of the settings (Figure 5). The students' overall perceptions of these three units as teaching–learning environments were both similar and positive, especially with respect to the clarity and 'goodness-of-fit' of course aims with teaching and assessment approaches (*clarity*); *assessment* for understanding; and the supportiveness shown by *staff* and *student* peers. In each case, the lowest score was for the subscale 'choice', which reflects the typical pattern for first-year undergraduate courses, where a predominant goal is generally to try to bring all the students towards a common baseline of knowledge and understanding, as a secure foundation for work in subsequent years. However, across the three units, it should also be noted, the scores for *teaching for understanding* and the effectiveness of *feedback* were somewhat lower. The score for perceived *interest*, enjoyment and relevance was also a little lower in B1F than in B2F and B3F.

Congruence of assessment and feedback
The assessment regimes in the three first-year course units differed in certain respects though all combined, in varying weightings, coursework assessments with

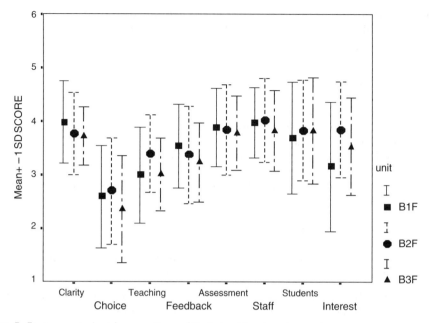

Figure 5. First-year students' perceptions of their teaching–learning environments.

terminal exams involving multiple-choice (MCQ) and short-answer questions. In the final-year units there was much greater variation, ranging from an approach based wholly on exams in one unit to assessment based entirely on coursework in another and a mixed economy in the third. Despite these many differences, nonetheless, as Figures 4 and 5 indicate there were similar and quite high questionnaire ratings by the students in all six units of the extent to which assessment required understanding.

However, what was also striking in the questionnaire data was the emergence of feedback as a significant facet of this dimension of congruence. On the scale 'feedback', ratings tended to be lower, especially in some of the course units. Indeed, an item-by-item analysis of the responses of final-year students revealed consistently positive scores for clarity about what was expected in the set work, encouragement to think about how best to tackle the set work, and provision by staff of support needed to help in completing the set work, and these were confirmed by the interview data:

S1: I think [the two lecturers] really help because when we got the [assignment] question I was like, 'What's that?!'
S2: So was I.
S1: And then [one of the lecturers] said, 'We'll have a tutorial'. And he took us through step by step what exactly should be in it, and how we get the information [. . .] So he have us all the help we needed for it.

--

S1: [The module coordinator] has got something on the website on how to answer the questions and giving example answers.
S2: Yeah, it's all the past exam questions from something like '98 onwards.
S1: Yeah, lots of links to other websites [. . .]

However, the questionnaire scores tended to be much lower for agreement with the statement 'The feedback on my work helped me to improve my ways of learning and studying' and for 'The feedback given on my set work helped to clarify things I hadn't fully understood' (McCune & Hounsell, 2005). The interviews with final-year students showed some of their concerns:

S1:   We don't have much kind of guidance on how to do essays.

S2:   Like none!

S1:   But we don't get any kind of, sit down and explain, 'cos the last time I wrote anything was GCSE when I was sixteen. 'A' levels are so specialized that you kind of forget how to write essays, and yet they are important and yet you don't get feedback [. . .]

S3:   Or perhaps if we had some more of them.

S4:   Yeah, start them early so we'd had practice by now.

--

S1:   [For essays] they used to give a mark sheet and it's got, like, structure, bibliography and references [. . .]

S2:   Yeah, it's got like five tick boxes.

 I: What about the comments?

S2:   Few and far between. Definitely.

S1:   It definitely depends on who's marking it, though. Some will just put 'very good', 'liked it', or some will put reams and reams of text.

The analyses of the first-year student interviews show similar dissatisfaction with the adequacy of feedback, particularly in two of the course units.

S1:   I totally got the wrong end of the stick. [. . .] I read the instructions, and I felt there were hidden things that you had to put [in the assignment] that they didn't explain. And I got 8 out of 20, and I've got nothing written on my [feedback] sheet at all.

S2:   Mine's the same. I got 10, and it's got NO comments on it whatsoever.

S1:   And they tell you to do it in double-spacing, so they can write things in, but they never do . . .

S2:   I mean, if we're getting half marks, it must have a lot wrong with it . . . [S1: Exactly.] But it's not telling us anything.

--

 I: Did you get some feedback on these exams that you've had?

S2:   We don't really get feedback on it – you get a mark – but even in coursework you just get a mark and maybe a couple of ticks or [S1: 'Good'] or 'put this in capital letters instead' or something, and that would be it.

S1:   You don't really get any feedback on anything.

However, the source of the students' discontent was not just the quantity and helpfulness of feedback. Their dissatisfaction extended in some cases to delays in receiving feedback and uncertainty about what the ground-rules were for buttonholing tutors in search of further guidance:

If you get [your coursework assignments] back then you should be able to learn from your mistakes. But they come back too late for you to learn from your mistakes, to help you with your actual exam. Cause that happened last year. I think it was right up until about the last week before we got some information back. And I thought well, what's the point?

--

I understand that they have so many to mark in a short space of time, but it would be nice if they could put more information into the marking. But if they can't it would be good to know if you have a question regarding your laboratory report, that needs further explanation, who to go, whether you should go and see X PhD student, or if you should go and see the lecturer who was in charge of that practical, or if you should go and discuss it with your tutor.

Despite these concerns, nevertheless, it should be made clear that, overall, the provision of guidance and feedback was widely variable rather than uniformly unsatisfactory, and the following illustrative comments offer an important counterweight to the less positive earlier ones:

> The majority of it is written down. They do go over it but if you are in doubt it is always in your laboratory manual. It really clearly states what you're supposed to do and if you're having trouble getting the information you have just got to go to your textbook or go and ask somebody.
>
> --
>
> S1: You've got your [unit handbook] that tells you all your references and learning objectives for each lecture.
> S2: And the lecture actually itself, and then afterwards it's like discussions been done and then you've got the reference and I think there is objectives as well in this.
> S3: And even answers to the problems that we've done. And the discussions afterwards. If you miss anything during the lesson you have it. [. . .]
> S4: It's really demanding because you have to think and you have to do a lot of work for it, but in the end, they also give you the basis for you to succeed, I think.

In the interviews with first-year teaching staff – and in obvious contrast to the student interviews – any comments on the provision of feedback are relatively scarce. This would seem to suggest a pervasive lack of awareness, on the part of the staff, about the strength of student concern about feedback, or perhaps a reluctance to endorse a student view of its importance. The comments made by staff about assessment vary quite a lot from one interview to another, reflecting to a significant degree the extent to which assessment roles are differentiated. In B3F, for example, the lecture-givers mark the exam questions relating to their lectures, while postgraduate or postdoctoral demonstrators mark the practical work, and formative assignments set in tutorials are marked by the lecturers responsible for those tutorial groups. One theme, however, which recurs across the three course units is an awareness of the need to balance quality and economy in assessment methods and procedures. It is therefore conceded that while it is difficult to devise MCQs which address higher-order learning outcomes, they do have a significant contribution to make (in combination with other assessment methods) in coping with the pressures of student numbers and constraints on resources:

> I'm not 100% happy with using a lot of multi-choice assessment but it does make it feasible to handle a large group of students. And they do do laboratory reports, so they do actually have to write something which I think is actually quite important 'cos they need to be able to construct and synthesize ideas, which a lot of them find quite, they find that itself quite a challenge. So, I think it's important to keep some report writing in the module. But I think the way it's assessed works reasonably well because it does mean that, by having the mid short test halfway through, sometimes you can pick up problems, and also it can sometimes give students a bit of a wake up call.

Congruence with students' backgrounds and aspirations

A distinctive feature of the three first-year units (and one they share with most first-year courses in contemporary mass higher education) was the diversity not only of the backgrounds and prior knowledge of the students concerned, but also of their aspirations and onward intentions – most strikingly in B2F, where some would go on to pursue one of a range of bioscience-linked degree programmes, while others had subject commitments that lay elsewhere. Given that diversity, the extent of congruence with students' backgrounds and aspirations in courses such as these was a dimension which merited attention in its own right.

Various strategies were in evidence across the three course units to assist them in engaging with the students' diverse needs and interests. These included tutorial systems or group-based practical activities designed to promote peer interaction and support, self-test question banks and supplementary learning–teaching resources, as well as staff who, as we have already noted, were generally perceived as approachable and supportive (Hounsell *et al.*, 2006). Nonetheless, there were various indications in the student interviews of the challenges entailed in achieving a consistently high degree of satisfaction with this dimension of congruence. While the students from traditional backgrounds had generally found their first year as undergraduates relatively plain sailing, some of their non-traditional counterparts had struggled to cope with study demands:

> I worked for eight years and then decided to go back to Uni. When I came here it was basically hell because I had no Biology knowledge, quite small Chemistry knowledge, so the first term was a bit of a nightmare – lots of work, much, much more work than I thought was involved. [. . .] The second term is much better. We actually have got to rely on what we did for the first term, so it's kind of levelled out.
>
> --
>
> I spoke to Dr X briefly and he said that really if you want to do well, then you do need to be working all the time practically and, for me, as well that's just not physically possible. I spend three hours commuting a day and I have a part-time job, so I literally maybe can do . . . just nowhere near that! [laughing] It's just not going to happen.
>
> --
>
> [There are] a lot of international students in the course [who] struggled really hard in the first semester. It was very, very frustrating when we kept hearing all the lecturers saying 'And you will have done this in A-level.' [All agreeing] We haven't done A-level! I can do the extra research, but it takes a lot of time, and when lecturers don't realize that you're doing that and they're just skimming through everything, it is very frustrating.

It is also important to note that teaching staff were aware of the challenges posed by these more diverse student intakes, but were also mindful of the practical constraints on the extent to which the students' needs could be appropriately met:

> It's very difficult to get a feel for what they're like in lectures there, because it's quite a sort of anonymous way of teaching. They turn up and they are well behaved – that's really about as far as it goes. And I see their examination answers, and there's clearly [. . .] you get a feeling for just how switched on and how into this part of the subject they are, and there's enormous variability I find. Some are really very good for first-year students and some are really very poor. So, the range is enormous. [. . .] I know from teaching it at other years, other higher levels, that quite a few people, who continue to do biology, haven't done biology at school. So, biology in level 1 is their first contact with biology . . . so, for that reason I suppose it's not surprising that some people find it more difficult to get into than others.
>
> --
>
> You know there are a large number of students in the class. So you don't really get any kind of feeling of, of coherence etc. You know they seem to work quite well together, but that's quite a difficult thing to judge when you're standing in front of a hundred odd people. And I think you might, that might be something that might be more apparent in practical classes. That's one of the reasons why we do try and have the same group of students in the tutorial group and they'll be in that tutorial group for all their different modules on that programme. I think the idea is to give them a feeling of belonging to a group.

Congruence of course organization and management

An increasingly common feature of large-enrolment first-year courses in contemporary mass higher education is that teaching and assessment are undertaken by course teams, often from a mix of backgrounds. In these units, the size of teams varied from four to nearly thirty, and they included mainstream and associate lecturers, postdoctoral laboratory demonstrators and postgraduate teaching assistants, together with varying levels of administrative and clerical support.

There were also differences between the three units in the extent to which roles were differentiated (e.g. distinguishing teaching, assessment, learning support and course management roles) as well as in the breadth and focus of effort (compare, for example, having responsibility for practicals over a whole semester or year, where effort is distributed, to responsibility concentrated around four successive lecturers).

There are of course manifest advantages in deploying a large and disparate course team with compartmentalized roles, not least in terms of being able to draw on a breadth and depth of collegial expertise, flexibility in scheduling of classes and accommodating leave, and economies to be had in hiring postgraduates and others to cope with a burgeoning demand for tutorial and practical classes. However, there are also potential limitations and drawbacks, three of which were evident in the interviews with students. First, a large and disparate course team can exacerbate (or at least, fail to ameliorate) a sense of *impersonality and distance*:

> Half the lecturers I probably couldn't recognize them if they walked past me. I wouldn't even say that that person taught me something in biology because the lecturers are constantly changing and you don't get any personal relationship with them.
>
> --
>
> S1:   How many lecturers did we have in that course?
> S2:   Yeah
> S1:   Seven, eight, nine?
> S2:   Loads.
> S1:   So you know, they would come for two or three lectures and then go . . . Sometimes I did not even know their name, to be honest. [. . .]
> S3:   We get these assessments kind of 'What do you think of this lecturer?' at the end of [the preceding module], you could hear everyone, sat there in the lecture theatre going 'So which was that lecturer? What did they lecture on?' . . . Such a rush of different people.

A second potential limitation is that as *lines of communication* become attenuated, so the possibility increases of messages not being passed on:

> S: I was discussing with Dr X, after the practical, the nature of the calculations involved . . . and I was saying that I'd realized that after going through step by step, that I could actually condense all those steps into a formula and just do one calculation to summarize the whole thing and asked whether it mattered whether I did it step by step or with the formula, did he mind? He said 'No, either. There will be no penalization for whichever way you did it.' So I did the first calculation step by step, to show I knew how to do it and then I did the second one with the formula and I got only half marks in my second calculation for not explaining my calculations — even after I'd specifically asked Dr X that that wouldn't be a problem. I'm assuming it's nothing to do with him, but it's just the [doctoral] student who marked it obviously wasn't aware of that.

And thirdly, there are risks of *inconsistency in practices* which can give rise to perceived inequities (as in tutorial provision in one of the course units), or a sense of student disappointment or even frustration that *exemplary practices* on the part of some members of staff seem to remain invisible to other colleagues, and so are not more widely promulgated. In all three course units, steps were taken by module coordinators to obviate such risks by dint of careful advance briefing or training, but these were not always successful.

> S1: It would be good if every lecturer gave out handouts.
> S2: Yeah.
> S1: It certainly makes it a lot easier in the lectures to actually listen.
> S3: Especially when you're coming to revise as well. Having a full set of notes rather than what you've tried to write down through the lecture.
>
> --
>
> S1: Sometimes they say 'Be more concise' but then another time I thought 'Well I'll try being more concise this time' and actually I got less for doing that! So then the next time I thought 'I'll go back to my other way' and it worked better! So it's been confusing.
> S2: I think every time they are corrected by different people anyway. Some of the correctors have said 'You should do it like this' when the person before had said to do it the other way, so then w   get marks taken off because we try to make an effort.

The challenges entailed in harnessing and coordinating the efforts of large and disparate course teams did not go unnoticed or unacknowledged by staff themselves, who also saw practical limits on what might realistically be done:

> The report-back sheet [an assignment pro forma] generates a mark which goes back to the students. However, although all the markers are asked to annotate the report sheets, some don't. And it's a bit frustrating when a student comes and says, 'This says "Excellent", [but] I've got 15 out of 20. If it's "excellent", why haven't I got a higher mark?' . . . And they're right. I mean, 15 out of 20 is 'pretty good'.
>
> --
>
> Team-taught courses have their pluses and minuses. Students are often very worried by team-taught courses because they find it hard to carry material over from one lecture into the next. They find it hard to see the thread that runs through the course. If you are aware of that, and you work hard at trying to pull things together, then I think that team-taught courses are very good, because you can have somebody who really knows about some particular topic. [. . .] But one has to bear in mind that there are cracks between [*laughs*] that people can fall down.
>
> --
>
> I guess that's part of the problem from our side. I'm not sure all of us have a complete view of [the course unit]. The course coordinators have to, to some extent, who each have their input to it. I'm not convinced we spend enough time as a body, getting everyone together to review where we are and where we're going. [. . .] You try to go along to meetings when meetings are called, but you're not always available, and since it's such a large course with so many people, having everyone there every time is not [feasible].

Concluding comments

The study from which the above findings derive sits firmly within the evolving tradition of research into contextual influences on learning which was outlined in the opening sections of the chapter. Indeed, in its approach to research, the study shares with the seminal work of Ramsden and Entwistle the defining features highlighted earlier: a mixed-method research design, an alertness to the subject dimension, a focus on teaching–learning environments as perceived and experienced, and learning processes and outcomes as a criterion of impact. Moreover, the study can also be seen as advancing our understanding of teaching–learning environments, in a number of important respects.

The first of these has to do with the introduction of the concept of ways of thinking and practising in a subject. Considerable further research would be necessary to confirm the validity and utility of this novel construct and to further an understanding of its quintessential characteristics. Nevertheless, it does seem to be a valuable complement to well-established differences in approaches to learning, offering a promising means of encapsulating key facets of high-quality learning in the later years of undergraduate study, while also interconnecting with newly emerging sociocultural perspectives on learning as participation in a disciplinary community of discourse (see for example, Northedge, 2002, 2003).

Second, the study shows the conceptual and analytical potential of congruence, building on Biggs' model of constructive alignment, in pinpointing and illuminating key contextual influences that could facilitate or constrain the quality of students' learning. One important dimension of congruence which emerged from the findings was the provision of guidance and feedback to students, the perceived adequacy of which varied greatly. Findings from other recent studies point to similar student concerns about formative feedback across a range of subject areas, institutions and higher education systems (Carless, 2006; Krause, Hartley, James, & McInnis, 2005; QAA, 2003), particularly but not exclusively in the earlier years of undergraduate study. Two other dimensions of congruence – congruence with students' backgrounds and aspirations, and congruence of course organization and management – were found to be applicable principally to the first-year course settings, where they were associated with large and diverse intakes of students taught and assessed by course teams whose make-up could also be large and diverse and whose roles could be distributed. These twin features can set daunting pedagogical challenges, especially in an era of reduced resources per student (DfES, 2003), as was evident in the experiences of the students interviewed in the present study, and was also acknowledged by many of the teaching staff interviewed. Cohort size and diversity also pose a considerable research challenge, since there can be variations in perceptions and experiences across classes *within* a given course unit that are related to the particular tutors or lecturers concerned, the composition of the student group taking those classes, and the conjunction between them. Indeed, it may be difficult to establish what the collective experience of such a teaching–learning environment might be, from the perspectives of the various students and staff involved except where, as in the present study, the research team is large enough to make possible an appropriately broad sampling strategy.

Lastly, this study offers a salutary reminder that, just as undergraduate teaching–learning environments can metamorphose in ways that give rise to new or heightened sources of influence on the quality of students' learning, so too must our research perspectives and strategies evolve to take account of a shifting ecology. In the present study, an engine of transformation was the coming of mass higher education foreseen by Trow. Following behind, however (but only just beginning to make its presence felt as the data for the present study were being gathered) was the application of the newer information and communication technologies to learning – with a budding impact on interactions between tutors, students and learning–teaching resources. In due course, this too will transform how teaching–learning environments are understood and investigated.

Acknowledgements

This chapter reports on work carried out not only by us but also by our colleagues Velda McCune, Judith Litjens and Jennifer Nisbet, and their contribution is gratefully acknowledged. Further information about the ETL Project, including members of the full project team, can be found at http://www.tla.ed.ac.uk/etl.

References

Anderson, C., & Day, K. (2005). History subject overview report. Universities of Edinburgh, Durham and Coventry: ETL Project. http://www.tla.ed.ac.uk/etl/publications

Becker, H., Geer, B., & Hughes, E. (1968). *Making the grade: The academic side of college life*. New York: Wiley.

Biggs, J. (2003). *Teaching for quality learning at university* (2nd ed.). Buckingham: SRHE and Open University Press.

Biggs, J. B. (1996). Enhancing teaching through constructive alignment. *Higher Education, 32*, 347–364.

Bruce, C., & Gerber, R. (Eds.). (1997). Special issue: Phenomenography in higher education. *Higher Education Research and Development, 16*(2).

Carless, D. (2006). Differing perceptions in the feedback process. *Studies in Higher Education, 31*(2), 219–233.

Department for Education and Skills. (2003). *The future of higher education* (Cm 5735). London: The Stationery Office.

Entwistle, N., McCune, V., & Hounsell, J. (2003). Investigating ways of enhancing university teaching-learning environments: Measuring students' approaches to studying and perceptions of teaching. In E. De Corte, L. Verschaffel, N. Entwistle, & J. van Merrienboer (Eds.), *Powerful learning environments: Unravelling basic components and dimensions* (pp. 89–107). Oxford: Elsevier Science.

Entwistle, N., Nisbet, J., & Bromage, A. (2005). *Electronic Engineering Subject Overview Report*. Universities of Edinburgh, Durham and Coventry: ETL Project. http://www.tla.ed.ac.uk/etl/publications

Entwistle, N., & Ramsden, P. (1983). *Understanding student learning*. London: Croom Helm.

HEFCE (2005). *Higher education in the United Kingdom*. Bristol: Higher Education Funding Council for England.

Hounsell, D. (1997). Understanding teaching and teaching for understanding. In F. Marton, D. Hounsell, & N. Entwistle (Eds.), *The experience of learning* (2nd ed., pp. 238–257). Edinburgh: Scottish Academic Press.

Hounsell, D., & Anderson, C. (2005). *Ways of thinking and practising in biology and history: Disciplinary aspects of teaching and learning environments*. Paper presented at the Higher Education Colloquium, Centre for Teaching, Learning and Assessment, Teaching and Learning within the Disciplines, University of Edinburgh, 10–11 June 2005. http://www.tla.ed.ac.uk/etl/publications

Hounsell, D., McCune, V., Hounsell, J., & Litjens, J. (2006). *Biosciences Subject Overview Report*. Universities of Edinburgh, Durham and Coventry: ETL Project. http://www.tla.ed.ac.uk/etl

Krause, K., Hartley, R., James, R., & McInnis, C. (2005). *The first year experience in Australian Universities: Findings from a decade of national studies*. Melbourne: University of Melbourne, Centre for the Study of Higher Education. http://www.cshe.unimelb.edu.au/

Marton, F. (1981). Phenomenography: Describing conceptions of the world around us. *Instructional Science, 10*, 177–200.

Marton, F., & Booth, S. (1997). *Learning and awareness*. Mahwah, NJ: Erlbaum.

McCune, V., & Hounsell, D. (2005). The development of students' ways of thinking and practising in three final-year biology courses. *Higher Education, 49*, 255–289.

Miller, C., & Parlett, M. (1974). *Up to the mark: A study of the examination game*. London: SRHE.

Northedge, A. (2002). Organizing excursions into specialist discourse communities: A sociocultural account of university teaching. In G. Wells & G. Claxton (Eds.), *Learning for life in the 21st century. Sociocultural perspectives on the future of education* (pp. 252-264). Oxford: Blackwell.

Northedge, A. (2003). Enabling participation in academic discourse. *Teaching in Higher Education, 8*(2), 169-180.

Parlett, M. (1977). The department as a learning milieu. *Studies in Higher Education, 2*(2), 173-181.

QAA (2003). *Learning from subject review, 1993-2001: Sharing good practice*. Gloucester: Quality Assurance Agency for Higher Education, ISBN 1 84482 006 8. http://www.qaa.ac.uk

Ramsden, P. (1984/1997). The context of learning in academic departments. In F. Marton, D. Hounsell, & N. Entwistle (Eds.), *The experience of learning* (2nd ed., pp. 198-216). Edinburgh: Scottish Academic Press.

Ramsden, P., & Entwistle, N. (1981). Effects of academic departments on students' approaches to studying. *British Journal of Educational Psychology, 51*, 368-383.

Reimann, N., Land, R., & Meyer, J. (2006). Economics Subject Overview Report. Universities of Edinburgh, Durham and Coventry: ETL Project. http://www.tla.ed.ac.uk/etl/publications

Scouller, K. (1998). The influence of assessment method on students' learning approaches: Multiple choice question versus assignment essay. *Higher Education, 35*, 453-472.

SFC (2004). *Higher education in Scotland: A baseline report*. Edinburgh: Scottish Funding Councils for Further and Higher Education.

Snyder, B. (1973). *The hidden curriculum*. Cambridge, MA: MIT Press.

Thomas, P., & Bain, J. (1984). Contextual dependence of learning approaches: The effects of assessments. *Human Learning, 3*, 227-240.

Trow, M. (1973). *Problems in the Transition from Elite to Mass Higher Education*. (Reprint of a paper prepared for an OECD Conference on mass higher education in Paris in June 1973). Berkeley, CA: Carnegie Commission on Higher Education.

Tynjälä, P. (1998). Traditional studying for examination versus constructivist learning tasks: Do learning outcomes differ? *Studies in Higher Education, 23*(2), 173-189.

Watkins, D., Dahlin, B., & Ekholm, M. (2005). Awareness of the backwash effect of assessment: A phenomenographic study of the views of Hong Kong and Swedish lecturers. *Instructional Science, 33*, 283-309.

Student Learning and University Teaching, 113–133
BJEP Monograph Series II, 4
© 2007 The British Psychological Society

The
British
Psychological
Society

www.bpsjournals.co.uk

8 – Early career learning at work and its implications for universities

Michael Eraut*

University of Sussex, UK

This paper first briefly summarizes the findings of a study of the mid-career learning of professionals, technicians and managers in the health, engineering and business sectors funded by ESRC's research programme on The Learning Society. This is followed by a discussion of the findings of a recently completed longitudinal study of the Early Career Learning at Work of newly qualified nurses, graduate engineers and trainee chartered accountants. Finally, it discusses the implications of these projects and other related research for learning in higher education.

Both projects shared the same three research questions:

(1) What is being learned?
(2) How is it being learned?
(3) What factors affect the level and direction of learning efforts?

These questions raised difficult methodological problems because of the important role of tacit knowledge in professional practice, the informal nature of most learning and the barriers posed by the close association in respondents' minds of learning with formal class-based teaching (Eraut, 2000). Thus, the experiences and findings of the first project had a strong influence on the design of the second project, which also expanded the third question to include factors affecting the use and extension of prior knowledge brought into employment from higher education and other life experiences.

Summary of the mid-career learning project

Evidence for the first project was collected through two sets of interviews about 6 months apart. 120 respondents from 12 organizations took part in the first interviews, and 88 in the second interviews. Given the problems of eliciting information about

*Correspondence should be addressed to Professor Michael Eraut, Sussex School of Education, The Sussex Institute, Essex House, University of Sussex, Falmer, Brighton BN1 9QQ, UK (e-mail: m.eraut@sussex.ac.uk).

DOI:10.1348/000709906X162424

learning, our strategy for the first interviews was to ask first about the nature of the respondent's job, recent tasks, duties and problems; secondly, to ask the nature of the competence/expertise needed to do it and thirdly, to ask how the necessary expertise was acquired and the extent to which it was changing. Finally, if it had not already become apparent, questions were asked about different sources of learning. Respondents were also asked to elaborate on salient learning episodes or exemplify general statements about learning. The second interview focused on the factors affecting our respondent's learning and expanding issues arising from the first interview. A fuller account of this project can be found in Eraut, Alderton, Cole, and Senker (2000). Our principal findings were as follows.

Learning from experience

Most of the learning described in the interviews was non-formal, neither clearly specified nor planned. It arose naturally out of the demands and challenges of work – solving problems, improving quality and/or productivity or coping with change – and out of social interactions in the workplace with colleagues, customers or clients. Much learning at work derives its purpose and direction from the goals of the work, which are normally achieved by a combination of thinking, trying things out and talking to other people. Sometimes, however, people recognize a need for some additional knowledge or skill that seems essential for improving the quality of their work, expanding its range or taking on new duties. Learning goals are then identified which they pursue by a combination of self-directed learning and taking advantage of relevant learning opportunities as and when they appear. Although this can involve some formal training being undertaken, it almost always requires learning from experience and from other people at work.

Learning from other people

The most common form of learning from other people takes the form of consultation and collaboration within the immediate working group: this may include teamwork, ongoing mutual consultation and support or observation of others in action. Beyond the immediate work environment, people sought information and advice from other people in their organization, from customers or suppliers or from wider professional networks. This was often done on a reciprocal basis. Only a minority made frequent use of written or audio-visual materials like manuals, videos or computer-based training. The rest tried to circumvent materials by getting the information they needed from other people.

Work-based learning is needed to follow-up off-the-job training

Working for qualifications and attending short training courses were important for some people at particular stages in their career. However, even then, work-based learning was important in developing the ability to use what has been learned off-the-job. This was especially true for short courses, which have very little impact unless they are appropriately timed and properly followed up at work. Generally, initial training was judged better when it was both broad in scope and involved periods in the workplace as well as in the classroom. Mid-career management and professional qualifications were judged highly effective because they were able to build on prior experience at work. Management courses involving small groups and projects played an important role in helping people shift their thinking from an operational to a strategic level.

The crucial role of the line manager

The critical factors affecting the level and direction of learning efforts are: the microclimate of the workplace, the self-confidence of the worker and the role of the local manager. The local manager influences both the climate and the individual dispositions through proactive attention to social relationships, mutual learning and good feedback, and influences learning opportunities through organizing work to provide the appropriate level of challenge and support for groups and individuals and to ensure participation in an appropriate range of work activities. However, local managers are rarely trained for this important aspect of the job. To appoint managers and develop them for this role would be a highly significant move towards the promotion of learning in the workplace.

Design of the investigation of early career learning at work

This project was part of the second phase of the ESRC funded Teaching and Learning Research Programme and ended in June 2005. Its better funding enabled a more ambitious design based on a longitudinal study of learning in the first 3 years of employment by newly qualified hospital nurses, graduate engineers on company accreditation schemes preparing them to become chartered engineers, and trainee chartered accountants, who combined an 'apprenticeship' in accounting with outsourced training for professional examinations. These three professions were chosen because they play key roles in the UK economy and public services and have contrasting approaches to professional formation. The graduate accountants and engineers are formally contracted trainees whose employers have systems of organized training support. While engineers have related degrees, trainee accountants require generic skills acquired during higher education, but not relevant degrees. The newly qualified nurses have completed 3-year diploma courses, which allocated 50% of their time to placements in practical settings; but, despite official requirements for induction and mentoring, their learning needs are often neglected.

The value of the greater funding for the second project was that it allowed four visits to each participant over a 3-year period, and enabled us (1) to observe our participants at work before interviewing them and (2) to conduct short opportunistic interviews with significant others in the workplace, including managers and mentors. These observations of the workplace activities and context helped us to ground interviews in the observed working life of tasks, relationships, situational understandings, implicit theories, cultural artifacts, etc., thus increasing the chance of eliciting the complete range of what is learned and what is tacitly required to do the work. By starting interviews with questions about what we had seen, it was easy to move on to what we had not seen while still maintaining a *discourse of description*, before asking for their views and feelings about what they had described. Without such observational triggers, we were likely to receive responses in the *discourse of justification*, the espoused theory rather than the theory in use (Argyris & Schon, 1974). In addition, the opportunistic interviews with managers and mentors enhanced our understanding of their expectations of our participants and of other aspects of the work environment.

Including observations can affect the recruitment of participants for several reasons. Although our researchers were not interfering with the work, some employers (particularly in accountancy) were neither easily persuaded that our 1–2 day visits did not remove participants from work for more than 1–2 hours, and that there were likely to be concomitant advantages for their learning, nor convinced that our promised sector reports would highlight how the learning, and possibly also the retention, of newly recruited staff could be enhanced. There were also sensitivities about observation and the presence of clients was a cause for concern in all sectors. In nursing, this was dealt with by local Research Ethics Committees, which was time-consuming but eventually successful. In accountancy, each client had to be approached for each visit by the accountant in charge of the visiting team but requests were only made if they felt that acceptance was probable. In engineering, problems only arose where there was a considered to be a risk of commercially sensitive material or negative opinions being leaked. In general, people trusted us to uphold our ethical code, but were unsure if their bosses would do the same.

We started with 40 nurses, 36 engineers and 14 accountants and retained 20, 34 and 11 until the third year. These numbers may seem small, but our methodology was qualitative and every participant was located in a different workplace. We ended up with 265 interview transcripts from these participants and almost as many field notes from observations, and a further 154 transcripts of short interviews with managers and mentors. Our approach to this challenging data analysis problem is discussed in detail by Steadman *et al.* (2005). They involve:

> Problems with maintaining *consistency of coding:*

> Compromises between having a *common system* to provide valid comparisons across professions and allowing for *legitimate sector differences*.

> Linkages between *theory, coding,* the processes of *inference* from data and the *interpretations* that create the project's findings.

What is being learned in these workplaces?

This apparently simple question is fraught with difficulty. The challenges of tacit knowledge and implicit learning discussed by Eraut (2000) are only part of the problem. Investigating the transition from higher education to the workplace involves working with different types of discourse and epistemologies. What counts as knowledge in higher professional education is largely determined by recognized theoretical frameworks, research-based evidence, publication and citation. What counts as knowledge in the workplace is largely determined by what is believed to be feasible and what is believed to achieve desired outcomes at an affordable cost. However, much working knowledge is embedded in working practices and discourses without even being recognized as knowledge.

My epistemological position

Both knowledge and learning can be examined from two perspectives, the individual and the social. These can be considered as analogous to the particle and wave theories of light. An individual perspective on knowledge and learning enables us to explore both differences in what and how people learn and differences in how they interpret what they learn. A social perspective draws attention to the social construction of knowledge and contexts for learning, and to the wide range of cultural practices and products that provide knowledge resources for learning.

In universities, knowledge is primarily associated with publication in books and journals, and subject to quality control by editors, peer review and debate. This *codified knowledge* is then given further status by incorporation into educational programmes, examinations and qualifications. The guardians of the codified knowledge system are the universities and publicly funded research councils, even though an increasing number of scientific publications now come from other organizations (Gibbons *et al.*, 1994). The model of knowledge creation is that of a discipline-based community knowledge base to which individual authors and groups of co-authors add new contributions, an interesting combination of social and individual perspectives. Each publication of status has editors and referees controlling *acceptance*, using criteria that include recognition of previous work, originality and credible evidence and argument. Journals of a more scientific nature use the criterion of *truth* according to the norms of the community from which the publication draws its readership. Some people in higher education regard these criteria as problematic, while those outside higher education are more likely to be concerned about their relevance.

Cultural knowledge that has not been codified plays a key role in most work-based practices and activities. There is considerable debate about the extent to which such knowledge can be made explicit or represented in any textual form; and the evidence gathered so far suggests that its amenability to codification has been greatly exaggerated (Eraut, 2000). What does appear to be generally acknowledged is that much uncodified cultural knowledge is acquired informally through participation in social activities, and much is often so 'taken for granted' that people are unaware of its influence on their behaviour. This phenomenon is much broader in scope than the implicit learning normally associated with the concept of socialization. In addition to the cultural practices and discourses of different professions and their specialties, one has to consider the cultural knowledge that permeates the beliefs and behaviours of their co-workers, their clients and the general public.

Personal knowledge is the individual-centred counterpart to cultural knowledge, which Eraut (2004) defines as what individual persons bring to situations that enables them to think, interact and perform. The rationale for this definition is that its defining feature is the *use* of the knowledge, not its *truth*. This allows one to investigate the effects of personal knowledge without necessarily being able to represent that knowledge in codified form, thus incorporating aspects of personal expertise, practical wisdom and tacit knowledge. For example, it includes not only personalized versions of public codified knowledge and understandings that affect how it is used but also everyday knowledge of people and situations, know-how in the form of skills and practices, and memories of cases and episodes. I also include aspects of self-knowledge, attitudes and emotions. Evidence of personal knowledge comes mainly from observations of performance and, since one apprehends performance holistically, this implies a holistic rather than a fragmented approach to knowledge.

Skills can be considered as both a form of cultural knowledge and a form of personal knowledge, according to the focus of attention. The term also tends to be used at two levels. One level is used to describe actions believed to be based on procedural memory alone, although the knowledge needed to decide when to use that skill will include situational understanding, which is not a skill. Such skills are likely to be either classified as technical or treated as taken for granted cultural attributes. While there is a body of codified knowledge about such skills, one cannot perform the skill by simply 'learning the words'; it could even be a hindrance. The other level of usage relates to processes, such as teamwork, leadership or problem solving, which are constructed from a mixture of procedural knowledge and other forms of knowledge. There is a danger that labelling these capabilities as 'skills' will implicitly deny both their complexity and their possible dependence on personal expertise.

Teamwork and group problem solving introduce the issue of the knowledge constructed by teams, which makes their combined capability greater than that of all their members acting individually. This will include mutually developed under-standings that permeate their discourse, mutual adaptation and collaboration in rapid response situations, mutual awareness of differences of perspective and expertise that broaden and deepen their problem-solving capability, and agreed processes for making decisions. While no doubt drawing on cultural resources, their new knowledge is likely to be too situated and too team-specific to merit description as cultural knowledge. It is neither codified nor purely personal. Hence it cannot be adequately covered by any of the three definitions. No doubt other exceptions will also emerge when this analysis is further pursued.

Since our methodology was designed to elicit what our respondents had learned to enable them to perform their various tasks and roles, all their responses indicated the nature of their personal knowledge. Some of the evidence pointed to the appropriate use of codified knowledge and some to the use of other cultural knowledge. However, our analysis needed to be more detailed in order to be useful, hence in each project we developed a typology of what was being learned. The process was tackled in three phases and involved the whole course team (4 in the first project and 7 in the second project), whose expertise spanned the professions concerned:

Starting phase (after the first set of interviews but before coding of the transcripts):
● Ascertain or deduce key aspects of observed or reported decisions and actions.
● List types of awareness or understanding required for these decisions and actions.
● Study related literature on professional knowledge, skills or competencies.

Middle phase:
● Develop a coding system to accommodate the above set of categories.
● Apply the coding system to the transcripts, making notes of any difficulties encountered.
● Adjust the coding system to accommodate these difficulties.

Concluding phase:
● Check the typology with a wide range of people for comprehensibility, relevance, clarity, coverage and lack of overlap.
● Use of the typology by doctoral students on different projects, noting the difficulties they encountered and any resultant challenge to aspects of the typology.

Our final product is presented in Table 1 below.

One important feature of these categories was that few of them appeared to describe learning that reached an end-point. The possibility of yet further learning was always present. Many of them were more appropriate for lifetime learning than for a short period of early career or mid-career learning. Therefore, we decided to call

Table 1. A typology of workplace learning trajectories (Eraut *et al.*, 2005a)

Task performance	**Role performance**
Speed and fluency	Prioritization
Complexity of tasks and problems	Range of responsibility
Range of skills required	Supporting other people's learning
Communication with a wide range of people	Leadership
Collaborative work	Accountability
	Supervisory role
Awareness and understanding	Delegation
Other people: colleagues, customers, managers, etc.	Handling ethical issues
Contexts and situations	Coping with unexpected problems
One's own organization	Crisis management
Problems and risks	Keeping up-to-date
Priorities and strategic issues	
Value issues	**Teamwork**
	Collaborative work
Personal development	Facilitating social relations
Self evaluation	Joint planning and problem solving
Self management	Ability to engage in and promote mutual
Handling emotions	learning
Building and sustaining relationships	
Disposition to attend to other perspectives	**Decision making and problem solving**
Disposition to consult and work with others	When to seek expert help
Disposition to learn and improve one's practice	Dealing with complexity
Accessing relevant knowledge and expertise	Group decision making
Ability to learn from experience	Problem analysis
	Formulating and evaluating options
Academic knowledge and skills	Managing the process within an
Use of evidence and argument	appropriate time scale
Accessing formal knowledge	Decision making under pressure
Research-based practice	
Theoretical thinking	**Judgement**
Knowing what you might need to know	Quality of performance, output and
Using knowledge resources (human,	outcomes
paper-based, electronic)	Priorities
Learning how to use relevant theory	Value issues
(in a range of practical situations)	Levels of risk

them *learning trajectories,* recognizing that these particular trajectories were far from linear. Changes in the level and direction of learning cause discontinuities in some trajectories, while others remain active or inactive, so that at any one time:

- *Explicit progress* is being made on several of the trajectories that constitute lifelong learning.
- *Implicit progress* can be inferred and later acknowledged on some other trajectories.
- Progress on yet other trajectories is *stalling,* or even *regressing*, through lack of use or because new practices have not yet been adopted.

We have tried to avoid the term *'competency'* because it carries many meanings and connotations. One problem is that some people use it to describe very detailed behaviours, while others use it to describe broad attributes. In both cases, it refers to a person's capability or personal knowledge and is treated as an individual characteristic. However, the term *'competent'* is not individually defined but socially defined, and refers to being able to meet a socially defined standard of performance (Eraut, 1998). Judgements of competence vary according to context and over time, and are influenced both by allowances for the experience of the performer and by the prior experience and perspective of the judge(s).

Professional qualifications, in particular, require both a specified amount of practical experience and the demonstration of competence in certain aspects of performance by successful candidates. The assessment process may require either that a particular level of competence is reached in each aspect or that the performance as a whole is satisfactory or both. Irrespective of the formal specification, assessors tend to use some combination of the two and allow strength in one aspect to compensate for weakness in another. Although the award of qualifications is generally assumed to be aligned with such competence, this is virtually impossible to achieve in practice. Trainees in most professions are allocated to a series of placements, through which they are expected, with suitable support, to acquire the specified level of competence. However, the learning affordances of each placement vary considerably according to the local context, and these differences will affect what each trainee learns and the profile of their competence at the point of qualification. The use of learning trajectories addresses both variations in competence and continuity of learning by tracking aspects of trainee performance before, during and after qualification.

A second advantage of using learning trajectories is that they can reduce the need to base qualification decisions on limited samples of performance under conditions of high anxiety. Mapping progress over time is measuring the ability to learn from experience, probably a better predictor of future performance than a final assessment.

Another advantage is the opportunity to include the context of performance in the learning record. What is learned is affected by the context and conditions for learning, and acquired competence does not usually transfer across contexts without significant further learning. Hence, it is important to include information about the context and conditions in the performance record in order to indicate the domain of a professional's current competence.

The implication of this need for amplification of the record is that 'points' on these learning trajectories are best considered as windows on episodes of practice in which the aspect of learning portrayed by the trajectory played a significant part. Each window should include the following information about the performance:

- The setting in which it took place, and features of that setting that affected or might have affected the performance.
- The conditions under which the performance took place, for example, degree of supervision, pressure of time, crowdedness, conflicting priorities and availability of resources.
- The antecedents to the performance and the situation that gave rise to the performance.
- The other categories of expertise involved.
- Any difference from previously recorded episodes.
- Indicators of expertise in the domain of the trajectory having been maintained, widened or enhanced.

The last point draws attention to the complexity of learning and performance in professional work. It is unusual for a performance to use knowledge from only one trajectory, and the seamless integration of personal knowledge from several trajectories may itself be an important learning challenge that goes beyond progress in several separate trajectories. The holistic nature of any complex performance should never be neglected.

How is this knowledge being learned?

After many experiments and discussions, we finally settled on an approach to classifying the learning we observed. The breakthrough arose from two distinctions. The first was to classify learning processes according to whether their *principal intention* distinction was working or learning. Most of the informal learning found in our previous project on mid-career learning (Eraut *et al.*, 2000) occurred as a by-product of normal working processes, for which working was clearly the principal object, and these processes were also prominent in our data for early career learners. Early career professionals were more involved in processes for which learning was the main goal, but this still contributed only a small proportion of their learning.

The second distinction arose when we became dissatisfied with including processes, which were clearly bounded and relatively time consuming, in the same list as very generic and often quite short actions, such as asking questions, observing or reflecting. These actions could occur many times in a single process, and were found within almost every type of process, often several at a time. When we separated these more generic shorter actions from processes perceived as either working or learning, we obtained the much tidier typology that we finally adopted and refined. Table 2 has three columns, each with a set of subcategories.

Table 2. A typology of early career learning (Eraut *et al.*, 2005a)

Work processes with learning as a by-product	Learning actions within work or learning processes	Learning processes at or near the workplace
Participation in group processes	Asking questions	Being supervised
Working alongside others	Listening	Being coached
Consultation	Observing	Being mentored
Tackling challenging tasks and roles	Getting information	Shadowing
Problem solving	Learning from mistakes	Visiting other sites
Trying things out	Reflecting	Independent study
Working with clients	Locating resource people	Working for a qualification
Consolidating, extending and refining skills	Giving and receiving feedback	Conferences
		Short courses

Our conclusion was that, given favourable conditions, learning in the workplace can be enhanced by improving opportunities for productive engagement in the work processes listed above. Working alongside a colleague for a period of time enables one not only to learn by asking questions and receiving feedback about shared activities and events as and when they happen, but also to pick up aspects of their reading of situations and ongoing monitoring and decision-making that are largely tacit and beyond their powers of explanation. Working in groups with people who have different kinds of expertise helps one to understand the nature of that expertise and make better use of it.

'Designated Mentors' were provided by all our partner employers, but were mainly confined to the first year for nurses. However, most mentoring was provided by helpful others, who were not designated mentors, in a manner similar to what Nielsen and Kvale (1997) called 'distributed apprenticeship'. Official mentors hardly figured in accountancy, where decentred support from those immediately available worked very well. In nursing, some official mentors provided a lifeline for their novices, while others were either allocated to a different shift or, unwilling to take the role seriously. Specially organized learning from supervisors, coaches or mentors requires that those who provide the support have both the appropriate skills, and the will and the time to use them properly.

Learning factors and context factors

The most important aim of our research was to discover what constituted favourable conditions for all these types of learning because this could lead to more effective interventions. The first variables to capture our attention were *confidence* and being *proactive* in seeking learning opportunities. We then noted that confidence arose from people successfully meeting *challenges* in their work, while the confidence to take on such challenges depended on the extent to which they felt *supported* in that endeavour. Thus, there is a triangular relationship between challenge, support and confidence (Eraut *et al.*, 2000). The contextual significance of the word 'confidence' depended on which aspects of this triangular relationship were most significant at any particular time. Often, it came close to Bandura's (1995) concept of *self-efficacy*, relating to their self-perceived ability to execute a particular task or successfully perform a role. However, especially in the early stages, it could also refer to their confidence in their colleagues' support.

We later added further elements to each apex of this triangle (see Figure 1) to reflect other factors found to be significant for the learning of early career professionals:

- *Feedback* has a huge effect on performance and motivation.
- *Commitment* to work and colleagues is generated through *participation* in-groups and appreciation of the *value of the work*.
- *Personal agency* recognizes participants' own sense of choice, meaningfulness, competence and progress (Thomas, 2000), which is not necessarily aligned with their employer's priorities.

Challenge and value
of the work

Feedback and support

LEARNING
FACTORS

Confidence and commitment
Personal agency

Figure 1. Learning factors (Eraut *et al.*, 2005a).

The second project enabled us to find out more about the nature of participants' work, and the learning culture of their workplaces, and hence to extend our model to include a second triangle (see Figure 2). This mirrors the first triangle but focuses on the *context factors* that influence the *learning factors*.

The allocation and structuring of work was central to our participants' progress because it affected (1) the difficulty or challenge of the work; (2) the extent to which it was individual or collaborative and (3) the opportunities for meeting, observing and working alongside people who had more or different expertise, and for forming *relationships* that might provide feedback and support. For novice professionals to make good progress, a significant proportion of their work needed to be sufficiently new to challenge them without being so daunting as to reduce their confidence. Their workload needed to be at a level that allowed them to respond to new challenges reflectively, rather than develop coping mechanisms that might later prove ineffective, and they needed to *participate* in an appropriate range of work activities. Finally, concerns about meeting their employers' and their own *expectations* of their *performance* and *career progress* arose from inadequate feedback of a normative kind, and weakened their sense of agency and commitment to their organization.

The use of this two triangle model to depict the main factors affecting learning and their mutual interaction in the first year of each profession is demonstrated below. Findings on learning in the two subsequent years can be found in Eraut *et al.* (2005a, 2005b).

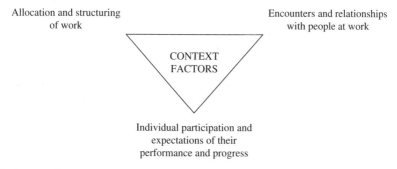

Figure 2. Context factors.

Trainee accountants in their first year

The accountancy organizations managed to provide appropriately challenging work for most of their new trainees for most of the time. This was achieved by structuring the majority of the work into audit visits lasting from two days to a month, within which tasks of gradually increasing complexity were first observed and then assigned, and a strong community of practice that provided continuity across audit teams (see Figure 3 below). Supporting learning was seen as a good investment because it increased the capabilities of novice professionals very quickly, made them more useful and gave a good return for intensive early support. The cost of trainees' time was included in audit contracts, so they were expected to pay their way within a few months. These both added to their sense of inclusion and created clear expectations for their seniors to provide the necessary support. Other reasons why support was most readily available in accountancy were that:

Figure 3. Context factors for the learning of first-year accountancy trainees.

(1)   Senior trainees were close at hand and often worked alongside the novice.
(2)   Teams were quite small, sometimes very small, and their objective was a jointly constructed product – an audit report for a specific client.
(3)   There were clear, usually non-negotiable, deadlines, and valuable time would be wasted if trainees got stuck and caused delays, however small their tasks were.
(4)   It was normally possible for more experienced trainees to pause or find a convenient stopping point in their own task to answer a question or advise on a problem.
(5)   Their seniors knew from their own recent experience that such help would be needed and providing it was a taken for granted part of the organizational culture.

The short length of many audits makes it necessary to have a strong organizational culture and a community of practice, through which expertise is shared and practice is sufficiently common to provide continuity of learning across audits. The overt nature, legal status and clear structure of audit documents give them an important role as mediating artifacts, around which both work and learning revolve. Thus, the work patterns of audit teams, continuity of practice across different audits of gradually increasing length and difficulty, and the structure of the audit documents themselves provide strong scaffolding for learning. Newcomers can usually envisage the intended product by looking at the previous year's audit and monitor progress by examining the latest version of the current audit file. Most of their support is provided by more experienced trainees, who were themselves novices only a few months earlier; hence, they feel capable of asking them silly questions and appreciate their negligible background knowledge of business.

Regular contact and increasing interaction with clients not only creates awareness of the value of audits, but also enables them gradually to acquire the skill of connecting business transactions with accounts and understand different types of business. The need to keep to tight schedules and adjust plans whenever an unexpected problem arises creates a strong climate of mutual cooperation and a sense of joint achievement, even though the team is temporary.

Unlike the other groups we studied, trainee accountants were studying for professional examinations and were given several months of 'college work' organized by contracted independent trainers and periods of study leave before exams. They found much of this study both relevant to their work and valuable, but this did not always become immediately apparent. Their trainee contracts required them to pass several examinations and those who failed their first-year examinations were usually dismissed.

Accountants were the most likely group to get immediate feedback, because their completed tasks were checked and incorporated into the audit document and they could easily monitor their own progress by the increasing complexity of the tasks they undertook (see Figure 4 below). However, this was not accompanied by good normative feedback on their strengths and weaknesses or general progress. As a result, trainees developed a stronger commitment to their work teams and colleagues than to their employing organization.

Factors affecting the early learning of graduate engineers

Some engineering companies had difficulty in providing the appropriate level of challenge, because much of the work did not lend itself to tasks requiring different levels of expertise that could be easily matched to trainees' needs. Thinking of alternative strategies for designing and allocating work was not a priority, but some local managers came up with new ideas. Our partner engineering companies operated on a long time scale. Hence, their Graduate Engineers (GEs) were mainly involved in major construction or research and development projects whose time scales were measured in years rather than weeks or days. The exception was when some engineering companies took advantage of their graduates' relative IT expertise by asking them to explore the value of new packages, for example.

Graduate Engineers were usually working near other more experienced team members in an open plan office. Tasks were usually part of a medium to long-term project, hence there was more opportunity to wait for a convenient time to ask a question and find the best person to approach. Within a few months, graduate engineers had become aware of who had what expertise, how well disposed they were to answering questions and how well they explained the key aspects of the problem, and this extended beyond their own team and sometimes, through the Intranet, beyond their own site. It was up to them to hunt down and use the most appropriate sources of support, which might or might not include their manager or mentor. Hence, we have described them in Figure 5 as hunter-gatherers of knowledge and resources.

Engineering teams had a rather looser structure, tasks were longer and a wider range of expertise was often involved. People spent more of their working time on their own with occasional meetings of small subgroups with related tasks. However, their open

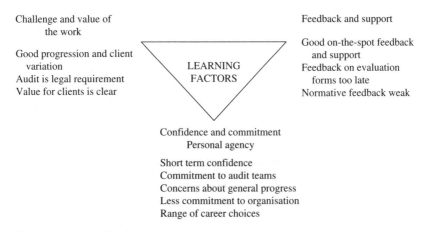

Figure 4. Learning factors for first-year accountancy trainees.

Allocation and structuring
of their work

Project teams (long term)
Open plan offices
Social links around workplace
Intranet
Strong CPD programmes
Little direct client contact
Work suitable for trainees is scarce

Relationships at work

Ask anything culture
Loose links in large teams
Informal contact with neighbours
Develops wider networks
Hunter-gatherers of resources and
expertise
Broader context of project often
missing

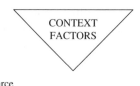

CONTEXT
FACTORS

Participation and expectations

Learning is serious business
Work expectations often unclear
Have to do whatever turns up
Limited peripheral participation
within their project

Figure 5. Context factors for the learning of first-year graduate engineers.

plan offices and informal social meeting at lunch, by the coffee machine or after work, provided a context in which graduate trainees could meet a wide range of people whom they then felt capable of approaching later, either to get advice or to find out whom to get it from. Learning was a serious business in engineering companies and this was demonstrated by their strong programmes of CPD courses, readily accessible to GEs, and by their appointment of at least two mentors for each GE, one for internal guidance and one for their progress towards becoming Chartered Engineers. However, many GEs had little or no client contact and very little opportunity to become acquainted with the broader context of the project on which they were working.

Work suitable for first-year GEs was scarce in some companies, but this was not recognized as a problem in need of attention. Thus, although GEs had excellent access to expertise and showed considerable skill in tracking it down, lack of challenging work often rendered this superfluous. As Figure 6 indicates, few mentors interpreted their roles in a proactive way, hence the quality of support for learning was dependent on

Challenge and value of
the work

Variable types and levels of
challenge
Depends on work available
Isolation fromclients resented
Chartered status valued only
by some

Feedback and support

GEs suss out most helpful
people in close range
GEs track down company
expertise beyond their office
Many designated support
roles, few of them active
Quality of support varies
with immediate locality
Normative feedback weak

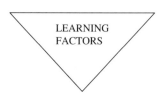

LEARNING
FACTORS

Confidence and commitment
Personal agency

Confidence ebbs with lack of challenge
Commitment to chartered status ebbs if
not valued in local workplace
Concerns about general progress
Range of career choices

Figure 6. Learning factors for first-year graduate engineers.

those experienced engineers in their immediate locality. Normative feedback through appraisals was weak; unlike the accountants, they got little immediate feedback on their ongoing work. Few of the people they encountered seemed to be concerned about feedback and GEs without access to obvious cues about their progress felt rudderless. This was exacerbated by their discovery that, although they had been recruited onto an accredited programme for those wanting to become Chartered Engineers, Chartered status was valued by only a few of their senior colleagues.

The most critical features of this learning environment stem from the type of work allocated to trainees, the looser structure of the work environment requiring trainees to be very proactive and the frequent lack of normative feedback which might assist trainees in adapting to these circumstances and challenge their managers to give greater thought to the work they allocate to trainees.

Factors affecting the first-year learning of newly qualified nurses

A high proportion of the wards where our newly qualified nurses worked were crowded and extremely busy, constantly challenged to find bed space for new patients and sufficient time from appropriately skilled staff to cope with their patients' needs. They were frequently short of staff, used a lot of agency and temporary staff, and had a skill-mix on the margin of safety. Novices' practical and emotional capacity to survive in these environments depended on their ability to learn many vitally important new practices very rapidly, while coping with a very challenging job. Their survival strategies are perhaps best described as 'trying to learn in a pressure cooker'. Hospital managers were concerned about the impact on retention; but it was the ward managers who had the maximum influence on the learning context. Some made learning a major focus of their work because they recognized its importance for morale and retention, while others were too overwhelmed to give it much attention. Thus, learning cultures could often differ greatly between wards in the same hospital.

The transition from student to staff nurse was typically seen by newly qualified nurses as being massive. At the start of their ward experience, they recounted four main areas of concern: striving to achieve technical tasks like drug rounds; being accountable and responsible; 'doing everything' and getting to know new people and equipment. They found themselves having to learn many new clinical skills, learning what to look for when monitoring patients and, above all, *learning to prioritize*, with or without helpful advice from more experienced colleagues. Taking on ultimate responsibility for patients and presenting themselves as competent, confident and calm nurses, while struggling to survive, caused anxiety and stress. This was recognized and supported in some wards, but ignored or repressed in others.

Although the need for support was very great (see Figures 7 and 8), newly qualified nurses found it difficult to get, because those able to provide support were busy. Qualified nurses were not working to a common outcome, but working in parallel with a different group of patients. The level of cooperation depended on the skill mix in the ward (if this was inappropriate, more experienced nurses were badly overstretched), the disposition of the senior nurses and their ability to keep an eye on nurses working nearby while still attending to their own patients. This almost tacit supervision was more difficult when the ward layout restricted inter-visibility. The ability to spread one's attention widely, and prioritize according to one's perception of an ever-changing situation, is a critical aspect of nursing expertise for senior nurses.

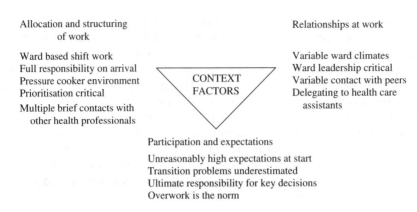

Allocation and structuring
of work

Ward based shift work
Full responsibility on arrival
Pressure cooker environment
Prioritisation critical
Multiple brief contacts with
other health professionals

Relationships at work

Variable ward climates
Ward leadership critical
Variable contact with peers
Delegating to health care
assistants

CONTEXT
FACTORS

Participation and expectations

Unreasonably high expectations at start
Transition problems underestimated
Ultimate responsibility for key decisions
Overwork is the norm

Figure 7. Context factors for nurses in their first-year after qualification.

Another factor in nursing was the need to acquire new skills rapidly. Usually, the most appropriate method was coaching; but this meant that a 'coach' had to be released from his/her ongoing responsibilities for a significant period of time. This requires that either a senior nurse, or the coach herself, has to negotiate some cover for the coach's patients. In some wards, the mentor was expected to take on this coaching role, whereas in others, it might be the local expert or the person who volunteered or just decided to help on the spur of the moment. The consequence was a well-planned skill development system in some wards, but a dearth of coaching in the others.

Nurses were more likely to be taken for granted than our other participants, both because they were already qualified and because they were less often observed by others. Moreover, complex clinical and communication skills had to be acquired to attain a reasonable level of performance. However, in many wards, they were more likely to get negative feedback on one mistake than positive feedback on everything they did well. Constructive feedback in areas where their performance was adequate but capable of being improved was most likely to occur when membership of a ward community provided access to significant social and emotional support. Such support appeared to be a necessary condition for a positive learning climate, but it was not

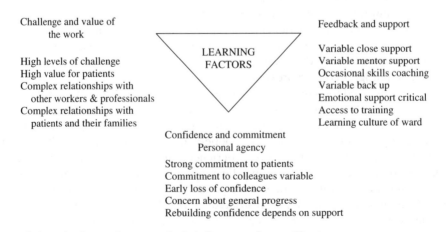

Challenge and value of
the work

High levels of challenge
High value for patients
Complex relationships with
other workers & professionals
Complex relationships with
patients and their families

Feedback and support

Variable close support
Variable mentor support
Occasional skills coaching
Variable back up
Emotional support critical
Access to training
Learning culture of ward

LEARNING
FACTORS

Confidence and commitment
Personal agency

Strong commitment to patients
Commitment to colleagues variable
Early loss of confidence
Concern about general progress
Rebuilding confidence depends on support

Figure 8. Learning factors for nurses in their first year after qualification.

always sufficient. Strong learning support and leadership from senior nurses was also necessary. A small number of wards provided neither social nor learning support, though individual nurses were sometimes able to transcend this largely negative climate. Some ward managers understood that the best way to improve their skill mix and the quality of their collective care was for novices and early career nurses to develop their capabilities as rapidly as possible. Others did not see this as a form of investment or were just too daunted by the problem of trying to implement it.

The combination of very high challenge, very high value and unreasonably high initial expectations is both risky and emotionally draining. Retention problems are predictable. Good back-up, strong support for rapid learning and a positive and supportive ward climate are essential. Continuing feedback on both specific skills and general progress is important for sustaining morale throughout the early career stage, but often in short supply. Management development and support needs to be directed towards these issues, if progress is to be made.

Implications for higher education

Student learning in general higher education

Hitherto, I have been contrasting higher education contexts with workplace contexts, while conveniently forgetting that higher education is itself a workplace. Both teachers and students work in higher education and much of that work is structured. Indeed, I would argue that the dominant structure for students is the work that they are expected to do, not the learning they are expected to achieve. Hence, my key questions for those who structure and support student work are:

- What learning affordances are created by these structures and modes of support?
- To what extent are the theoretical frameworks and empirical findings on learning in other workplaces also applicable in higher education?
- What resources would be essential or desirable for enhancing these new kinds of activity?

My paper is not long enough to include detailed accounts of the learning of early career accountants, engineers and nurses; but one of the most striking features is the wide range of people from whom those working in supportive environments are able to learn. In accounting and nursing, these include their peers and colleagues only a few months or a year or two ahead of them. Higher education makes very little use of students as sources of learning support and has only just begun to think about physical and electronic resources that might enhance productive inter-student learning.

The planned, rather than incidental, use of students as learning resources could significantly expand the potential range of learning affordances in the HE workplace, thus enabling the possible use in higher education of the learning processes listed in Table 2 above. We also need to bear in mind the learning and contextual factors in the two triangle model, in particular: the relationships, the scope for individual and group agency, the challenge and value of the allocated work and the additional work involved in helping others to learn. Within this broader frame of reference, nearly all the processes and activities in Table 2 become feasible, if not always desirable. Moreover, learning the skills required for this much wider range of working processes would be a considerable asset for students' future work after graduation.

Problem solving is perhaps the most used process of the work processes in Table 2; but is normally treated as an individual activity in science, mathematics and some social sciences. Typically, lecturers go through problems without seeking to discuss how the expert knows what to do. Problem-based learning as a group activity is now quite common in professional courses, where it helps students to access the literature, to connect concepts and theories to practical situations and to induct students into professional discourse and case-based learning. However, there is also scope for problem-solving groups to be used for studying applied aspects of science and social science for developing skills relevant to both higher education and subsequent employment.

Perhaps the greatest challenge facing higher education today is developing skills of critical reading and thinking, clearly structured and argued writing in a number of genres, group-work, giving and receiving feedback, and transfer of concepts and ideas to new situations in a much larger proportion of graduates than at present. Currently, students seeking to develop those skills get relatively little support, perhaps participation in a seminar where the stronger students adopt a more rigorously critical approach and some feedback on written work that addresses skills as well as content. There is also no opportunity to get feedback and advice in mid-stream while they are engaged in note-making or drafting an assignment. However, working alongside more experienced people in workplaces outside education may give opportunities to address issues in the midst of the working process, both by better understanding how one's neighbour does things and by being able to get advice just when it is most needed and then try it out to see how it works and/or whether you understood it properly.

Analogous opportunities in higher education might be developed by small groups of students doing joint or parallel work in stages, and discussing their ongoing progress at regular intervals, perhaps mentored by a more experienced student. Such work could also be supported by tools that trigger reflection and self-evaluation and/or by observing a more experienced group of students. Problems and issues arising from these discussions could be then brought to a lecturer for further debate in a forum with other student groups. My guiding principle is first to think about how some desired learning might be handled in a learning-oriented work environment, then to consider how that idea might be implemented in a higher education setting.

Progression in both the general skills discussed above and the understanding and application of key theoretical perspectives could be tracked by learning trajectories similar to those discussed in an earlier section. Reporting episodes in the manner suggested above could do justice to the complexities of these skills and avoid reducing them to constructs represented by a single number on a scale. The use of such trajectories would also be an invaluable preparation for any new initiatives focused on developing these key aspects of learning because they would provide invaluable evidence about the nature of the problem and the variety of ways in which it was manifested.

Additional implications for initial professional education

There are yet further implications for Professional Education, concerning the transition from education to workplace settings. In professions like Nursing, which have a series of placements within their initial period of training, the alternation between education and workplace settings set up expectations for mutual relevance which are easily disappointed if the time gap between the introduction of a theory topic and its practical application is too long (Eraut *et al.*, 1995). It can also be difficult for students to recognize the theoretical knowledge embedded in many practices when it only enters the daily discourse at a superficial level that requires little understanding. A further problem is that few people understand the magnitude and complexity of the further learning entailed in using theoretical knowledge in practice settings, especially when neither HE nor employers accept responsibility for supporting such learning. Eraut (2004) has argued that such a transfer involves six distinct but not necessarily independent steps:

- The extraction of potentially relevant knowledge from the context(s) of its acquisition and previous use.
- Understanding the new situation, a process that often depends on informal social learning.
- Recognizing which areas of knowledge are relevant to the new situation.
- Focusing more precisely on what knowledge is needed for a particular assessment, decision or action.
- Interpreting and/or transforming that knowledge to suit the new situation and context.
- Integrating the various relevant aspects of knowledge prior to and/or during performance.

The evidence suggests that this is best done in practice settings, possibly involving HE staff. There could also be better preparation in HE through informing the students precisely where and when they might expect to use the theory they had just been taught (Eraut *et al.*, 1995; Eraut, 2004).

Another area of confusion is the role of theory itself. There is often a failure to distinguish between the different types of theory taught in higher professional education. Professions both appropriate theories from science and social science and create their own theories both in the academy and in their professional practices. These theories may be based on empirical research and conceptual frameworks peculiar to the applied field, the elaboration of practitioner maxims and practical principles or what can best be described as a preferred view or ideology of the profession, that is a theoretical justification of its purposes and practices in terms of moral principles, views of society and occupational beliefs about the effectiveness of various practices.

This last type of theory plays an important role in sustaining professional identity and will usually derive partly from ethical principles articulated by philosophers and partly from the cultural assumptions about the role of that profession that prevail (or used to prevail) in that particular society. However, there is also a downside because of a strong tendency to create theories of practice that are ideologically attractive but almost impossible to implement. This usually happens when professionals are urged to adopt practices that involve much greater levels of time and effort than service users and/or the public purse can possibly finance. Hence, there is a significant gap between the theories of practice taught by former practitioners, based on how they would have liked to have practised, and the activities performed by current practitioners. This contrasts with a common workplace stance in which current practice is uncritically accepted as an inevitable reality, and any impetus towards improving the service provided by an occupation is lost. The so-called 'theory-practice gap' often turns out to be a gap between ideal practice and actual practice.

Theory is much less prominent in practice settings, but nevertheless silently influential. Theories are often embedded in work activities, which are transacted in a discourse that rarely mentions them. Moreover, they are not necessarily imported from higher education. Practitioner theories can be detected both in shared practices and in personal approaches to practice, and both shared and personal theories may be explicit or tacit. Argyris and Schon's (1974) exposure of common contradictions between 'espoused theories' and tacit 'theories of action' cites several examples of what I would describe as professional reluctance to abandon ideals that practitioners find difficult to implement under normal working conditions. Hence, theories of action that fall short of these ideals are used but rarely discussed.

Not surprisingly, one of the main differences between HE settings and workplace settings is the discourse. This difference is caused not only by these ideological issues but also by the action-based emphasis of practice-based thinking, which require rapid responses informed by prior experience whenever possible (Eraut, 2000). This helps to explain our finding that newly qualified nurses had to rapidly acquire a substantial repertoire of such responses before beginning to renew their interest in theory. This often coincided with the beginning of their second year, when they began to be allocated sicker patients with more complex conditions for which routine responses were less appropriate.

Implications for higher education teachers

Finally, we briefly consider the implications for learning the role of a lecturer in HE. The organization of teaching in separate classrooms minimizes naturally occurring opportunities for mutual observation. The increasing use of teaching assistants in higher education opens up the possibility of an organized apprenticeship approach; and even without that initial experience, aspects of apprenticeship could be used in the first term of a new lecturer's contract. For example, early experience could be very usefully acquired by co-planning a sequence of lectures with an experienced colleague, contributing progressively larger components of those lectures and collecting feedback from students on the various aspects of the course. Learning to conduct seminars might be helped by co-teaching with a co-novice, each alternating periods of teaching with periods of observation. The early career professionals we observed in our research needed to learn from experts, peers and clients, and this should also apply to new lecturers. This might work best, if they were given a choice of possible learning processes and expected to choose and try out those they thought would work best for learning from experts, peers and students.

Other forms of learning we observed that would be equally important for lecturers were:

- Self-management skills like prioritization and time management.
- Building networks of contacts for finding out how to get things done.
- Building networks of contacts for getting advice on the culture and micro-politics of the department/school/faculty.
- Developing greater independence and sense of agency in others, in this case students.
- Giving and receiving feedback.
- Consolidating, expanding and refining one's repertoire of skills.
- Trying out new ideas, possibly in conjunction with a colleague.

Changing the context helps to see familiar problems in a different way and suggests different approaches to tackle them, and even different priorities for change.

References

Argyris, C., & Schon, D. A. (1974). *Theory in practice: Increasing professional effectiveness.* San Francisco: Jossey Bass.

Bandura, A. (1995). *Self-efficacy in changing societies.* New York: Cambridge University Press.

Eraut, M. (1998). Concepts of competence. *Journal of Interprofessional Care, 12*(2), 127–139.

Eraut, M. (2000). Non-formal learning and tacit knowledge in professional work. *British Journal of Educational Psychology, 70,* 113–136.

Eraut, M. (2004). Transfer of knowledge between education and workplace settings. In H. Rainbird, A. Fuller, & H. Munro (Eds.), *Workplace learning in context* (pp. 201–221). London: Routledge.

Eraut, M., Alderton, J., Boylan, A., & Wraight, A. (1995). *Learning to use scientific knowledge in education and practice settings.* London: English National Board for Nursing, Midwifery and Health Visiting.

Eraut, M., Alderton, J., Cole, G., & Senker, P. (2000). Development of knowledge and skills at work. In F. Coffield (Ed.), *Differing visions of a learning society* (Vol. 1, pp. 231–262). Bristol: The Policy Press.

Eraut M., Maillardet F., Miller C., Steadman S., Ali A., Blackman C., & Furner, J. (2005a). *Early career learning at work.* End of Award Report, ESRC.

Eraut M., Maillardet F., Miller C., Steadman S., Ali A., Blackman C., & Furner, J. (2005b). *An analytical tool for characterising and comparing professional workplace learning environments.* Paper for BERA Annual Conference.

Gibbons, M., Limoges, C., Nowotny, H., Schwartzman, S., Scott, P., & Trow, M. (1994). *The new production of knowledge.* London: Sage.

Nielsen, K., & Kvale, S. (1997). Current issues of apprenticeship. *Nordisk Pedagogik, 17*(3), 130–139.

Steadman, S., Eraut, M., Maillardet, F., Miller, C., Furner, J., Ali, A., & Blackman, C. (2005). *Methodological challenges in studying workplace learning: Strengths and limitations of the adopted approach.* Paper for BERA Annual Conference.

Thomas, K. W. (2000). *Intrinsic motivation at work: Building energy and commitment.* San Francisco: Berrett-Koehler.

British Journal of Educational Psychology, 135–146
BJEP Monograph Series II, 4
© 2007 The British Psychological Society

The
British
Psychological
Society

www.bpsjournals.co.uk

Reflections on papers 1, 3, 7 and 8

Hazel Francis*
Institute of Education, University of London, UK

Introduction

In his introductory chapter, Entwistle outlines the body of work lying behind the papers in this volume and adds his own summary of significant concepts in a framework of relationships between them. Much of the work has aimed to investigate what is happening on a wide variety of local and cross-national sites with respect to the nature of student learning under existing educational provision. Much focuses on descriptive information from students about themselves, their learning experiences and the nature of their learning achievements. What the research most certainly is not, is comparative or experimental investigation of the effects of different instructional programmes on the amount of student learning. It cannot therefore be evaluated in the same way. Nevertheless, I think that, as a large and coherent body of research that has already affected teaching in higher education, it should be evaluated, especially since there is a huge public interest at stake in the provision and evaluation of higher education. How, then, might one look at a collection of studies that are disparate as to immediate aims and research methods but link an overall aim of better understanding of student learning with two major inter-dependent themes, namely of variation in the nature of learning and of variation in learning experience in different learning environments? My tentative answer is to start from what evaluation might achieve and I believe that two goals must be attempted. The first is to check how far particular arguments or accounts of on-site research are insightful and convincing and the second is to check on any argument for extension of findings to other possible sites. Anything that can be validly concluded might have implications for research on and within Entwistle's framework and for at least some aspects of pedagogical provision and practice in higher education.

In taking this perspective, I have been much influenced by two publications by Lee Cronbach and his associates in a consortium at Stanford University in the early 1980s (Cronbach *et al.*, 1980; Cronbach & Shapiro, 1982). The consortium members were themselves involved in evaluation projects commissioned by the US government and various funding bodies, and were able to reflect on what they had learned from their different disciplinary bases. They were critical of the paucity, power to mislead and

*Correspondence should be addressed to Professor Hazel Francis, Institute of Education, University of London, 20 Bedford Way, London WC1H 0AL, UK (e-mail: h.francis@ioe.ac.uk).

DOI:10.1348/000709906X170290

low-cost effectiveness of information gained from experimental research that was based on a random allocation model with its search for general and generalizable findings based on statistical inference and numerical data. In educational provision, any programme delivery is a complex venture in a complex setting, where a great deal may already be known about the likely effects of intervention and where it is usually impossible to prevent leakage of information about new ventures and thus to make the clean comparisons between treatment groups hoped for from random selection. Moreover, the delivery of any intervention is not so clear and invariant as to allow assumptions about equivalence between treatments on selected research sites. Thus, doubt is thrown on the wisdom of reliance on random selection and adequate sample size to draw valid conclusions within the research and to make dependable inferences about generalizability beyond it. However, these and other criticisms did not lead Cronbach and his associates to abandon the importance of quantitative data or rational thought in the design of research programmes and in the defence of any conclusions or recommendations drawn from on-site research.

Thus, the direction of reform retained the logical argument that underlies the random allocation model and used it to suggest steps that might be taken to meet the problems arising from oversimplification of educational phenomena. Attention was given to the aspects of variation both within instructional delivery (what we might see as different learning environments) and between educational sites (instances of institutional and cultural contexts). Comparisons between these within a research programme might well affect expectations of benefit and thoughts of suitability for any prospective site outside it. For example, it would not be wise for a headmaster to adopt a recommendation for teaching based on an overall positive outcome of a research programme, if his school could not carry it out in the same way as the research schools whose outcomes contributed most to the overall findings or if his school or local area cultures were markedly different from theirs. He would do better to find out what happened in any of the schools that were like his. This approach put the nature as well as the amount of learning into the evaluation frame and positively sought descriptions of variation in programme delivery, in learners and in sites. Worthwhile research therefore would not necessarily look for the same educational recommendations for all sites but rather for well-defended advocacy for suitably comparable conditions. But for this wisdom to be possible, research reports would require quite detailed attention to qualitative as well as quantitative descriptions of difference and similarity between site, programme delivery and outcome.

It seems to me that this opens up the importance of description and analogy rather than measurement and generalization in designing and using educational research, and stresses the potential value of in-depth, on-site investigation for insights into the teaching–learning process. In addition, because of implicit comparison between what has happened and what might happen, it stresses the value of a thorough understanding of what is going on, whether or not any change is proposed or investigated. In this context, it appears to me that the body of research included in Entwistle's summary of research on teaching and learning in higher education is rich in insights and methods of trying to understand what is going on. It can therefore be valued as work that, if understood well by providers and tutors, can promote useful thinking and practice in higher education. What it cannot do, and what is probably impossible anyway, is formulate oversimplified recommendations that have unthinking application across the huge variation in site and endeavour that characterizes the sector.

In starting with this evaluative perspective, I have so far said nothing about the substantive nature of the work that Entwistle has referred to as a body of research on teaching and learning in higher education. In his introduction, Entwistle firmly and neatly positions the research perspective for this volume in the direct investigation of student learning in educational contexts and away from the development and application of psychological theories of learning. Since my brief is to reflect on his introduction and on the three papers in this section, I should like to consider this positioning and its implications before attending to what at first sight seem to be very different chapters, when my own perspectives on learning will emerge to some extent.

The nature of learning environments in educational settings

As to the nature of learning within education, there has been a long tradition of describing it in psychological terms by educationists, but with a notable lack of attention from psychologists since the early decades of the last century. Working in the developing discipline of psychology, those who elected to study learning did so from research into the conditions of human and animal learning and into the nature of human thinking as skills or abilities to be brought to bear on various kinds of generic learning tasks. These endeavours eventually entailed close encounters with information technology, artificial intelligence and neuroscience, but not with education. Thus, psychology, except for work concerned with children with special educational needs, came to offer little in the way of either applicability or understanding to the improvement of educational practice. However, according to Entwistle's account, learning as the ordinary person uses the term has been seriously investigated in educational contexts for some 30 years by researchers from different disciplines, including psychology. This must be especially welcomed with regard to higher education at a time of considerable change and expansion. Entwistle's summary of work in this field is an excellent introduction to the papers that follow, the more so since the authors themselves contributed to this history.

The general aim of this work has been to understand student learning in higher education, particularly with regard to the students' experiences of learning and the effects of learning environments. As he indicates, an important feature of Entwistle's own work has been the portrayal of the immediate learning environment of the teaching–learning process within an encompassing course and institutional environment. This is a differently oriented and more complex picture than that behind the notion of powerful learning environments as developed, for example, by De Corte (De Corte, 2000). Such work, influenced by constructivist psychology with its emphasis on the learner as a problem solver, sets out to manipulate instructional design to require learning through problem solution. But the fact that such an optimistically constructed instructional delivery, which should in theory work well but does not always do so in practice, has led to numerous studies adopting a less psychologically confined conception of the learning environment (see Konings, Brand-Gruwel, & van Merrienboer, 2005 for a useful discussion). This takes on board the variations in student and teacher conceptions of learning, and in their perspectives and understandings in relation to student–teacher engagement in some form of learning experience and the need for their matching or harmony. The work portrayed by Entwistle in his introduction has already laid the foundations for exploration of these issues and the contribution of this volume to research into learning in educational contexts is very timely.

Learning environments are not quite the same thing as educational contexts, albeit the terms might be used interchangeably under some circumstances. The term learning environment is itself neutral as to the presence or absence of intentional educational provision, though for mankind it always entails aspects of both physical and social worlds of experience. Educational contexts are characterized by deliberate design and control of such aspects in order to promote particular learning achievements. Within such contexts, the question arises as to the nature and significance of variation in learning environment. How important research into this question is for higher education must depend on the educational values driving the provision. More of that anon, but for the moment I believe it can be said that Entwistle's personal attempt to identify concepts that have emerged as important from the research he has summarized, together with his identification of relations between them constitutes a most helpful way of descriptively theorising the field.

Moving on from Entwistle's introduction, the three papers commented on below highlight different aspects of educational contexts of direct relevance in the field of higher education – the immediate practice of tutoring (Perkins), the subject field involved (Hounsell and Hounsell) and professional training (Eraut). But in addition, they address to different degrees and in different ways the essential nature and experience of immediate learning environments within these educational contexts.

What can we learn from theories of difficulty and 'trouble spots'?

Perkins' paper is an excellent example of relating psychological, in this case constructivist, notions of the nature of learning to a particular issue in academic subject content. The experience of teaching, when learners encounter particular difficulty in academic work, is the immediate focus of the paper, the implied but obvious learning environment being the immediate exchange with tutors in an academic course context. The topic of sorting out the nature of subject content difficulty for students is developed beautifully clearly and the various illustrations used to identify particular theories of difficulty will be recognized by tutors and students alike.

It is interesting to find that a theory of difficulty is distinguished from a theory of pedagogy. This distinction is made by taking it for granted that we all know what 'pretty good' pedagogy is (or if we don't, we can find out) and by asking what can be obtained from a theory of difficulty to add whatever extra is needed to achieve 'really good' pedagogy. At the heart of this extra is the attempt to identify what in particular it is in the subject content that causes 'trouble spots', rather than attributing fault to the learner or to any aspect of the conditions of teaching and learning. Perkins uses the term 'explanation' to apply to tutors explaining to themselves the content causes of difficulty, not to the possible further step of explaining content to students. This may be important, since a tutor's own understanding (explanation to the self) would be expected to influence the planning of subject presentation and of the interaction of student with topic, whereas the second possible use of the term would be expected to be a part of an account of student-teacher exchange in the actual process of teaching and learning as distinct from the planning. For this reason, I see the paper as sitting firmly in the context of concern about improving learning environments, but insufficiently in the context of the actual work of student learning in dealing with the problematic content. To be fair to Perkins, he seems to suggest this in his concluding section deliberately ending his particular argument at this point. Moreover, in the paper referred to by Entwistle (Perkins & Blythe, 1994), he describes some aspects of dealing with what constitutes student learning for understanding.

From identifying trouble to dealing with it

A possible way into the problem of dealing with trouble spots in actual teaching–learning interaction is to ask what actually counts as 'explanation', whether to the self or another? Now it may seem odd that one of the best approaches I have seen to chewing over this question comes from some work that I must confess I found difficult, being unfamiliar with the language of cybernetics in which it is couched. Pask (1975, 1976) published work entitled *Conversation Theory*, based on the endeavour to research what is happening mentally when someone is learning something. In order to do this, he proposed to build on the technique of engaging in verbal conversation with a learner, discussing with the learner the way he or she learns in the actual process of learning. His strategy, in order to control for tutor or observer variation and bias in explanation and understanding, was to design machine systems that could function as informer or questioner with regard to a topic when the learner engaged with them – hence the cybernetics. This work formed the basis for his characterization of learning conversations in which tutors must demonstrate their understanding in the process of teaching, while students must demonstrate theirs in some form of 'teach-back'. At the heart of the work on learning conversations is a question that is central to the issue of dealing with 'trouble spots' where students and tutors, alike, must engage in helping the other to appreciate their own understanding of subject content – "What does it take to show that someone has learned something, in the sense of understanding it?" Pask saw the essential test of understanding to be explanation of the content and structure of the topic under consideration, together with explanation of how this account has been arrived at and why it is to be preferred above others. To what extent this double level of explanation is actually asked for in educational contexts is both a moot and researchable point.

The theoretical approach to the work examines in a generic sense what is *necessarily* entailed in learning by an individual and then extends this to the situation of two individuals learning from each other. By extension, learning could be supported and demonstrated within a group or network. This captures the duality of learning as individual and social action, and also as natural and sociocultural experience. With regard to the individual learner, the essential of learning begins with building in memory a repertoire of experienced actions and consequences that increasingly forms a basis for making informed choices of action in new situations. Variation in experience (a link with Marton's paper in this volume) allows fine tuning of what is known and opens up novel opportunities of learning. Learning is demonstrable in terms of consistency and appropriateness of action in relation to consequence. If we have learned something, we can show our understanding to *someone well positioned for similar understanding*. This condition is particularly important with respect to the learner's prior knowledge and experience and to the possession of a common language of communication. Obviously, this includes natural language, but it may also include specialized versions such as disciplinary-based genres, machine languages and any commonly understood non-verbal means of expression. Provided that this includes use of the same ways of expression, we can show by what we say or draw, as well as by our actions, that we know what to do and not to do, where and when to do it or not to do it, and how to do it, and that we have chosen that way rather than any other.

We can readily see that this skeletal account captures the basic experience of learning as we use the word in everyday life, but in educational contexts, where the immediacy of the material situation involved in understanding subject content is often lacking, the importance of how language is used must be stressed. Teaching–learning *conversations* may depend too heavily on 'tell me', at the expense of 'show me what to do and how to do it'. Language depends for its function on basic agreement that a form of expression serves for 'show me', whether used at, or distant from, a place where demonstration might happen. Using language in this way can count as explanation in verbal terms and underpins much teaching, but unless the underlying structure of 'show me', namely the pattern of actions which demonstrate the learning, is captured in the verbal explanation, the latter is but ashes. The answer to 'why do you think or do it that way?' is likely to be 'Because you told me to' rather than 'Because, for these reasons, it gives the most satisfactory result'. Students need to be provoked by tutors into the understanding entailed in why they should, or should not, act or think in one way rather than another. This may be a particular feature of at least some of the 'trouble spot' scenarios referred to by Perkins. Unfortunately, teachers do not always have that depth of understanding themselves and they experience difficulty at certain points in the same way as their students, but finding trouble spots in student learning could alert them to their own as well as their students' difficulties with understanding. They might then be helped by discussion with colleag s or by in-service support.

From understanding trouble to anticipating it

'Pretty good' and experienced teachers who have taught a given content to a variety of students for some time may have found points where content has been particularly challenging and help their students to become aware of it, but inexperienced tutors and students generally may not adequately recognize that they have hit such a difficulty until problems surface later or critical assessment suggests weak or insufficient under-standing at some previous point. So can work on 'trouble spot' difficulty, whether about the identification of the nature and cause, or about how to deal with it, also play a role in promoting recognition of difficulty? Past experience of assessment of student learning, both ongoing and final, could be a useful guide. The role of ongoing assessment can be particularly important if it really explores students' understandings during learning, as Pask suggested, while it might also function as an ongoing 'trouble spot' detector to guide tutors.

This suggests to me that 'really good' pedagogy requires more than identifying the content difficulty in order to approach a particular task of teaching; it also requires actually relating such understanding to the tutor's usual approach to teaching, if only to be alert to other as yet unidentified sources of difficulty. This implies that the teacher is simultaneously a learner of subject content and also of how students are 'getting on with the work'; it should come as no surprise to find reports elsewhere in this monograph that approaches to teaching may reflect the three major approaches to academic learning (deep, surface and strategic) described in Entwistle's introduction. Thus, a possible surface approach to teaching might accompany well-designed, well-resourced and well-delivered courses but would nevertheless not aim to understand why student learning turns out in the way it does. Similarly, a strategic approach might aim to maximize attainment measures without necessarily aiming to maximize student understanding of the subject. Only with a deep approach, could we expect to find that aim of understanding student learning at trouble spots that would mark really good pedagogy.

Turning to students, much work depends on understandings achieved earlier, but precisely because of its underpinning of future work, the subject content involved in 'trouble spots' requires special recognition. It may seem odd but while some students sense during learning that they do or do not understand something adequately, others do not. This may have something to do with their willingness to test their own learning by explaining it to themselves, but it may also relate to earlier experiences of learning and teaching, and to tutorial response to their work. It is indisputable that personal histories of learning in school will have led students to expect difficulties with understanding from time to time and that failure to recognize them, or to adequately resolve them at the time, will not lead to failure or disaster at final assessment unless they happen frequently; provided that assessment of their learning results in a sufficient grade they will move on. Although most examiners would claim that they attempt to award better grades to work that shows fuller or greater understanding, assessment may depend a great deal on being able to reproduce parts of what is to be learned without enough understanding to make a firm base for future work. Some learners, who have come through schooling depending heavily on reproductive learning, or believing that this is what is required from them, may feel a general unease that they do not perform better, but are not likely to sense that particular unease that comes with recognition of difficulty over understanding at 'trouble spots'. The upshot is that by the time they enter higher education, not all students are able or prepared to recognize for themselves when they have met a point of critical difficulty in subject content, where they would do well to seek better understanding. Without labouring the point, this might well indicate a possible expansion of research on student approaches to learning, just as the question of tutor anticipation of trouble spots seemed to relate to approaches to teaching.

Perkins' paper indicates, at least to me, that he has persuasively identified a difficulty in the teaching-learning process and shown it to be widespread enough to merit serious investigation, not only into what constitutes subject content difficulty but also into how tutors might deal with it. The topic is located within Entwistle's framework and invites on-site research into its importance in relation to various academic disciplines, the role of ongoing assessment and the quality of student learning. However, it carries a direct message in clear language to tutors in higher education to consider their pedagogical practices in relation to the more difficult content aspects of what they teach and to ensure that they understand them completely themselves.

The extent to which higher education can make teaching provision to meet the kind of ongoing assessment required for demonstrating learning is a serious challenge for providers and tutors alike.

Teaching and learning environments in academic educational contexts

Some insights into the nature of this challenge come from Hounsell and Hounsell's excursion into the particular subject field of biosciences in order to explore the students' and teachers' experiences of aspects of teaching-learning environments in three universities with different histories of development. This work deals with a broader picture of academic work than the immediate engagement in work on a topic, although the finer grain of such experience as 'trouble spots' must lie within it. The scope of the concern is clearly defined and related to work reported in Entwistle's paper, notably the work by Biggs on the notion of alignment of curriculum objectives, teaching methods and assessment in the pursuit of teaching and learning for understanding rather than reproduction. It builds on this by looking to 'congruence' between features within immediate teaching-learning environments as an important influence on students' approaches to learning. The sharper focus is on the relationship between teaching for understanding, feedback and assessment in first and final year undergraduate courses.

I intend to comment on what I see as the two main findings in the report, but how much faith can I place in them? The sample size is large enough to take the accounts of experiences within the three sites and between the years within the sites quite seriously. The combination of questionnaire and interview data is powerful in that the findings would be much less persuasive if either stood on its own. The questionnaire provides a structure to be interpreted, a skeleton awaiting flesh; the interview data supply the flesh of interpretation, but on their own would yield a shapeless mass. So I find the work persuasive and worthy of serious consideration, if only to open up a wider consideration of the issues in other subject fields and other university sites. As a former university teacher, I must confess to a sense of reading about reality that might bias my judgment – but at least I have come clean and the reader must make what he or she chooses on that score.

The first of the two major findings I feel deserve attention arises from the comparisons within first and final years. What the first-year environments have in common is similarity of teaching strategies to achieve the aim of bringing all students to a common base of learning as preparation for work in the later years. In terms of student experience, there was considerable reported satisfaction with the clarity and congruence of teaching and assessment, and with tutor and peer support. Possible causes for concern were less satisfaction with feedback from tutors and with teaching as falling short of in terms of aiming for understanding. Final-year students' courses differed from first-years' in the considerable difference between and within them in terms of teaching strategies and the work undertaken, but this did not affect the generally high satisfaction with aspects of the teaching/learning environments except for the experience of feedback. Generally assessment was more favourably viewed than feedback. How then did this come about?

The interview data yielded information about what counted as feedback and assessment in the environments concerned. Whatever form it took, assessment was scheduled to happen after learning was supposed to have been achieved. It was timetabled, expected for every student, and reasonably clearly described to them in terms of what to expect. In that it tested for understanding how to deploy acquired knowledge and skill, it could be said to test for understanding, and to be congruent with course aims and content. But it did not test for understanding *during* learning in order to help the learner to acquire knowledge.

This was where feedback might have been helpful, but what was reported as feedback was not intrinsic to learning. It consisted largely of advice on strategies of coping with tasks and of post-task comment to individuals on their work and was experienced as not being sufficiently informative. One can only think that it fell far short of tutorial evaluation of student's 'teach-back' as envisaged by Pask for testing students' understanding of what they were learning. It suggested that tutors would have difficulty in identifying and dealing with 'trouble spots'. Tutors themselves reported little on feedback, but gave some indication that both assessment and feedback had to be balanced against other calls on their time. Hounsell and Hounsell questioned whether the aim of teaching for understanding was being achieved as completely as it might have been. Clearly, there is a challenge to tutors and course teams to consider how they might best achieve more intrinsic feedback and to universities to consider the implications of resource allocation and staff–student ratios for the quality of teaching and learning.

The second major finding comes from students' reported experiences in their final year of undergraduate work. The nature of university study in biosciences (but not only in these) is to present students with ways experts in their fields pursue the development and reporting of their work. As the students in the reported research progressed through their studies, they were expected to shift from a reliance largely on secondary texts and tutor-mediated knowledge to considerably more work on primary texts and their own practical investigations. The paper reports the difficulties students said they encountered in the early stages of their final year as they recognized the nature of this change in expectations. Hounsell and Hounsell see this as a very significant feature of higher education – the induction of students into the workplaces and practices of seekers after knowledge. This is not a simple extension of schooling, but a qualitative change in education; one which has roots in some aspects of school experience but which gains momentum in the first year of undergraduate learning and makes its fuller demands in the final year, preparing students for further work in higher education or research centres or for professional life which at its best demands continued thoughtful learning.

An example of students' difficulties in dealing with a similar change in expectations, in postgraduate work, was reported by myself and a colleague, where we explored students' reading of primary texts and research papers and the difficulties they said they encountered with them on a Masters degree course (Francis & Hallam, 2000). A major feature of the difficulty was coping with the language of a research community, socialized into its own practices and ways of working. At the beginning of the course, students reported not having the same command of the subject research field genre as their tutors in their attempts at communicating their learning, but this lessened with further tutorial engagement and practical research work. (Here I have to reflect that Pask's requirement of a common language to enable learning conversations must entail the notion that the language concerned is also developed in those conversations.)

This shift in the nature of university study draws attention to the university as a workplace in itself and as a collection of separately identified workplaces concerned with different subjects or disciplines. Hounsell and Hounsell develop the notion of ways of thinking and practising as characteristic of the work into which students are inducted and point to a richer concept of learning with understanding than what goes on in the head. This seems to me to be a hugely important insight into academic work. The concept of practice goes well beyond that of simply doing things and entails social purposes, meanings and styles of behaviour. It is congruent with usage in the way we speak of professional practice in fields such as medicine and law. It enriches the concept of teaching and learning environments and has value in relation to efforts to improve the quality of learning and teaching in different academic courses. It offers a way in to considering professional training, which is the topic of Eraut's work.

From the academic setting to the professional workplace

Eraut's paper takes the reader out of the academic learning context into the wider world of early career professional practical training. It is based on empirical work that was designed in the light of previous investigations into mid-career learning and focuses on three careers – nursing, engineering and accountancy. In these contexts, academic knowledge (described by Eraut as codified knowledge) is not regarded as much for its truth-value as for its utility in the relevant profession. What is valued, once in the workplace, is the largely unwritten knowledge of how to do the job and to do it well. Thus, learning is motivated by the perceived needs of the work and occurs not in a relatively formal interaction with one or more tutorial figures, but in the day-to-day interaction with a variety of people such as colleagues, clients, mentors and managers. Eraut reports empirical work that tries to formalize a picture of how this happens and how it relates to earlier and off-site more academic training. Is the picture a faithful representation? Can we use it?

Since the study was based on observations of trainees at work, all in different workplaces, and on subsequent interviews with them and with a selection of managers and mentors, a relatively small number of trainees in each career context formed the research sample. For picture-building this presents no problem. The picture can be tested later against other samples if need be, but the methodology does restrict the level of engagement in learning that can be reported on. The method tells something of what is learned or being learned, what problems are perceived and encountered and of the support mechanisms available, but it cannot touch the detailed analysis implied in the approach to difficulty and explanation developed by either Perkins or Pask. The effect of this constraint is seen in the rather general typologies of learning trajectories and early career learning, though the emphasis on on-going learning, rather than end-state learning, comes out well. Since the main aim is to identify conditions that promote, rather than hold up, learning in the workplace, an essential step is the elicitation from the data of what to counts as important in regard to learning. Guided by results of the previously mentioned study of mid-career learning, the analysis of current data yielded findings of the importance of looking for learning, meeting challenge and finding feedback and support from others. With these factors identified, it was possible to look for conditions in the workplace that supported or impeded learning. That these factors turned out to be useful ways of looking at conditions in different professional contexts is not surprising. As Eraut indicates, their validity is supported by a psychological literature and by earlier work and I doubt whether any reader will be able to find ground for arguing against them. That they yield different balances of findings from different work contexts is the real nub of the research and the sum of the picture drawn out of it.

Even if the picture of the effects of the context on learning is faithful across the actual research sites, this does not allow us to generalize to others. It simply gives us what promises to be a useful way of looking at them and an invitation to replicate or challenge them. Perhaps more importantly, it gives those involved in early career training a 'thought toolbox' to examine their own practices. There is no immediate generalization of applicable findings but, very importantly, there is a clarification and challenge that might lead to more thoughtful and productive practice on a range of sites.

Eraut uses it to think about higher education, overriding his earlier distinction between the 'codified' knowledge of university-based learning and the cultural knowledge of workplace knowledge by pointing out that academic learning is itself located in a workplace – a workplace of colleagues engaged in a common enterprise but with different experiences, roles and responsibilities. Higher education students are apprentices in the business of knowledge construction and use, and they learn within the subject-specific knowledge cultures established through academic research history. This puts a great deal of flesh on the bones of the notion of a learning environment. Questions arise about the way student learning might be best supported by fully exploiting the availability of other personnel who are fellow or former students, library and laboratory staff, and, most importantly, researchers in the relevant field. Eraut usefully spells out some of the implications for course design and tutorial practice, but the main point is the recognition that student learning takes place within the values and practices of the acquisition and use of knowledge that pertain to various academic and professional disciplines. Codified knowledge only makes sense within the context of its cultural roots and use. This is also one of the messages in the Hounsells' paper.

Significance of the research overall

Thanks to the research reported in this volume, we have a good idea of what kind of educationally valued teaching–learning provision higher education might aim for and it is largely expressed in terms that are accessible to a wide range of providers in government and in university administration and to the academic workforce and the students they serve. There is clearly not a general recommendation of some specific practice to cover all aspects of teaching and learning, nor even of a limited range, but there is a general challenge to identify those aspects of teaching–learning environments which could be improved to maximize benefit within different disciplines and courses, and there are different descriptions which allow tutors and others to draw analogies with their own situations to help meet the challenge.

But if this body of work impresses with the faithfulness of its reporting of student experiences in the educational contexts selected for study, what of its significance for higher education?

Influences on approaches to learning

The research into students' approaches to learning suggests these may be habitual (derived from experience and from expectation of continuing along the same lines) or varied (responding to personal interest or tutor-influenced expectations). All approaches may therefore be seen as strategic behaviour by students (whether or not ill-judged). The behaviour students adopt within their approaches will depend to a large extent on information about what to learn and how to go about it. Moreover, and most importantly, their learning will depend on how they are expected to demonstrate it, and thus on information about the nature and purpose of assessment and on the actual practices of assessment and feedback. Some responsibility for maximizing the use of any particular approach must therefore lie with tutors and the system within which they operate. Students need information beyond what knowledge or skill they are expected to learn and how to go about acquiring it. Most importantly they need to know whether or not feedback and assessment require them to demonstrate understanding of knowledge, how it is established and how it might be challenged. This implies a quality of learning conversation between students and tutors that cannot be obtained if the curriculum suffers from content overload with respect to the time available for learning and teaching. In addition to improving tutorial practice, some content pruning may thus be called for to encourage strong and healthy growth in the effort to acquire knowledge and skill. Entwistle's overview suggests a range of other possible sources of interference with this growth.

Educational aims and values driving provision

Teaching practices in traditional university education have included provision of learning environments, as well as variation in learning experiences, that have attempted, however imperfectly, to promote well-understood discipline-based knowledge and practice, and thus to serve the purpose of producing well-qualified professional practitioners and researchers in various fields of importance to society. All the papers in this volume place a premium on the promotion of learning with understanding, intelligent practice and critical thought; and they therefore seek to identify teaching and learning environments that make these highly probable features of students' experiences of learning. However, both the papers by the Hounsells and by Eraut point to the wider issues raised by change from traditional, relatively small-scale and sharply-focused higher education, to the mass provision more common today. With its considerably larger student population and its wider variety of courses and purposes, this raises huge problems for providers in terms of finance and resources. The quality of learning valued in this volume may not be the most important feature of higher education in the minds of all providers. It would be easy to assume that the teaching practices valued in traditional higher education, with serious attempts to maximize student learning with understanding, are an unnecessary luxury when the value of provision for the many is set against the concerns of a few, but such an assumption would undermine the aims and value of provision for all. The concern for improving the quality of student learning through improvement in teaching–learning environments that lies behind the work reported in this volume applies to *all* educational contexts, and some of it goes a long way to identifying the false dichotomy between academic and other work that feeds discriminatory views. Higher education has always prepared students for work in society, though for a limited range of vocations. An expansion to preparation for other occupations in life is a necessity as modern conditions demand a more thoughtful, informed and skilled workforce, but if society is to be served well by this workforce then all students must be served well in higher education.

However, it cannot be taken for granted that government and higher education providers share the concerns for the benefit of students and society expressed by the authors of this volume. If higher education provision is dominated by an aim to maximize student numbers, whatever their learning, or by an aim to foster factual knowledge and automated skills without a critical approach to deploying them, different demands will be made on tutors and other resources, and differently qualified students will emerge. This is not an issue of quantification of learning through mark scales in degree examinations; it is a question of the quality of the learning experience and of what is learned. It will be a serious loss for individuals and society if the fate of the research reported here is not to be used to improve the nature and quality of student learning, but to point sadly at what might have been.

References

Cronbach, L. J., Ambron, S. R., Dornbusch, S. M., Hess, R. D., Hornick, R. C., Phillips, D. C., *et al.* (1980). *Toward reform of program evaluation.* San Francisco: Jossey-Bass.

Cronbach, L. J., & Shapiro, K. (1982). *Designing evaluations of educational and social programs.* San Francisco: Jossey-Bass.

De Corte, E. (2000). Marrying theory building and the improvement of school practice: A permanent challenge for instructional psychology. *Learning and Instruction, 10,* 249–266.

Francis, H., & Hallam, S. (2000). Genre effects on higher education students' reading for understanding. *Higher Education, 39,* 279–296.

Konings, K. D., Brand-Gruwel, S., & van Merrienboer, J. J. G. (2005). Towards more powerful learning environments through combining the perspectives of designers, teachers, and students. *British Journal of Educational Psychology, 75,* 645–660.

Pask, G. (1975). *Conversation, cognition and learning: A cybernetic theory and methodology.* Amsterdam: Elsevier.

Pask, G. (1976). *Conversation theory: Applications in education and epistemology.* Amsterdam: Elsevier.

Perkins, D. N., & Blythe, T. (1994). Putting understanding up front. *Educational Leadership,* 4–7.

Student Learning and University Teaching, 147–150
BJEP Monograph Series II, 4
© 2007 Paul Ramsden

The
British
Psychological
Society

www.bpsjournals.co.uk

Reflections on papers 2, 4, 5, 6 and the conference as a whole

Paul Ramsden*
Higher Education Academy, UK

The conference out of which this monograph grew stimulated in me again the kind of childlike excitement and openness to ideas that makes academic work the most satisfying of endeavours. In my present role as chief executive of the Higher Education Academy, I am much occupied with the ways in which we can apply the best available evidence in improving students' experiences of learning in higher education. For that reason, I am keen to comment on these papers from the perspective of a user of the research they exemplify.

Each of us knows that the student experience has multiple dimensions – from lectures to paid work to libraries and leisure and sports. However, it is also true that the quality of their experience is dominated by the ways in which students are exposed to the subject matter they study. 'Satisfaction' with higher education, as measured in for example the National Student Survey, is most strongly associated with the quality of teaching that students experience. Put it another way: students' experiences of teaching and their teachers are more central both to their enjoyment and to the outcomes of their learning than the standard of facilities or indeed the effectiveness of assessment. Speaking more formally, it is the nature of the relation between the student and the subject matter that is crucial to a high-quality experience; and this relation is, from the perspective of the student, shaped by the opportunities provided through teaching and curriculum.

A large number of national initiatives have been put-in place in the UK over the past 10 years aimed at improving the student's experience of learning. These range from the idea of a professional association of lecturers, through to pressures for required training in university teaching, the establishment of subject centres to provide discipline-based support, attempts to separate teaching from research in the hope of raising the former's status, and on to the enhancement-led approach to assuring quality in Scotland and the enormous (circa £350 million) project to establish teaching excellence centres in England.

Few of these initiatives have been informed directly by research evidence; evidence-based policy has been less widespread than appeals to evidence to justify existing policy.

---

*Correspondence should be addressed to Professor Paul Ramsden, The Higher Education Academy, Innovation Way, York Science Park, Heslington, York YO10 5BR, UK (email: paul.ramsden@heacademy.ac.uk).

DOI:10.1348/000709906X162415

Ironically, however, the kind of research embodied in the present monograph has had an enormous, though indirect, effect on policy and practice. It has inspired lecturers to think critically and creatively about how their teaching makes it possible for students to learn. It has enabled those who support the development of good teaching in universities – whether as designers of programmes in teaching, or as managers of departments or university-wide initiatives, or as instigators of national projects – to generate the conditions in which a focus on the quality of student learning becomes habitual.

Ference Marton's influence on these developments in practice is impossible to overestimate. What we need to help lecturers make learning possible is not detailed analysis of the best ways to organize learning, or training in basic competence in teaching – valuable as these are. More importantly, we need an understanding of the different ways in which subject matter (the 'object of learning') may be dealt with and how students experience those differences. The context created by the lecturer and the programme helps to shape the quality of students' understanding. The theory of variation implies that the most valuable conditions for learning arise when teaching is so structured that in relation to a particular concept or topic, the student's experience of invariance and variance in the subject matter is appropriately organized. How content is organized is critical in determining the conditions of learning. In the classic surface approach to the content, the student cannot discern the structure of variation. It is the teacher's task to create the conditions in which the student may distinguish that structure.

It is then a small step to the work of Prosser and his colleagues. In the simplest terms, organizing the conditions in which lecturers can think critically about the contexts of learning they create for students is equivalent to helping students discern variations in the object of learning. The aim is to develop a student-focused approach, which concentrates on the relation between the object of learning and the student, rather than a teacher-focused approach, which concentrates on what the teacher does. The former is compatible with a critical, questioning and inquiry-led attitude to teaching. However, a defining characteristic of teaching in higher education is its close affiliation with research. In universities, the search for new knowledge traditionally goes hand in hand with the process of making knowledge accessible to students. The most fascinating insight is that variation in the ways in which academics understand their subject matter is associated with their experiences of teaching. Understandings that are more complex are linked to a student-focused approach and less complex ones to a teacher-focused approach.

This promises at last to settle the difficulty of understanding the nexus between research and teaching in higher education and to explain the observation that good university teaching (itself disposed to critical inquiry about student learning) is frequently perceived to be associated with the research. Clear articulation of important aspects of the subject matter being taught and how they relate to each other, and the capacity to situate one's understanding of the subject matter in the field as a whole, are characteristic of the successful researcher. In this context, it is interesting to observe that there is a positive association between RAE scores and students' experiences of good teaching in the analysis of the 2006 NSS results. Perhaps the policy makers who would encourage a greater separation between teaching, research and professional practice may need to think again.

Vermunt and Richardson provide, in their respective papers, overviews of the complex relationship between the quality of the student learning in higher education and the educational context. One of the highlights of this field of research has been the influence of work on the learning environment on practice; policy and practice in the design of curricula and assessment has been transformed by the application of research into the effects of context on students' experiences and learning outcomes. Practical issues of graduate employability and work-related skills increasingly dominate the policy agenda for higher education in the UK; and it is noteworthy that transferable and generic graduate skills are fostered by the same kinds of experience that encourage deep approaches to learning. Traditional notions of critical thinking and the capacity for independent judgment beyond the narrow confines of curriculum have gained fresh currency.

Vermunt's special contribution has been to examine the ways in which the self-regulatory skills that are appropriate for lifelong learning in the workplace and beyond are encouraged by certain environments. 'Powerful' teaching and learning environments encourage integration of theoretical and practical knowledge and provide progressively more opportunities for self-regulation in students' learning. Vermunt points out that realizing this form of curriculum implies a change in how many academics conceptualize teaching. A question arises from this conclusion as to where the responsibility for improving student learning lies within a university or a higher education system. Governments do not decide; the Higher Education Academy does not decide; the vice-chancellor does not, nor indeed the Dean or the Head of the school, or the individual lecturer. Who does decide?

Richardson helps us towards the answer in his succinct overview of developments in the use of survey instruments to provide evidence of relations between students' perceptions of the academic environment and their approaches to learning and studying. Studies of students' experiences of e-learning, problem-based curricula and distance learning consistently confirm the robust nature of the concepts embodied in the Australian survey of students' experiences (the Course Experience Questionnaire) and the revised Approaches to Studying Inventory. A very interesting issue identified by Richardson is the question of the underlying structure of the relationship between context and approach. The inference from the empirical analysis would appear to be that students' approaches are driven by their perceptions and that their perceptions are equally influenced by their capacity to adopt appropriate approaches.

This is a particularly important conclusion in relation to practice. We may refer again to the NSS, whose results suggest that UK higher education students are least positive about aspects of the learning environment associated with assessment and feedback on performance. For example, while 86 per cent of respondents agreed that 'staff are good at explaining things', 57 per cent agreed that 'I have received detailed comments on my work' and only 51 per cent agreed that 'feedback on my work has helped me clarify things I did not understand'. If perceptions determine approaches, but not vice versa, and if perceptions are hard-wired to tangible aspects of context such as the number of comments on assessments, then it may seem that the research evidence would support a major intervention on the part of universities to provide better quality and more feedback.

But if the causal path runs both ways, and if experiences are associated with, but not determined by the environment – both of which conclusions are entirely consistent with theoretical basis of the last 25 years of research on students' experiences of learning – then . . . what? A different, more circumspect and more difficult technique may be necessary. The task could require efforts to change students' expectations of feedback and to help them understand the usefulness of the information they already obtain, *as well as* attempts to change the context. It may also suggest a need to intervene before students enter higher education, since their study behaviours and approaches are associated with their prior experiences of all kinds of education.

Richardson's concludes that researchers and practitioners should think more flexibly and creatively about the ways student experiences are manifested in learning outcomes provides a positive ending to this brief discussion of the practical implications of this work. It continues to be a paradox of research on university students' learning that the more its context is resolved, the more it becomes clear that individual experience governs its quality. At the end of the day, it is the learners themselves whose experiences determine the quality of the outcomes they achieve. Academics and academies can help make learning possible, but fallible students, thank goodness, will continue to remain the architects of their own destinies.

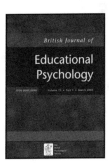

The
British
Psychological
Society

Media Training Courses

Working with the media?
Want to gain some valuable tips & experience?

Whether you are a complete beginner or looking to update your skills, you will find our training sessions stimulating and enjoyable.

An Introduction to Working with the Media

A one-day immersion in the media – newspapers, magazines, radio and television – with lots of hands-on experience. This course is designed to give a general introduction to how the media operates, as well as introducing some of the skills necessary in media liaison. e.g. press release writing and interview techniques.

Broadcast Interview Skills

A one-day course that covers everything required for speakers to feel confident about taking on broadcast interviews. It will focus on radio interviews, but will also cover TV interview techniques.

Delegates will be provided with plenty of practical opportunity to get in front of the microphone and to gain experience of actually being interviewed.

All courses take place in London and include lunch and course materials.

Registration form and further details from:
Dawn Schubert
Administrator, Publications & Communications Directorate
Tel: 0116 252 9581; E-mail: mediatraining@bps.org.uk

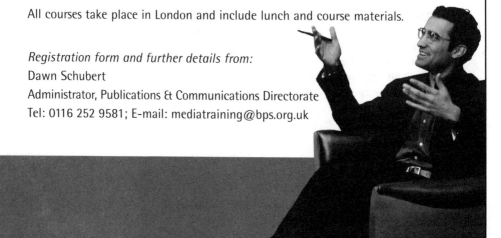

The best psychology, to your inbox - free!

Sign up for The British Psychological Society's free, fortnightly e-mail:
vital resource for students, lecturers…in fact, anyone interested in psychology.

www.researchdigest.org.uk